JAMES
GERBER

219-633-4969

Database Design Methodology

Database Design Methodology

Database Design Methodology

M. Vetter
(IBM ESRI)

R.N. Maddison
(The Open University)

ENGLEWOOD CLIFFS, NEW JERSEY   LONDON   NEW DELHI
SINGAPORE   SYDNEY   TOKYO   TORONTO   WELLINGTON

British Library Cataloguing in Publication Data

Vetter, Max
   Database design methodology.
   1. Data base management
   2. File organization (Computer science)
   I. Title
   001.6'442   QA76.9.D3

   ISBN 0—13—196535—2

Library of Congress Cataloging in Publication Data

Vetter, Max, 1939—
   Database design methodology.

   Bibliography: p.
   Includes index.
   1. Data base management.   I. Title.
QA76.9.D3V47   001.6'42   79—13876
ISBN 0—13—196535—2

ISBN 0—13—196535 2

PRENTICE-HALL INTERNATIONAL INC., *London*
PRENTICE-HALL OF AUSTRALIA PTY., LTD., *Sydney*
PRENTICE-HALL OF CANADA, LTD., *Toronto*
PRENTICE-HALL OF INDIA PRIVATE LIMITED, *New Delhi*
PRENTICE-HALL OF JAPAN, INC., *Tokyo*
PRENTICE-HALL OF SOUTHEAST ASIA PTE., LTD., *Singapore*
PRENTICE-HALL, INC., *Englewood Cliffs, New Jersey*
WHITEHALL BOOKS LIMITED, *Wellington, New Zealand*

Printed in the United States of America

   82 83 84 85 5 4 3

Contents

Contents

2

Test 10-17-83

3,4

Contents

Preface

The developments of database facilities and applications in recent years have created a need for, and made possible, a basically new approach to database design. Designers need methods of successfully analyzing the kinds of information that will flow to and from users and be represented as data in computerized systems. Their aim is efficient, cost-effective and logically right data models. They must implement, not merely to meet current and likely applications within available and anticipated technology, but also build in flexibility to meet any future evolution without expensive reprogramming or restructuring.

Database analysis and design is passing from the phase of research and a collection of techniques that have been shown as useful in practice. We discuss the various theories and techniques, bringing together the most promising into a single comprehensive systematic procedure for analysis and design, yet indicating that ours is not the only way.

By coordinating that which is currently available from many sources this book will assist in the improved use and expansion of existing DBMSs. More importantly it provides guidelines for the evolution of future DBMSs which may as yet be only reasearch ideas.

* The design method proposed in this book, and which we and others believe to be necessary, is therefore new. It differs from other approaches by developing an application—independent analysis of the information in an organization to produce a structure which is also software- and hardware-independent.

* The design procedure is based on proven theory and the combination of tools proposed is unique. It applies set theory, functions, the theory of graphs and normalization rigorously to the database design process. We show every principle by example and state the general.

We explain how to develop a conceptual data model which reflects the inherent properties of the information, independent of current applications and of technical limitations and will stand the tests of time and evolution. From this stable reference point are developed specifications of the interfaces and data structures to be used for all kinds of DBMSs so that future changes, large or small, external or internal, general or specific are as easy as possible. Different types of structures and interfaces can exist together.

Database terminology varies: by and large we have followed the American National Standards Institute Computers and Information Processing Standards together with conventions of school, college and university mathematics and computing.

The book is aimed at a wide readership:

* Data processing professionals such as data analysts, systems analysts, database designers, database administration staff and programmers seeking promotion may learn from the mixture of theory and practical examples.

* Students and teachers of university or similar courses in computer science should also appreciate the compilation of fundamentals which otherwise would have to be gathered from many books, journals, reports and conference proceedings.

The table of contents summarizes the structure of the book; this is expanded in the introductory Chapter 1 which outlines how the various topics are developed and how they fit together. There are questions and exercises at the end of each chapter, as well as references and bibliographies for further study. Solutions are in an appendix.

The material for this book comes from courses developed and taught at the IBM European Systems Research Institute (ESRI) in La Hulpe, Brussels, the AMAGI Research Institute in Itoh, Japan and the Swiss Institute of Technology in Lausanne; and also from various papers given at international conferences in Japan and Europe.

Comments and suggestions from colleagues and reviewers have been invaluable in shaping and refining the structure of our approach. In particular we are most grateful to Professor C.A. Zehnder (Swiss Institute of Technology), Professor P. Wilmes (University of Louvain, Belgium), members of IBM ESRI and to Dr. M.J. Beetham and the Open University Student Computing Service Research Computing Advisory Service.

Any errors or omissions are ours however, and any suggestions for the book's improvement would be welcomed.

M.V.

R.N.M.

Database Design Methodology

1

Aims

1.1 INTRODUCTION

Operational and management information, when represented as data usable in many ways, is a valuable resource. Particularly it is so if it can be easily and quickly used to meet all possible requirements - answering the unexpected as well as the routine.

This means an organization should design the way that its data is held so that it can easily be used for any application and so new applications can be added without requiring any extra work on previous ongoing ones.

A database is a collection of data stored and organized so that all user requirements can be met.

By a user we mean an individual or group that has requirements involving providing or receiving information. This excludes application programmers and computer systems staff.

The structure, design and control of a database normally need a database administrator (DBA). This is a person or team that controls and manages the database. The technical responsibilities of the database administrator are to
- identify the needs of the organization and of users
- define, implement and control the data storage including the structure and self-consistency
- define and control access to the data
- coordinate the data resources of the whole organization, ensuring user and management cooperation.

The job needs tactful politics to ensure success. Policies and procedures have to be established to guarantee effective protection and to control use of the data. Coordination and agreement are also needed over the choices of the overall information areas to be covered.

1

Traditionally organizations are divided into departments, divisions, groups and sections with responsibilities for particular aspects. The <u>functional areas</u>, i.e. groups of related business system activities and processes, may or may not be the same as the departmental structure.

The <u>information subject areas</u> are those overall groups of kinds of information to be held and communicated by computer. These information areas will cover the information common to the functional areas whose staff use the computer. E.g. employee information is a possible information subject area; it will be used in functional areas such as payroll and personnel. Similarly sales information is an information area that is used in activities such as sales order processing and other activities for accounting and production planning.

The database administrator's responsibilities require actions that are far beyond the activities required of a data processing department implementing traditional file-based computer systems. Briefly we review such systems to show the difficulties.

Such systems were each tailored to meet specific operational application requirements. These requirements were identified and documented by systems analysts. Their corresponding application programs were each designed and coded almost independently. They each used files of records structured individually to meet the needs of the application.

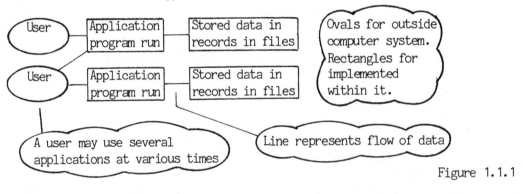

Figure 1.1.1

Little thought was given to holding the data in structures that could easily be used in new ways, e.g. in a new application that associated together data from several types of record in previously unrelated files.

Gradually more application programs were added. For effectiveness on the computers of the 1960s and 1970s some processes had to be <u>batched</u>, i.e. a group of similar transactions were processed together. Because one application process needed data in files sorted one way e.g. by customer account number and another by e.g. invoice number, many sorting and merging programs and processes were also needed. This involved many versions of the data in files on magnetic tapes. Such data could only be accessed sequentially. Computer runs had to be done in correct sequence and weekly or monthly. The availability of disk storage made possible record access in any sequence (called random access) by application programs. The applications were programmed in terms of logical records that were stored by the operating system as say five per physical block on disk.

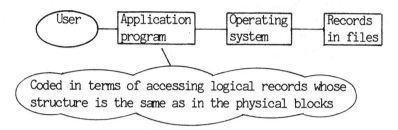

Figure 1.1.2

For the moment _logical_ means as apparently structured, e.g. for handling by an application program.

But the data structures were still chosen to fit individual applications. The choices of what types of data items were in which record types and what pointers from one record to another existed were highly application dependent.

Database management software

The 1970s saw an extra software interface, a database management system (DBMS). This is between the application programs and the accesses to the physically stored data. So the application programs can be coded as though they view the data in seemingly different structures from the actual physical structures. There is no sorting, merging or sequential file processing.

Because of their enormity database management software packages are usually general purpose. They are developed by a computer manufacturer or software house. In fact they contain several interfaces for reasons described later.

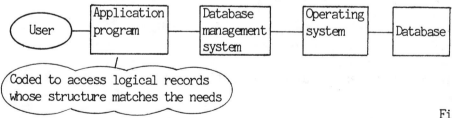

Figure 1.1.3

In this arrangement a physical block of data on disk storage may contain a mixture of data whose structure in detail is not deducible from the application program coding.

The above leads to these concepts, the first four being desirable features of a database management system
   - all information within the subject areas relevant to users should be storable

- each application can be programmed as though only the kinds of data that it needs are present
- new applications and new types of data can be added without disturbing the coding or operation of existing applications
- only the database management system directly interfaces to the physically stored data, the application programs do not
- particular computer equipment and software, including database management systems, can only do what they have facilities for. The limitations may constrain the designer.

We shall gradually develop these ideas.

Subjects of interest

To the database designer and administrator the areas of interest about information and data are as follows
- the real world and its information, e.g. ABC is a manufacturing organization
- that information concerning the real world that is within the areas relevant to users, e.g. J. Smith orders 5 engines from ABC's salesman, but not J. Smith's height. We call this the mini world.
- ideas in people's minds about such information, e.g. there are orders concerning quantities of parts for customers. This gives a number of associated types of information called a conceptual data model for reasons below
- ideas about the flow and use of such types of information, e.g. the orders are processed in the Sales Order Processing section, giving a functional model
- the ways of representing all such information types as data meeting computer constraints, e.g. having certain named data items such as Order-date in a logical record type named Order
- the physical structure and representation of the actual data to be held on storage devices such as discs, possibly with transfers controlled by an operating system
- the logical structures of subsets used by applications
- the specification of application processes
- communication and transmission of data
- the control of resources, including the initiation and execution of processes by the computer
- security.

The conceptual data model describes the structure of all the types of data needed to represent the mini world information. A functional model describes the data flows and use for applications e.g. for purchasing.

Usually no user is involved with every type of information but the conceptual data model includes all types.

One of our central ideas is that developing the conceptual data model should be done independent of computer constraints. During this modelling the analyst should discover the structure of the information by talking to users and managers - never minding what can or cannot be done by the available database management system, computer and operating system. Only thus can users' requirements be documented satisfactorily. After finishing that conceptual modelling and getting users' and management agreement - and only then - the designer should start to think about the global logical model i.e. the way the data is logically structured in the computer system.

We hope you, the reader, are not put off by all the terms used. They will all be gradually explained in the next few chapters. For the moment
- logical means as apparently structured
- global means covering all types of information
- conceptual means as formed in the mind - free of any computer considerations.

To aid data modelling, the analyst and database administrator may need to use a computer system to keep records of the many types of data items involved. Some database management systems provide facilities for storing the names of the types of data items e.g. Employee-no, Order-date, and a description of each. This is called a data dictionary. A data dictionary can in principle hold the details of
- the global conceptual data model
- the global logical model
- each application program logical model
- access, integrity and resource controls
- the physical model.

The details should include how the data types are associated to carry meaning. The details should also include in which applications each type of data is used. Since the associations that are the essence of the meaning are stored, the data dictionary can be used to analyse what would be the effects of proposed changes in the data types and associations.

Only if a change occurs in the real mini world as modelled in the global conceptual data model should that model need to be changed. Thus only then should the global logical model change. Exceptionally the global logical model may also need changing if the current database management system that it fits is to be replaced by another, though strictly that is the development of a new global logical model for a different set of constraints. The usual case is a new software release with advantageous features. The coded form of a global logical model is called a schema. It is the way the data in the database is regarded as structured.

All computer systems need features for privacy and integrity - not just database systems. Security features cover access control - information should not be disclosed to or corrupted or destroyed by unauthorized people, e.g. some people may be able to create, modify, and delete an employee's data, others to read only, others only to do overall processes giving anonymous statistics.

All systems need accuracy - information should agree with reality. E.g. some data may have an 'owner' responsible for its accuracy and applications will

have data vetting checks. Integrity means the stored information should be
self-consistent and not get corrupted or lost by accident or malfunction. This
needs recovery arrangements to rectify the stored data after hardware and
software errors, power failures and other misfortunes.

Finally the system must be useful and easy to use. Information must be
received by the correct people at the right time. They must understand the data
they receive so they can act on the information. They must have confidence in
its quality. They must be able easily to obtain information that they need and
to feed to the computer system data representing new information. So the computer system must be reliable and easily usable to be useful.

Stages of design

The design and development of a computer-based information system has
various stages. Most projects should include the following activities. Arrows
denote the flow of information.

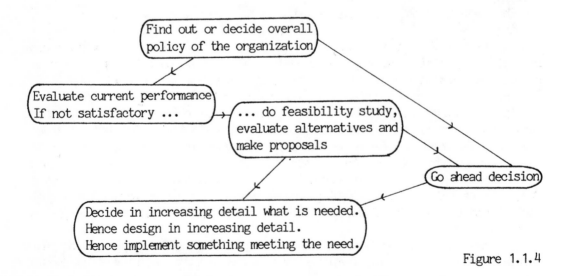

Figure 1.1.4

Analysis comes before design. For computer-based information systems the
last box above includes something like the following.

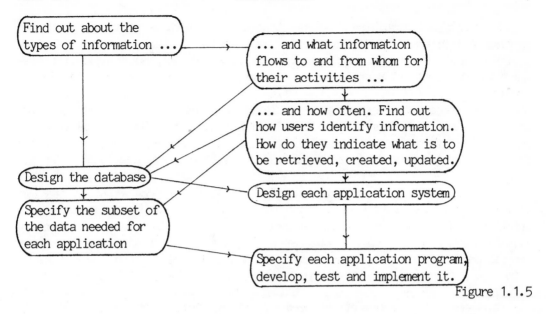

Figure 1.1.5

In the above the left side is mostly about types of information and types of data, i.e. data models. The right side is mostly about users' applications and systems, i.e. business functions and functional models.

Design aims

Before tackling the various stages and methods of analysis and design you need to appreciate the aim. The aim is to design a database
(a) to serve many applications
(b) so new types of data and new applications can be added easily
(c) so that as the pattern of use evolves the structure of the data as held on disk can be changed without affecting application programs
(d) so all types of information can be stored, even though no user knows about all the types of information
(e) that conforms to proposed or agreed standards
(f) that uses a particular software package, e.g. a database management system available on a particular computer.
These six considerations are always true.

There are also features of the organization that are likely to be true for ever. For example it employs staff and manufactures goods for sale.
The aim is to create a database design that embodies and is based on
- the consequences of the six ever-true considerations
- those statements about the organization's information that are true long-term.

This involves combining features that should be true about all computer systems and features of the particular organization. This book can help you learn considerations that may apply to all organizations, but cannot list features of your particular organization. However we can try to give realistic examples.

In one sense the objective of analysis and design is to identify those statements about the organization's information that are likely to be true for ever and then to design their consequences into the database. These include the six considerations above since they should apply to all organizations.

(a) There are many applications. Each application program needs its own view of that subset of the data types that it uses, i.e. its own interface or subschema. The coded form of the specification of the data types used by an application program is called a subschema. Roughly, it is a subset or structure that is derivable from the corresponding schema, but including only the types of data needed for the application. It is also called an external data model.

(b) New evolving applications need new types of data and new relationships to existing types of data.
Combining (a) and (b), it should be possible to
 - change an application subschema independent of the others (as (a))
 - add new subschemas for new applications
 - add new types of data to the schema without changing any of the subschemas for the existing applications.
These together are called logical data independence.

(c) As the pattern of use changes the database team need to be able to tune the physical structure to improve performance. They also need to add new types of data to the structure of the stored data. E.g. it should be possible to change seasonally the physical structure without affecting application programs or users. This is called physical data independence.
This means every application program has to work with every physical structure that the database team may create during the life of that application. In general the physical structures will be created long after the application program coding.

For example suppose there were twenty applications and ten physical structures. That would need 200 interfaces. Surely that should be cut down if each needs significant human work to implement. This is achieved by having one overall global logical model that describes all the types of data in the database. The 20 application programs are interfaced to the global logical model giving 20 interfaces called subschemas. The 10 physical structures are also interfaced to it. At different times the ten physical structures are the ways that all the types of data in the global logical model are stored. Thus only 30 interfaces are needed. Tuning means improving performance, e.g. by changing the physical model.

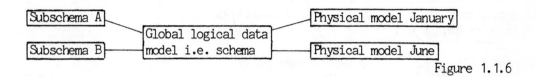

Figure 1.1.6

Using the term database control system (DBCS) to mean the software in use while applications are running, the flow between the user and the database is as follows.

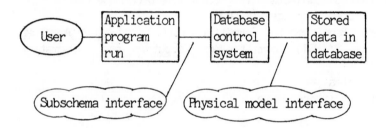

Figure 1.1.7

(d) There are several groups of users. Each group knows only some of the statements about types of information. E.g. sales staff cannot describe fully all the types of production information. So many partial pictures have to be gathered from documents and interviews and then combined together. Differences have to be reconciled. For example different people may use the names Part, Component, Assembly, Item, Material. The analyst must be sure whether or not these are the same.

It is far better to do such analysis free from any computer constraints. It is too difficult to get it right if during the modelling the analyst is forced to work within the rules and structures allowable by particular software. Indeed because such software can change it is wrong to do so when trying to develop a model that incorporates the long-term true statements about the organization's information. So the flow of ideas is as follows in building the models.

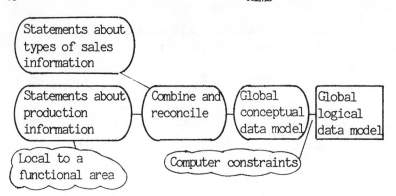

Figure 1.1.8

(e) Various organizations have proposed standards about models, schemas, subschemas, interfaces, representations, data descriptions, application programing languages and related subjects. Proposals have been made by
 - Conference on Data and System Languages (CODASYL)
 - Standards Planning And Requirements Committee (SPARC) of the American National Standards Institute (ANSI) Committee on Computers and Information Processing (X3)
 - authors of published articles
 - organizations for their own internal use.

(f) Various general purpose software schemes have been produced. Some of these are wholly or partly based on standards. Some of them, being produced before the standards get agreed, contribute to the development of the standards but then perhaps the final standards do not follow the earlier proprietary package. Sometimes the standards are not fully satisfactory and take years to become refined. There are many reasons that available software such as database management systems do not conform to standards fully. Such packages involve many compromises in their design and implementation.

In principle it should be possible to implement any conceptual data model on any database management system. In practice the development of a global logical model to fit a particular package is a specialized task, needing extensive familiarity with the package to produce good performance and flexibility. Indeed many packages do not include all the facilities needed.

Different computer constraints and database management system rules mean different global logical models and different physical models. As new versions of packages become available better models may be implemented.

All the above yields the following pattern of information and data models.

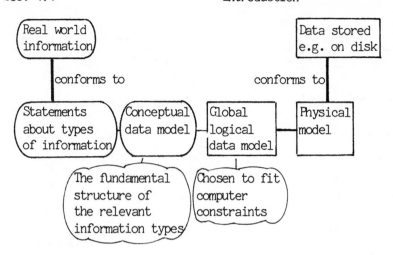

Figure 1.1.9

There is a corresponding structure of functional models.

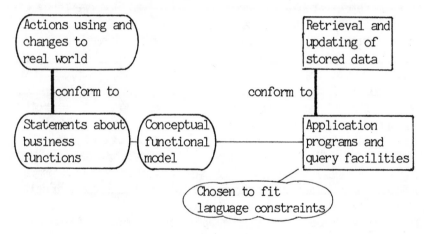

Figure 1.1.10

Database architecture

In 1970 the Joint GUIDE and SHARE Data Base Requirements Group proposed their requirements for a DBMS and introduced the entity record concept {1.5}. This concept corresponds roughly to the conceptual data model mentioned above. Since this model lays down rules independent of current practice it is sometimes called canonical. Five years later (i.e. 1975) the ANSI/X3/Standards Planning and Requirements Committee (SPARC) published a first proposal concerning the architecture of a DBMS {1.1, 1.2}.

Fig. 1.1.11 gives an overview of the whole architecture. It supports, roughly speaking, three distinct realms described by appropriate data models.

External realm
represented by several
external data models

Conceptual realm
represented by a
conceptual model

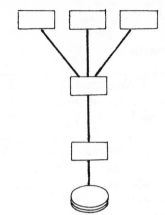

Internal realm
represented by an
internal model

Storage device

Figure 1.1.11

As shown, the ANSI/X3/SPARC architecture distinguishes between
- the conceptual realm represented by a conceptual model which corresponds essentially to the canonical representation mentioned above,
- the internal realm represented by an internal model which describes the apparent structure of all the types of stored data and
- the external realm represented by several external models, each of which provides a simplified model of the real world as seen by one or several applications. The term external model means the view of the user, application program or query language program during operations corresponding to business functions.

This three level architecture is nowadays widely accepted because it allows one to achieve a high degree of data independence. Data independence is provided by mapping the external models to a global logical model that approximates to the conceptual data model and then mapping the global logical model to the physical model as in later chapters. This includes
- storage structure independence which is the application program immunity to changes in the storage structure as described by the internal model
- growth independence which is the application program immunity to changes in the canonical representation as described by the conceptual model.

This mapping approach guarantees that an external model can change without affecting other external models. It also guarantees that an internal model can change (possibly required in the case of replacement of a disk or similar storage device) without affecting external models. Finally, it means that suitable data models can be used for different purposes, e.g. for the internal realm models which affect computer efficiency and for the external realm models which influence human efficiency. Throughout this book we shall use the ANSI/X3/SPARC terminology and refer to the canonical structure as the conceptual model.

It is true that few (if any) DBMS's actually available support a conceptual model. Nevertheless, a conceptual model independent of a DBMS is essential

because {1.10} it serves as the basis for

1 documenting and understanding the organization's data

2 defining the databases to be implemented with today's DBMSs in order to fulfil the organization's data requirements

3 planning the implementation schedule of the databases required by new computer systems

4 providing a mechanism to control use of the data

5 planning the migration from the traditional system approach to the database approach

6 planning the migration from one DBMS to the next generation of DBMS.

1.2 THE DESIGN PROCEDURE AS A WHOLE

Fig. 1.2.1 illustrates the content of this book and shows how it relates to the ANSI/X3/SPARC proposal. Chapter 1 (Aims) and Chapter 2 (Basic Mathematical Concepts) do not really belong to the design procedure as such but serve as an introduction to the subject and provide the mathematical knowledge required.

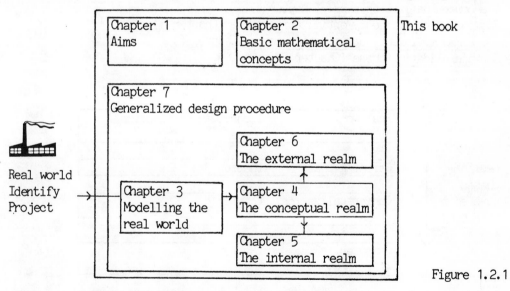

Figure 1.2.1

The real design procedure is covered by Chapters 3 to 7 which interrelate closely and should be read in that order. Chapter 7 (Generalized Design Procedure) represents a consensus that consolidates the content of Chapters 3 to 6. You should not conclude that the design procedure proposed in this book necessarily requires an ANSI/X3/SPARC database architecture. Such an assumption is not true. We have already pointed out that it is important to construct a conceptual model at a suitable level of abstraction, even if the DBMS available is such that this model will exist in manuscript or typescript form only. If

the DBMS does not support a true conceptual realm the database administrator
will then have to transform manually the conceptual design into a form that the
system does support. Appropriate guidelines will be provided in Chapters 5 and
7.

Fig. 1.2.2 shows the same idea in a slightly different manner, showing main
design objectives within the chapters.

No attempt has been made in this book to cover the project identification
(i.e. determination) phase. In other words the reader will not find an answer
to the question 'Which information subject areas of an organization should be
considered for a database?' A bibliography is provided at the end of this
chapter for you to find literature covering the identification phase. This book
tries to provide precise guidelines on how to define, structure, store and
present data once the portion of the real world one would like to consider
within a database is known.

The whole design process is divided into 5 phases
1 a <u>defining phase</u> (Chapter 3)
2 a <u>conceptualization phase</u> (Chapter 4)
3 a <u>computer efficiency optimization phase</u> (Chapter 5)
4 a <u>human efficiency optimization phase</u> (Chapter 6)
5 a <u>consolidation phase</u> (Chapter 7).

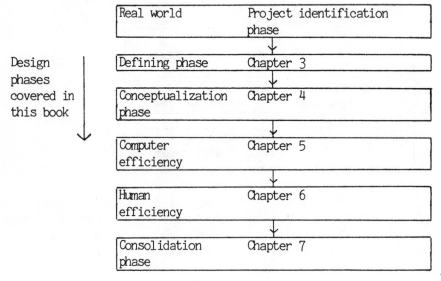

Figure 1.2.2

Design process

We now go on to discuss the content of chapters related to the real design process. This overview uses technical terms that are explained in the later chapters. If you are unfamiliar with the terms, do not worry, just skim the rest of this chapter and turn to Chapter 2.

The Content of Chapter 3

This chapter discusses how to define the information resources of an organization once the analyst knows which portion of the real world to consider.

Real world	Project identification phase	
Chapter 3	Defining phase	Modelling the real world
3.1	Primitives of the real world	Entities Entity properties Property values Entity relationships
3.2	Conceptual objects	Entity sets Relationship sets Entity attributes Relationship attributes
3.3	Representing conceptual objects by data	Entity key Diagrammatical and tabular representation of entity sets, relationship sets and attributes
Chapter 4		

Figure 1.2.3

As illustrated we first introduce what we consider as primitives of the real world: entities, entity properties, property values and entity relationships (Section 3.1). The identification phase provides these elements as input for the defining phase.

We then introduce the concepts of entity set, relationship set, entity attribute and relationship attribute (Section 3.2). These are usually called conceptual objects. They allow the analyst to classify ideas about the real world and to base the design process on firm theory.

Section 3.3 discusses how conceptual objects can be represented by means of data. We introduce a diagrammatical representation and a more convenient tabular representation.

The Content of Chapter 4

Chapter 4 is central to this book. It explains how to analyse associations between types of information. It discusses how to represent conceptual objects such that each single fact is only represented once. For example that a person has a salary and is located in London are two different facts and should be considered separately. The concept of single places for single facts is not only important to achieve a higher degree of data independence but also follows from basing the design process on a firm theory of conceptual objects.

Section 4.1 gives a procedure to produce a rough model of part of the real world.

Section 4.2 shows how this rough real world model can be transformed into a better model represented by a set of irreducible units called elementary relations (ERs). Elementary relations satisfy the requirement for a single place for a single fact. They have the advantage that further steps in the design process can be based on a firm theory.

Section 4.3 shows that the set of elementary relations represents a directed graph. This can be represented by a connectivity matrix. Applying the transitive law to the directed graph usually produces additional elementary relations. These additional elementary relations represent relationships which the analyst might have overlooked while specifying conceptual objects. In general it is possible to derive further elementary relations from any incomplete collection of such.

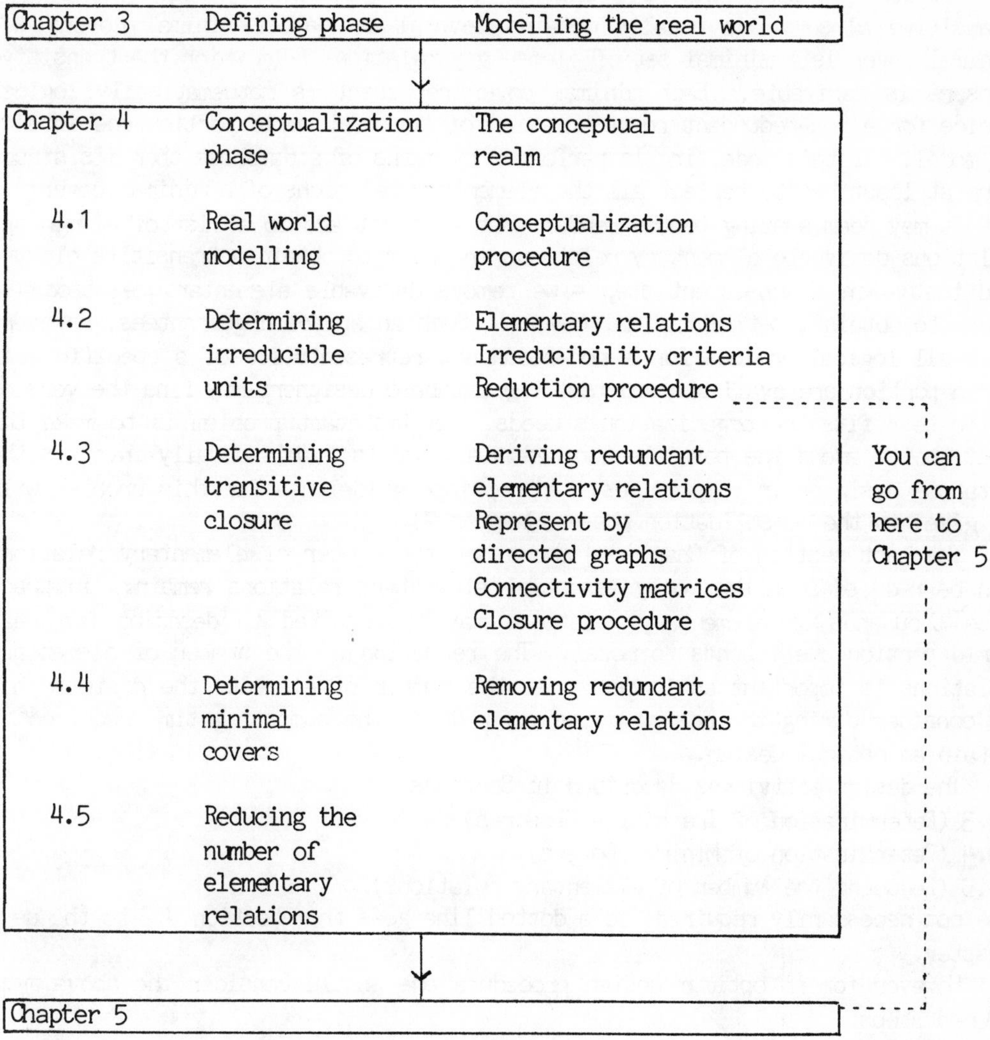

Chapter 3	Defining phase	Modelling the real world

Chapter 4	Conceptualization phase	The conceptual realm
4.1	Real world modelling	Conceptualization procedure
4.2	Determining irreducible units	Elementary relations Irreducibility criteria Reduction procedure
4.3	Determining transitive closure	Deriving redundant elementary relations Represent by directed graphs Connectivity matrices Closure procedure
4.4	Determining minimal covers	Removing redundant elementary relations
4.5	Reducing the number of elementary relations	

You can go from here to Chapter 5

Chapter 5		

Figure 1.2.4

The set of all elementary relations (including the derived ones) describes a specific portion of the real world exhaustively and is called a transitive closure. There is always a unique transitive closure for a given set of elementary relations. Section 4.3 presents a procedure applicable to a connectivity matrix to produce the transitive closure for a set of elementary relations.

Section 4.4 shows that by removing derivable elementary relations from a transitive closure one usually obtains several so called minimal covers. A minimal cover is a minimal set of elementary relations from which the transitive closure is derivable. Each minimal cover represents a mathematically logical choice for a non-redundant representation of the real world portion one intends to model. If this modelling is performed by means of a database then its structure at least has to reflect all the elementary relations of a minimal cover.

It may seem amazing to the reader that we first add to a list of elementary relations derivable elementary relations in order to obtain a transitive closure and that - in a subsequent step - we remove derivable elementary relations in order to obtain a set of minimal covers. Such an approach guarantees, however, that all logical choices for a non-redundant representation of a specific real world portion are available and that the database designers may find the version which best fits the organization's needs. An important problem is to make the best choice among the possible non-redundant models. This usually involves the database designer in compromises. Appropriate guidelines for this problem will be given in the consolidation phase (Chapter 7).

The last section of Chapter 4 shows how the number of elementary relations can be reduced such that only essential elementary relations remain. In practice thousands of elementary relations may be required to describe the real world portion one intends to model. The reduction of the number of elementary relations is important as it decreases the number of elements the designer has to consider during the design phase and reduces the computing time required to obtain an optimum design.

The design activities described in Sections
4.3 (Determination of Transitive Closures)
4.4 (Determination of Minimal Covers)
4.5 (Reducing the Number of elementary relations)
are not necessarily required, so a dotted line goes from Section 4.2 to the next chapter.

However for an optimum design procedure one should consider the above mentioned steps.

The Content of Chapter 5

Chapter 5 concerns computer efficiency. Elementary relations can be glued and stored together in order to minimize the number of accesses.

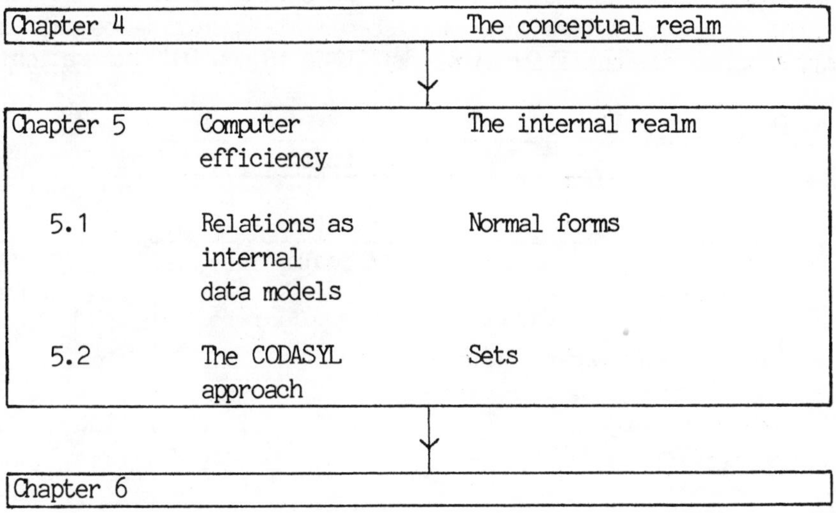

Chapter 4		The conceptual realm

Chapter 5	Computer efficiency	The internal realm
5.1	Relations as internal data models	Normal forms
5.2	The CODASYL approach	Sets

Chapter 6		

Figure 1.2.5

In Section 5.1 we first behave as if the designer were able to define the internal model by means of wider relations called n-ary relations. We show that the creation of n-ary relations has to follow certain rules. This is particularly true if the n-ary relations have to be consistent with a set of elementary relations as defined for the conceptual model and if these n-ary relations must not lead to problems in storage updating operations. Update means insert, modify and delete stored data. We show that the normalization criteria proposed by E.F. Codd, R.F. Boyce, W. Kent, R. Fagin and C. Zaniolo are extremely useful.

Section 5.2 discusses how to interpret an internal model described by n-ary relations for implementation with a CODASYL-based DBMS.

The Content of Chapter 6

Chapter 6 concerns human efficiency. This requires that data can be provided to a user in a suitable form - a form adapted to the user's skills and adapted to the problem to be solved. Through the 1970s experts have discussed whether the most suitable form uses hierarchical, network or relational data structures. We strongly believe that the answer is not 'either or' but 'as well as'. One should be able to transform a given stored data representation into any other form in order to facilitate data use. Thus some future DBMSs may support all of hierachies, networks and relations on the external realm.

This approach, called structure type coexistence, is promising because it may tremendously simplify the migration from past DBMSs to new DBMS generations.

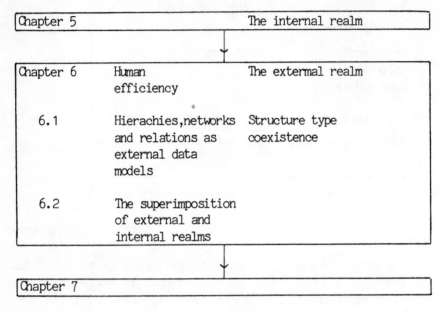

Chapter 5		The internal realm

Chapter 6	Human efficiency	The external realm
6.1	Hierachies,networks and relations as external data models	Structure type coexistence
6.2	The superimposition of external and internal realms	

Chapter 7		

Figure 1.2.6

Section 6.1 explains hierarchical, network and relational data structures and discusses the concept of structure type coexistence.

Section 6.2 covers some problems to be avoided at time of use. The user's retrievals and updates are <u>manipulations</u> of stored data corresponding to real world information. These manipulations have to conform to the user's view of part of the conceptual model. They also have to conform to models in the computer system, and the DBMS and application software must ensure the conformity, to maintain integrity and accuracy.

Thus the database administrator has to observe some important restrictions when designing external data models used for storage updating manipulations. These restrictions are because of the superimposition in which the external data models are mapped to the conceptual model which in its turn is mapped to the internal data model.

This means that any storage operation (retrieval or update) specified on the external model has to be reflected by means of corresponding operations on the internal model without destroying thereby the consistency with the conceptual model.

The Content of Chapter 7

Chapter 7 represents a consensus of the preceding chapters and consolidates their content.

Chapter 6		The external realm

↓

Chapter 7	Consolidation phase	Generalized design procedure
7.1	Consolidation phase	
7.2	Conclusion	

Figure 1.2.7

In Section 7.1 we first discuss a so called consolidation phase. The problem is as follows. In Chapter 4 we pointed out that it is usually possible to represent a specific real world portion by means of several non-redundant models called minimal covers. We also pointed out that an important problem - to be solved by the database administrator usually - is to find the minimal cover which best fits the organization's needs. For the consolidation phase we assume that the best solution is to choose the minimal cover (i.e. the global logical model) whose physical implementation requires fewest machine operations when mapping the internal model to the organization's most crucial external models, i.e. when running the commonest applications.

The procedure discussed in Section 7.1 allows the analyst to obtain precisely that minimal cover.

We would like to stress the fact that the consolidation phase like the preceding design phases does not require a DBMS with a three level architecture as proposed by the ANSI/X3/Standards Planning and Requirements Committee (SPARC). Most DBMS actually available only support a two level architecture (i.e. an external and an internal realm). Nevertheless it is desirable to obtain an internal model both which satisfactorily models the mini world (presumably defined by means of a conceptual model in manuscript or typescript form) and which requires fewest machine operations when mapping the internal model to the external models for the organization's most frequent applications.

EXERCISES

Solutions are in Appendix 2.

1 Information is difficult to define, though a well-understood concept. What features must computerized information have for staff to be able to act on it?

2 How does a database differ from a file of records on a magnetic tape, where the magnetic tape records are so structured that they can be used for the current application?

3 Give the term for each of the following.
(a) As apparently structured, for example the data structure as viewed by the database administrator or an application programmer, in contrast to the physical structure
(b) Covering all types of information for all users
(c) Independent of computer hardware and software constraints
(d) Stored information should not be lost or become inconsistent due to computer or human error
(e) Stored information should agree with reality
(f) People and organizations expect information about themselves not to be misused or disclosed in unauthorized ways
(g) The mechanisms for ensuring the moral right described in (f) above
(h) To obtain information from stored data e.g. by obtaining a copy of the relevant stored data item occurrences.
(i) To do any combination of store new data, modify existing stored data (i.e. change stored values), and delete stored data.

4 Distinguish logical data independence from physical data independence.

5 Why is it desirable to have a database design in which each fact is stored only once?

REFERENCES AND BIBLIOGRAPHY

1.1 ANSI/X3/SPARC: Interim Report: Study Group on Data Base Management Systems. Bulletin of ACM - SIGMOD the Special Interest Group on Management of Data, Volume 7, Number 2, 1975
1.2 ANSI/X3/SPARC DBMS Framework, 'Report of the Study Group on Database Management Systems', Tsichritzis, D.; Klug, A.: Eds., AFIPS PRESS, 210 Summit Avenue, Montvale, New Jersey 07645, 1978
1.3 Date, C.J.: 'An Introduction to Database Systems', Addison-Wesley Publishing Company, 1977 (2nd Ed), 1975 (1st Ed)

1.4 GUIDE: 'Establishing the Data Administration Function', GUIDE Establishing the Data Administration Function Project, June 1977

1.5 GUIDE and SHARE: 'Requirements for a Data Base Management System', The Joint GUIDE and SHARE Data Base Requirements Group, November 11, 1970

1.6 Iverson, K.: 'A Programming Language', John Wiley, 1962

1.7 Lyon, J.K.: 'The Database Administrator', John Wiley and Sons, 1976

1.8 Martin, J.: 'Computer Data-Base Organization', 2nd Ed., Prentice-Hall, Inc., Englewood Cliffs, New Jersey 07632, 1977

1.9 Vetter, M.: 'Hierarchische, Netzwerkfoermige und Relationalartige Datenbankstrukturen (mit ausgewaehlten Beispielen aus einem Fertigungsunternehmen)', Ph.D. Dissertation, ETH Zurich (Swiss Institute of Technology), Juris-Verlag, 1976

1.10 Walker, W.A.: 'Designing a Conceptual Data Model', GUIDE 45, Atlanta Georgia, November, 1977

Bibliography for the Identification Phase

1.11 Coleman, R.J.: 'MIS: Management Dimensions', Holden-Day, Inc., 1973

1.12 Couger, J.D.: 'System Analysis Techniques', John Wiley and Sons, 1974

1.13 Davis, G.B.: 'Management Information Systems, Conceptual Foundations, Structure, and Development', McGraw-Hill Series in Management Information Systems, 1974

1.14 IBM: 'Business Systems Planning, Information Systems Planning Guide', IBM Form Number GE20-0527, 1975

1.15 Langefors, B.: 'Information Systems - Theoretical Aspects of Information Systems for Management', Information Processing 74, North-Holland Publishing Company, 1974

1.16 Langefors, B.: 'Information Analysis and Data Base Structures Report TRITA - IBADB - 1012', Institution for Informations Behandling Royal Institute of Technology, Stockholm, 1974

1.17 Lundeberg, M.: 'Information Analaysis as a Practical Tool, General Support TRITA - IBADB - 4206', Royal Institute of Technology, Stockholm, 1972

1.18 Lundeberg, M.: 'On Information Systems Work. Further Development and Practical Application of a Theoretically Based Information Systems Work Methodology TRITA - IBADB - 4001', Royal Institute of Technology, Stockholm, 1972

1.19 Nissen, H.E.: 'A Method for the Description of Object Systems in Information Systems Work TRITA - IBADB - 4403', Royal Institute of Techno.ogy, Stockholm, 1972

1.20 Nissen, H.E.: 'Formalized Description of Object Systems. A Tool in the Development of Information Systems TRITA - IBADB 4204', Royal Institute of Technology, Stockholm, 1972.

1.21 Parkin, A.: Systems Analysis. Edward Arnold (Publishers) Ltd., London, 1980 ISBN 0-7131-2800-3

2

Basic Mathematical Concepts

Chapter 2 consists of two sections. Section 2.1 reviews some elementary concepts of the theory of sets that are needed for understanding the principles underlying database design.

Section 2.2 relates the theory to database notions. This subject is an important prerequisite for later chapters. The reader already familiar with the theory of sets is urged to study at least Section 2.2.

2.1 INTRODUCTION TO SETS

A set is a named and well defined collection of objects called <u>members</u> or <u>elements</u>. It can be defined
 - by listing all its members (<u>tabular form</u> or <u>extensive form</u> of a set) or
 - by stating the properties the members have to satisfy (<u>set builder form</u> or <u>intensive form</u> of a set).

The name of a set is usually written in upper case (capital) letter(s) or with an initial such letter. An element is usually written in lower case.

<u>Example 2.1.1</u>

The set of all students of a college may be named STUDENTS. For simplicity we suppose there are only four members, as here.

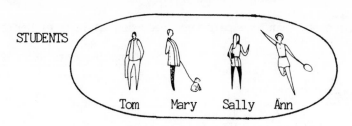

STUDENTS

Tom   Mary   Sally   Ann

Figure 2.1.1

We list them as
$$STUDENTS = \{Tom, Mary, Sally, Ann\}$$
i.e. the members are separated by commas and enclosed in curly brackets. This
listing of the members is called the <u>extensive</u> form. Curly brackets are used to
enclose a definition of a set.

The <u>set builder</u> form of STUDENTS is written
$$STUDENTS = \{x \mid x \text{ is a student of the college}\}.$$
This reads 'STUDENTS is the set of x's such that x is a student of the college.'
The <u>vertical bar</u> means 'such that'.

However
$$NICE\text{-}GIRLS = \{x \mid x \text{ is a nice girl}\}$$
is not a set since the expression 'nice girl' is not well defined.

A set is characterized by two facts
 - members occur only once in the list
 - the ordering of the members within the set is immaterial.
Thus
$$STUDENTS\text{-}A = \{Tom, Mary, Sally, Ann\}$$
$$STUDENTS\text{-}B = \{Mary, Sally, Ann, Tom\}$$
$$STUDENTS\text{-}C = \{Ann, Sally, Mary, Tom\}$$
are all identical.

The <u>list</u>
$$STUDENTS\text{-}D = \langle Tom, Mary, Sally, Ann, Tom \rangle$$
is not a set since it contains a particular element (e.g. Tom) twice.

Curly brackets denote a set whereas angle brackets denote a list.

In many situations duplicates are not allowed so as to ensure self-consistency of information, e.g. invoice numbers form a set since they are all
distinct. But the surnames of a group of people form a list because a name may
occur several times.

Cardinality of Sets

The number of distinct members of a set is called the <u>cardinality</u>.

The previous STUDENTS had 4 members. In 1964 there were 99 twins born in
the Sheffield Hospital for Women, according to some computing R. N. Maddison
did in January 1965. Since this excluded triplets and quads people said the

cardinality should be even. But one pair were recorded as born either side of the New Year.

Membership Denotation

The fact that Sally belongs to STUDENTS is written
$$\text{Sally} \in \text{STUDENTS}.$$
That Max does not belong is written
$$\text{Max} \notin \text{STUDENTS}.$$

Equality and Inequality of Sets

Two sets having the same members are called equal. We write
$$\text{STUDENTS-A} = \text{STUDENTS-B}$$
meaning each member of one set is a member of the other.
Inequality is denoted by $\neq$. For example
$$\{\text{Fred, Joe, Richard}\} \neq \text{STUDENTS-A}.$$

Null Set

A set containing no elements is called the null set. It is said to be empty or void and is denoted by the symbol $\emptyset$ or $\{\}$.
At the start of a financial period the set of people who have paid is empty (unless anyone paid in advance). The set is well defined at all times. Membership grows. The stored members of the set may be deleted at the end of the period, making it empty again.

Subset or set inclusion

Set A is a subset of B (or A is included in B) means each member of A is also a member of B. That A is contained in B is written
$$A \subseteq B$$
The word subset means either equality or inequality.
A proper subset means some of B do not belong to A, written
$$A \subset B$$
E.g. for STUDENTS = {Tom, Mary, Sally, Ann} the subset
$$\text{MATH-STUDENTS} = \{\text{Mary, Ann}\}$$
represents the students enrolled for mathematics. This subset is a proper subset.

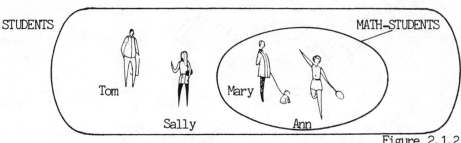

STUDENTS

MATH-STUDENTS

Tom

Mary

Sally

Ann

Figure 2.1.2

In general it is possible for all students to do a particular course, so it would be wrong modelling to insist that the mathematics students were a proper subset. Similarly, although some manufactured items were normally made only to be used as components in larger assembled items it would be wrong to insist they could not be for sale. Someday a customer might want such.

Disjointness of sets

If no element of set A belongs to set B and no element of set B is in set A then the sets A and B are disjoint. For example analysis of an organization would show that an order cannot be for more than one customer. So the sets of orders for different customers are disjoint, yet every order belongs to one such set.

The union of sets

The union of the sets A and B is the set of elements that belong to A or B or both, written

$$A \cup B.$$

Formally we write

$$A \cup B = \{x \mid x \in A \text{ or } x \in B\}.$$

Example 2.1.2

Let

$$\text{PHYSICS-STUDENTS} = \text{PHYS} = \{\text{Mary, Tom}\}$$
$$\text{CHEM-STUDENTS} = \text{CHEM} = \{\text{Mary, Ann, Sally}\}$$

be the sets of students doing physics and chemistry. The union is

$$\text{SCIENCE-STUDENTS} = \text{PHYS} \cup \text{CHEM} = \{\text{Mary, Tom, Sally, Ann}\}.$$

Note that Mary, who belongs to both, appears only once in the union, as in Fig. 2.1.3.

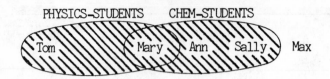

Shading represents the union.

Figure 2.1.3

The intersection of sets

The <u>intersection</u> of two sets A and B is the set of all elements that belong to A and to B, written

$$A \cap B.$$

For example

$$PHYS \cap CHEM = \{Mary\}.$$

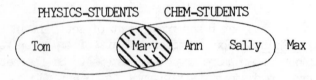

Shading represents the intersection.

Figure 2.1.4

Formally the intersection of A and B is written
$$A \cap B = \{x \mid x \in A \text{ and } x \in B\}.$$
Disjointness is equivalent to having an empty intersection.

The difference of sets

The <u>difference</u> of two sets A and B is the set of elements belonging to A but not belonging to B, written

$$A - B.$$

This idea is needed e.g. for orders delivered but not paid for. The formal definition is in Exercise 8 at the end of this section.

Example 2.1.3

Let

$$PHYS = \{Mary, Tom\}$$
$$CHEM = \{Mary, Ann, Sally\}.$$

The difference (i.e. the set of students doing physics but not chemistry) is
PHYS - CHEM = {Tom}.

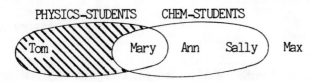

Shading represents the difference PHYS - CHEM.

Figure 2.1.5

The difference the other way round
CHEM - PHYS
means those doing chemistry but not physics, i.e.
CHEM - PHYS = {Ann, Sally}.

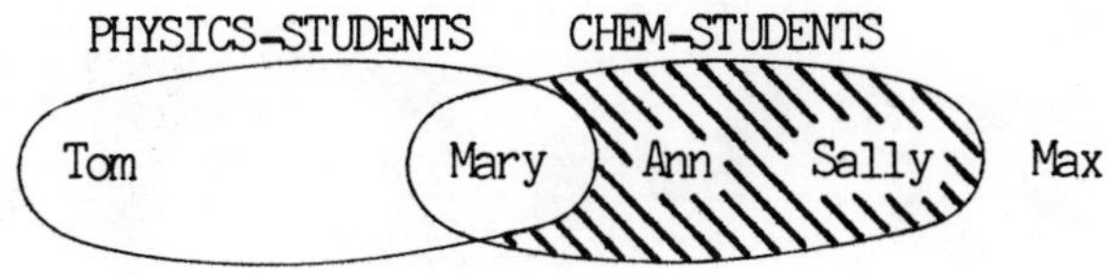

Shading represents CHEM - PHYS.

Figure 2.1.6

The universal set

The universal set, denoted by U or E (for entirity) means all possible ele-
ments in the context.
For the previous example
U = {Ann, Mary, Max, Sally, Tom}.
In diagrams the entirity can be shown by a surrounding rectangle, but it is
usually omitted where not needed.

The complement of a set

The complement of a set A is written A' meaning U - A, i.e. the elements not
in set A. E.g. the complement of items paid is those outstanding.

Shading represents A'

Figure 2.1.7

In english 'not' means complement, 'and' means intersection and 'or' means union when applied to members of sets. When unbracketed their precedence is in the order 'not', 'and', 'or'. E.g.

Not A and B or C

means

(((Not A) and B) or C).

The following rules, called <u>laws</u>, apply to the operations of union, intersection and complement.

Indempotent laws
$$A \cup A = A$$
$$A \cap A = A$$

Associative laws
$$(A \cup B) \cup C = A \cup (B \cup C)$$
$$(A \cap B) \cap C = A \cap (B \cap C)$$

Commutative laws
$$A \cup B = B \cup A$$
$$A \cap B = B \cap A$$

Distributive laws
$$A \cup (B \cap C) = (A \cup B) \cap (A \cup C)$$
$$A \cap (B \cup C) = (A \cap B) \cup (A \cap C)$$

Identity laws
$$A \cup \emptyset = A$$
$$A \cup U = U$$
$$A \cap U = A$$
$$A \cap \emptyset = \emptyset$$

Complement laws
   A $\cup$ A' = U
   (A')' = A
   A $\cap$ A' = $\emptyset$
   U' = $\emptyset$
   $\emptyset$ ' = U

De Morgan's laws
   (A $\cup$ B)' = A' $\cap$ B'
   (A $\cap$ B)' = A' $\cup$ B'

Figure 2.1.8

We show pictorially some of the less obvious laws.   Some others are in Exercise 9 at the end of this section. For a more formal treatment we recommend {2.8}.

Associative laws

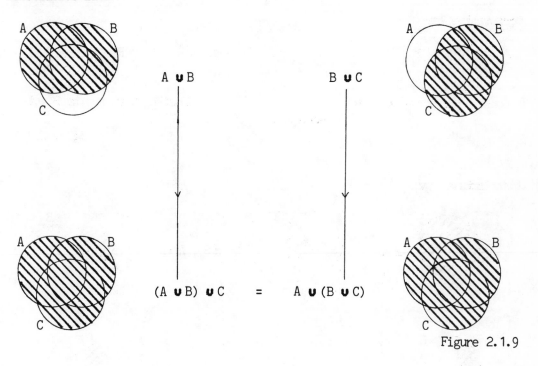

$A \cup B$ $B \cup C$

(A $\cup$ B) $\cup$ C   =   A $\cup$ (B $\cup$ C)

Figure 2.1.9

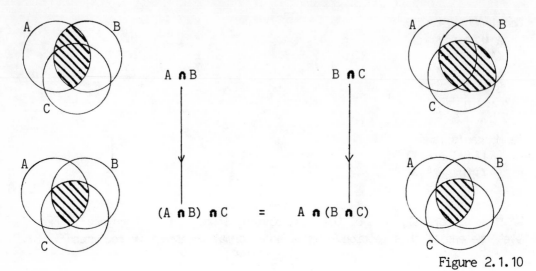

$$A \cap B \qquad\qquad B \cap C$$

$$(A \cap B) \cap C \quad = \quad A \cap (B \cap C)$$

Figure 2.1.10

Commutative law

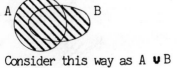 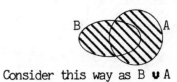

Consider this way as $A \cup B$ Consider this way as $B \cup A$

Hence $A \cup B = B \cup A$

Figure 2.1.11

Distributive law

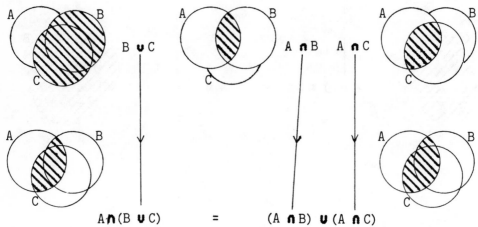

$B \cup C \qquad A \cap B \quad A \cap C$

$$A \cap (B \cup C) \qquad = \qquad (A \cap B) \cup (A \cap C)$$

Figure 2.1.12

De Morgan's law

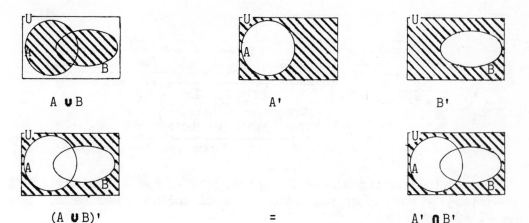

A ∪ B   A'   B'

(A ∪ B)'   =   A' ∩ B'

Figure 2.1.13

Ordered Pair

An ordered pair consists of two elements, say a and b. One of the elements, say a, is considered as the first element and the other as the second element. An ordered pair is written

<a, b>.

Angle brackets are used because it is a list of length 2.

The Cartesian product of sets

The Cartesian product (or product set) of two sets, say A and B, is the set of all ordered pairs <a, b> where a belongs to A and b to B. We write

A x B

and read it 'A cross B'. In symbols this is

A x B = {<a, b> | a ∈ A and b ∈ B}.

Example 2.1.4

Let

GIRLS = {Ann, Su}
BOYS = {Tom, Bob, Paul}

The Cartesian product of GIRLS and BOYS is all possible girl-boy friendships.

GIRLS x BOYS = {<Ann, Tom>, <Ann, Bob>, <Ann, Paul>,
               <Su, Tom>, <Su, Bob>, <Su, Paul>}

Each pair such as ⟨Ann, Tom⟩ is one element of the Cartesian product as Fig.
2.1.14.

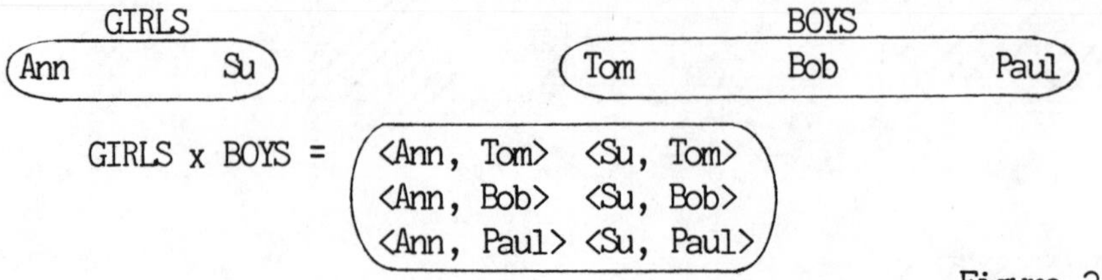

GIRLS   BOYS

(Ann   Su)   (Tom   Bob   Paul)

GIRLS x BOYS = (⟨Ann, Tom⟩ ⟨Su, Tom⟩
                  ⟨Ann, Bob⟩ ⟨Su, Bob⟩
                  ⟨Ann, Paul⟩ ⟨Su, Paul⟩)

Figure 2.1.14

A manufacturer of tights needs to say what size - large, medium, small - is
appropriate for every cross combination of height and hip measurements. This
has a similar structure.

Example 2.1.5

Let A = {a, b}. The Cartesian product of A with itself is
$$A \times A = \{⟨a, a⟩, ⟨a, b⟩, ⟨b, a⟩, ⟨b, b⟩\}.$$

Ordered n-Tuple

The concept of an ordered pair can be extended to an _ordered n-tuple_ -
spoken to rhyme with 'couple'
$$⟨a_1, a_2, \ldots a_n⟩.$$
For example the address 1250 Valley Street, Denver, Colorado 80123 is a
5-tuple of the general form
$$⟨Number, Road, City, State, Zip-code⟩.$$
In this structure the Number of the plot and the Zip-code can be the same - they
are both integers. The City and State can also be the same.

The Cartesian product of more than two sets

The concept of Cartesian product can be extended to more than two sets. The
Cartesian product of the five sets A, B ... E consists of all ordered 5-tuples
⟨a,b ... e⟩ where a belongs to set A, b to B ... In general for n sets
$$A_1 \times \ldots A_n = \{⟨a_1, \ldots a_n⟩ \mid a_1 \text{ belongs to } A_1 \ldots a_n \in A_n\}$$
This corresponds to every possible Number with every possible Road, every
possible City, every State and every Zip-code, not just the addresses that actually occur.

Example 2.1.6

Let

        COURSES = {Math, Chem, Phys}
    CLASSROOMS = {R1, R2}
    PROFESSORS = {Brown, Smith}.

The Cartesian product of COURSES, CLASSROOMS and PROFESSORS represents all possible course, classroom and professor combinations, i.e.

COURSES x CLASSROOMS x PROFESSORS =

                {<Math, R1, Brown>, <Math, R1, Smith>,
                 <Math, R2, Brown>, <Math, R2, Smith>,
                 <Chem, R1, Brown>, <Chem, R1, Smith>,
                 ... <Phys, R2, Smith>}.

The cardinality of this is 3 x 2 x 2 = 12 (i.e. the cardinality of COURSES times that of CLASSROOMS times that of PROFESSORS.

Binary Relation

In real life, pairs of objects can be associated. Of all possible pairs say of men and women some are actually associated in a particular way at a particular time while others are not. This is true of marriage, and also in associating people with people meaning who works under whom.

A binary relation (say R) of set A and set B is a subset of the Cartesian product A x B. It is written

                R(A,B)   or   R (A, B)

and satisfies

                R(A,B) $\subseteq$ A x B

Example 2.1.7

Let BOYS = {Bob, Paul} and GIRLS = {Ann, Mary, Su}. Then a binary relation can be defined

            BROTHER-OF = {<Bob, Ann>, <Bob, Mary>, <Paul, Su>}

meaning Bob is the brother of Ann and Mary and Paul is the brother of Su. Thus

            BROTHER-OF (BOY, GIRL) $\subseteq$ BOY x GIRL.

The order of the elements of a pair is important, e.g. <Ann, Bob> does not belong since Ann is not the brother of Bob.

Example 2.1.8

For another example the sizes of grey trousers currently in stock in a particular shop are certain combinations of waist and leg measurements

            GREY-TROUSERS-IN-STOCK $\subseteq$ WAIST x LEG.

This is a set of ordered pairs. The order is important - waist and leg measurements cannot be interchanged. Suppose at noon on Monday 2 July 1979 the sizes available were as follows.

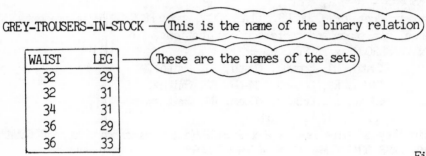

GREY-TROUSERS-IN-STOCK ──(This is the name of the binary relation)

WAIST	LEG
32	29
32	31
34	31
36	29
36	33

──(These are the names of the sets)

Figure 2.1.15

Such a table with two columns is a binary relation - binary meaning two columns. Its specification would be written
$$\text{GREY-TROUSERS-IN-STOCK (WAIST, LEG).}$$

Binary relations can be drawn in other ways - as diagrams and as graphs.

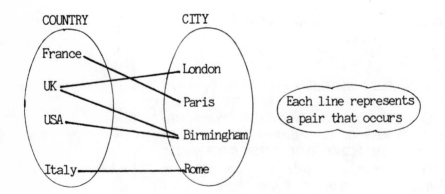

COUNTRY   CITY

France
London
UK
Paris
USA
Birmingham
Italy
Rome

(Each line represents a pair that occurs)

Figure 2.1.16

We could draw as a graph the relation
$$\text{PERSON (HEIGHT, WEIGHT).}$$

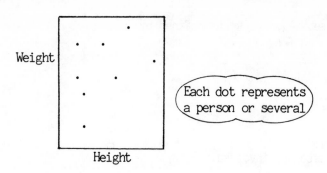

Figure 2.1.17

Two people can have the same height or the same weight or both, the dots represent the combinations of height and weight that occur. There is only one dot for two people who have exactly the same height and weight.

A binary relation is a <u>set</u> of ordered pairs, i.e. an ordered pair cannot occur twice.

The reverse of a binary relation

Every relation R from set A to set B has a reverse relation from set B to set A. E.g. if R says what leg sizes are available for a given waist, the reverse says what waist sizes are available for a given leg size.

The reverse relation is defined by
$$R^{-1} = \{<b,a> \mid <a,b> \text{ belongs to } R\}.$$
For example
$$\text{GREY-TROUSERS-IN-STOCK}^{-1} = \{<29,32>, <29,36>, \ldots <33,36>\}.$$

Relation

The concept of a binary relation can be extended to n-ary relations. For example what kinds of car (Make, Model, Year, Color) are available for sale at a dealer's can be represented as a relation
KINDS-OF-CAR (MAKE, MODEL, COLOR, YEAR).

MAKE	MODEL	COLOR	YEAR
Ford	Granada	Blue	1979
Vauxhall	Viva	Red	1978
Citroen	GS Club	Yellow	1979

Names of sets

Values from the sets

Figure 2.1.18

From such tables can be answered enquiries such as 'Are there any 1979 cars?'

A relation between the n sets A_1, ... A_n is defined by
$$R \subseteq A_1 \times ... A_n$$
and is written
$$R(A_1, ... A_n).$$

A relation is called
<u>unary</u> (or said to be of degree 1) if n = 1
<u>binary</u> (or degree 2) if n = 2
<u>ternary</u> (or degree 3) if n = 3
<u>n-ary</u> (or of <u>degree</u> n) if n sets are involved.

Functions

A function is a special kind of relationship between two sets, say A and B. Each member of set A is associated with exactly one member of set B. So for sets with finite cardinality a function is a subset of the Cartesian product A x B such that each member of A appears exactly once. A member of B may appear none, one or more times. Two or more members of A can be associated to the same member of B.

A function is denoted by
$$f: A \rightarrow B$$
which reads 'f is a function of A into B'.

The set A is called the <u>domain</u> of the function and B is called the co-domain. For a particular a ∈ A the corresponding b ∈ B assigned to a is called the <u>image</u> of a and is denoted by
$$f(a)$$
which reads 'f of a'.

Names of functions are usually written in lower case (i.e. small) letters.

<u>Example 2.1.9</u>

Let EMPLOYEE# = {E1, E2, E3, E4} and NO-OF-YEARS = {20, 30, 35, 50, 60}.

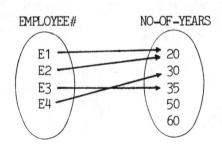

We have drawn arrowheads to help you think from E1 to 20, but eventually you can omit them in diagrams of occurrences as the association may be used either way.

Figure 2.1.19

Then
$$\text{Age-is: EMPLOYEE\#} \rightarrow \text{NO-OF-YEARS}$$

is a function of EMPLOYEE# into NO-OF-YEARS since to each element in the set EM-
PLOYEE# there is assigned a unique element of the set NO-OF-YEARS representing
the age of that employee. The function Age-is can be represented as a set of
ordered pairs such as

$$AGE-IS = \{\langle E1, 20\rangle, \langle E2, 20\rangle, \langle E3, 35\rangle, \langle E4, 30\rangle\}$$

or as Fig. 2.1.19.

For example the image of E1 is 20, i.e.

$$Age-is(E1) = 20.$$

We have used Age-is as the name of a function, with an initial capital
letter and a hyphen to distinguish it from such ordinary english words as 'age'.
There is also a set named AGE-IS.

Note that it is not required that for a function $f: A \longrightarrow B$ each element in
B appears necessarily as an image of some elements in A. The elements in B appearing as the image of at least one element in A are called the <u>range</u>. The
range of the function $f: A \longrightarrow B$ is denoted by

$$f(A)$$

and represents a subset of B, i.e.

$$f(A) \subseteq B.$$

Example 2.1.10

For the above function

$$Age-is: EMPLOYEE\# \longrightarrow NO-OF-YEARS$$

the range is

$$Age-is \ (EMPLOYEE\#) = \{20, 30, 35\}.$$

Notice that

$$Age-is \ (EMPLOYEE\#) \subseteq NO-OF-YEARS.$$

(Unfortunately confusingly, some people say 'mapping' for what we have
called a function. We say 'mapping' for any rule of association from elements
of a domain to elements of a codomain, including in particular where an element
of the domain is associated to more than one of the codomain. This is clarified
in Section 2.2.)

Functions of Cartesian Products

The domain and the co-domain of a function may each be subsets of Cartesian
products of any number of sets. Thus

$$f: A \longrightarrow B$$

with

$$A = \{\langle a_1, \ldots a_m\rangle\} \subseteq A_1 \ x \ \ldots \ A_m$$
$$B = \{\langle b_1, \ldots b_n\rangle\} \subseteq B_1 \ x \ \ldots \ B_n$$

represents a function so long as to each tuple in A there is assigned one and
only one tuple in B.

Such a function is usually denoted by
$$f: A_1, \ldots A_m \longrightarrow B_1, \ldots B_n.$$
The right side is an ordered collection regarded as a single group. So also
is the left side.

A realistic example is given in Section 2.2, page 49.

The product function or composition function

The product function or composition function is defined as follows. Assume
the functions $f: A \longrightarrow B$ and $g: B \longrightarrow C$ exist. Each $a \in A$ has an image $f(a)$ in
B – the co-domain of the function f. B is also the domain of the function g.
Thus, each $b \in B$ (and particularly each image $f(a)$ in B) has an image $g(b)$ in C.
This means that for each element $a \in A$ there exists a corresponding element
$g(f(a))$ in C.

In other words there exists a function of A into C. This function is called
the product function or composition function of f and g and is denoted by either
$$(g \circ f) \text{ or } (gf).$$
We say either 'g oh f' or 'g of f'. It means do f first then do g.

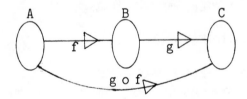

Figure 2.1.20

The image derived by the product function (g o f), e.g. (g o f)(a), is
defined to be the image derived by the function g applied on the image derived
by the function f, i.e.
$$(g \circ f)(a) = g(f(a)).$$
That is why we write gf not fg for doing f first then g.

Example 2.1.11

Let
$$EMPLOYEE = \{E1, E2, E3, E4\}$$
$$DEPARTMENT = \{D1, D2, D3\}$$
$$MANAGER = \{M1, M2, M3\}.$$

Furthermore, let the functions

$$\text{Works-for: EMPLOYEE} \longrightarrow \text{DEPARTMENT}$$
$$\text{Headed-by: DEPARTMENT} \longrightarrow \text{MANAGER}$$

be as in Fig. 2.1.21.

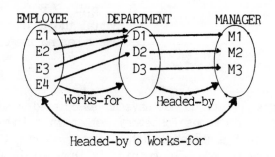

Figure 2.1.21

The product function

$$\text{(Headed-by o Works-for): EMPLOYEE} \longrightarrow \text{MANAGER}$$

i.e. the function

$$\text{Managed-by: EMPLOYEE} \longrightarrow \text{MANAGER}$$

can be computed by

$$
\begin{aligned}
\text{(Headed-by o Works-for)(E1)} &= \text{Headed-by(Works-for(E1))} \\
&= \text{Headed-by(D1)} \\
&= \text{M1} \\
\text{(Headed-by o Works-for)(E2)} &= \text{Headed-by(Works-for(E2))} \\
&= \text{Headed-by(D1)} \\
&= \text{M1} \\
\text{(Headed-by o Works-for)(E3)} &= \text{Headed-by(Works-for(E3))} \\
&= \text{Headed-by(D1)} \\
&= \text{M1} \\
\text{(Headed-by o Works-for)(E4)} &= \text{Headed-by(Works-for(E4))} \\
&= \text{Headed-by(D2)} \\
&= \text{M2}.
\end{aligned}
$$

Total and Partial Functions

We have said that in a function from set A to set B every member of A has associated exactly one member of B. Such mathematical functions can be applied to sets with infinitely many members, for example any number can be squared. Computing has to be restricted to procedures that will finish in a finite time. The term total function is applied to functions where given an input it is possible in a finite number of computing steps to either find the image or else report that the input is not a valid value in the domain.

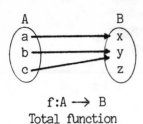

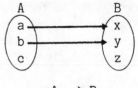

$f:A \longrightarrow B$

Total function

$g:A \longrightarrow B$

Partial function

because c has no image

Figure 2.1.22

By contrast, where some of A perhaps do not have an associated member of B we call it a <u>partial function</u>. This means for every member in A there is at most one (possibly none) member in B associated with it, as g above. (Strictly this is not a function as defined above.) The meaning is that within a finite time either

- the image of a given input will be obtained, e.g. from b (as input data to the procedure for g) the value y will be obtained; or else
- it will be reported that the given input has no associated image even though in the domain, e.g. from c; or else
- it will be reported that the input is not in the domain, e.g. from d (which does not belong to A).

Summary of Section 2.1

A set is any well defined collection of distinct member elements e.g. PARTS = {Nut, Bolt, Screw}.

No meaning is carried by the order in which the members are given. Each object either belongs or does not belong to each set. E.g. PARTS2 = {Screw, Nut, Bolt}. Equal sets have the same members. PARTS2 = PARTS.

A set is empty when it has no members.

The Universal set is all those elements discussed.

A subset is some of or all the members.

The intersection is those belonging to both of two sets.

The union is those that belong to either or to both.

The complement is those not belonging to the set.

The operations of intersection and union follow certain rules. They are commutative and associative. Each is distributive over the other.

A list can includes duplicates, e.g. <Bolt, Washer, Washer, Nut>.

An ordered n-tuple consists of n elements in appropriate order, the first element belonging to the first set and so on. The Cartesian product of n sets consists of all possible n-tuples. A relation is a subset of a Cartesian product: in information systems usually the tuples will correspond to real-world entity or relationship occurrences.

A binary relation is a pairing of elements of two sets, e.g. which small parts are components in which larger assemblies. The order of the two is important - it carries meaning. Hence the term ordered pair. It can be given as a table with two columns, a diagram or a graph. The meaning can be a sentence such as 'a owns b'. The reverse is also a binary relation, meaning b is owned by a.

In general a relation can have any degree. Each row of its table form is a member, consisting of associated values of whatever the columns represent. No information is carried by the order of the rows. Two rows cannot be the same, i.e. all rows are distinct.

A function is a rule that associates each member of a set A to a corresponding member of a set B. In some situations the rule may be represented by a set of ordered pairs or a subset of a Cartesian product.

Products (i.e. compositions of functions) are obtained by applying a second function, say g, to the result of a first function f, written g o f.

Total functions are computable. Partial functions allow members of the domain set A optionally to have either none or one image in B.

This section introduced the following mathematical concepts
 - Definition of a set
 - Cardinality of a set
 - Membership denotation
 - Equality and inequality of sets
 - Null set
 - Subset or set inclusion
 - Disjointness of sets
 - The union of sets

- The intersection of sets
- The difference of sets
- The complement of a set
- The universal set
- Laws of the algebra of sets
- Ordered pair
- The Cartesian product of sets
- Ordered n-tuple
- Binary relation
- The reverse of a relation
- n-ary relation
- Function
- Total function
- Partial function
- Product or composition of functions.

EXERCISES

1 Suppose each programmer is engaged on only one project at any time, or else is on leave (sick leave, annual leave ...). Does this mean the sets of programmers for the projects are disjoint?

2 Suppose each customer is served by either one sales person or no one if by post. How should customers be grouped into sets? Are the sets disjoint? Is their union empty?

3 Which if any of the following are the same?
A Orders paid and either delivered or loaded
B Orders paid and loaded together with those delivered
C Orders both paid and delivered or else loaded and paid
D Orders delivered and paid or else loaded
E Orders paid and loaded or delivered

4 In english which of the following does 'F and G or H' mean
A $(F \cup G) \cap H$
B $F \cup (G \cap H)$
C $F \cap (G \cup H)$
D $(F \cap G) \cup H$
E   Something else.

5 In english does "not" bind tighter than "and"? What does "A and not B or C" mean expressed in terms of intersections, unions, complements? Is "not B and A or C" the same?

6 Write out a table to show the following. Paste needs water. Wallpaper needs paste. Rooms need wallpaper. Windows need paint. Houses need rooms, windows and walls. Walls need bricks and wallpaper. Ceilings need paint. Brushes are needed for each of paint and paste.

7 Write out a relation showing the working days of December (not Saturdays or Sundays, Christmas Day or Boxing Day) assuming 1 December is a Monday. What is its degree? What is its cardinality?

8 (i) What is the formal definition of the difference of two sets A and B?

(ii) If BLDGS is a set of buildings and OFFICES and HOUSES are appropriate subsets, what is the expression for the buildings that are not houses or offices?

9 (i) Draw pictures to illustrate
(a) $(A \cap B)'$ and $A' \cup B'$
(b) $A \cup (B \cap C)$ and $(A \cup B) \cap (A \cup C)$.

10 (i) For the sets of girls and boys from Example 2.1.4
GIRLS = {Ann, Su}
BOYS = {Bob, Paul, Tom}
invent a relationship Has-boy-friend and occurrences such that it is a function. For simplicity arrange that each girl has a different boy-friend. Give the occurrences as a binary relation. If the reverse exists then give its occurrences. Can the reverse be a partial function? Can the product of Has-boy-friend and its reverse be formed?

(ii) What happens instead in Part (i) if Ann and Su each have Bob as boy-friend?

2.2 THE MEANING OF ASSOCIATIONS

The analyst must be able to distinguish and classify various kinds of information. This section distinguishes three kinds of association
- simple
- conditional
- complex
and relates these concepts to the theory of sets as discussed in Section 2.1.

In addition, the concept of roles is introduced. This allows designation of the meaning that a given set plays in a particular association.

Relations are one way of representing the associations between real life objects. For the moment we call the types of information associated with an entity its <u>attributes</u>. A more precise definition is developed in Section 3.2.

For example a sales order has a unique Order-number, it may or may not be delivered, it has a price and order date and is for a customer. These are five attributes. Each order has a value for each type of information; the values belong to corresponding sets. They are <u>types of</u> information.

ORDER#	DELIVERED	PRICE	ORDER-DATE	CUSTOMER
1289	Yes	12.64	8.9.79	Mass Paper
1290	No	70.58	8.9.79	Mini Kits

Figure 2.2.1

In practice the list of attributes for an order is longer – e.g. various quantities of various parts with various descriptions, prices and tax. Some of these attributes have associations between them, but for the moment we use the simpler attributes only. These five attributes take one value for each order. If that were not so we could not draw up a simple table with each row representing an order and each column an attribute.

Simple association

Each Order# has an associated Price.

ORDER#	PRICE
1289	12.64
1290	70.58
1291	12.64

Names of the sets to which values belong

Figure 2.2.2

This is a simple association. We write
$$ORDER\# \longrightarrow PRICE.$$
The meaning is that every member of the set Order# has exactly one associated Price. Price depends on Order#, i.e. quoting an Order# determines a Price. Because an Order# always associates to exactly one Price we say it is <u>to one</u>.

The association has direction. From Price to Order# is not a simple association since quoting a price e.g. 12.64 does not lead to exactly one Order#. Arrow diagrams must show the direction.

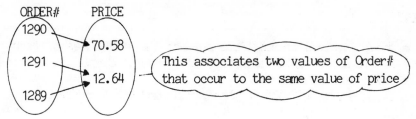

Figure 2.2.3

The structure of the table with five columns in Fig. 2.2.1 is four simple as-sociations each from Order# to one of the other attributes.

The relationship from Order# to Price is also a function. It is a subset of the Cartesian product Order# x Price but with the restriction that each Order# value appears exactly once in the ordered pairs

<1289, 12.64> <1291, 12.64> <1290, 70.58>

We draw it thus.

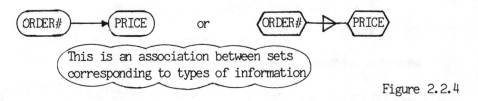

Figure 2.2.4

An association is said to be <u>simple</u> (i.e. of <u>type 1</u>) where each member in set A is always associated with <u>exactly one</u> member in set B. Thus simple as-sociations are total functions. They are a type of relationship of special in-terest for analysts. The name Price can also be used for the name of the func-tion or association.

Figure 2.2.5

A simple (type 1) association from set A to set B is denoted by

a: A $\longrightarrow$ B.

which reads 'a is a simple association from A to B'.

The set A is called the <u>domain.</u> The set B is called the <u>codomain.</u> Each member of the domain is associated with one of the codomain, two or more of the domain may be associated with the same member of the codomain.

The name of an association may be in either lower case (as "a" above) or in upper case. People who think about meanings as functions may use lower case. People who think of associations as relations may use upper case like relation names.

Example 2.2.1

The above involved associations between the attributes of each entity that belongs to the set of entities named Sales-order. Simple associations can also exist between sets of entities.

For example let HUSBANDS = {Adam, Bob} and WOMEN = {Eve, Mary, Su}. Consider

$$\text{HUSBAND-OF} = \{<Adam, Eve>, <Bob, Mary>\}.$$

Then

$$\text{HUSBAND-OF: HUSBANDS} \longrightarrow \text{WOMEN}$$

where every husband occurs in exactly one ordered pair is an example of a simple association. It is a total function. Nothing is implied about the reverse association from WOMEN to HUSBANDS.

Notice that because Adam cannot be associated with more than one woman

$$\text{HUSBAND-OF} \subset \text{HUSBANDS x WOMEN}.$$

i.e. HUSBAND-OF represents a proper subset of the Cartesian product of HUSBANDS and WOMEN. Thus HUSBAND-OF can be represented by a set of ordered pairs such as

$$\text{HUSBAND-OF} = \{<Adam, Eve>, <Bob, Mary>\}$$

or by the expression

$$\text{HUSBAND-OF (HUSBANDS, WOMEN)}.$$

which denotes a relation.

So far the associations between attributes have all been either from one attribute to another or from one entity set to another. The concept can be generalized to being from more than one attribute.

Example 2.2.2

Suppose an analyst trying to devise a conceptual data model of a manufacturing business looks round the stores and production areas and talks to the staff. Quickly the analyst will learn say that each product has a unique Part#. This applies to raw materials, partly assembled products and to finished products.

The analyst sees a box of 100 bolts of a certain size. Another size of bolts are in lots of 20. It seems that Lot-size depends on Part#. But the analyst must continually check his ideas with the future users. On enquiry the analyst is told that for example junction boxes can either be bought from supplier S1 in lots of 100 or can be made in the factory in lots of 50. Occasionally they are bought from supplier S2 in tens.

PART#	HOW-GOT	LOT-SIZE
12864	Buy from S1	100
12864	Buy from S2	10
12864	Make	50
12973	Buy from S1	20

Figure 2.2.6

Here lot-size is an attribute that depends on both Part# and How-got. It is a simple association i.e. a function from two sets to one set. It is a (total) function because quoting valid combinations of values for Part# and How-got leads to exactly one value of Lot-size. We write

Lot size: PART#, HOW-GOT $\rightarrow$ LOT-SIZE.

A name such as Lot-size may be used both for the function and for the set to which the values belong where this does not lead to confusion.

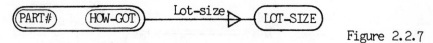

Figure 2.2.7

In an earlier example four attributes were each dependent on a single one, Order#. Similarly there can be more than one attribute that is dependent on two attributes like Part# and How-got.

For example Unit-cost may also depend on these - maybe making a batch of parts costs less than buying or maybe different suppliers have different prices. We can draw this.

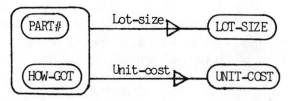

Figure 2.2.8

Lot-size is a function of PART#, HOW-GOT. With this structure and meaning the domain is a set of ordered pairs. Similarly the result of a function need not be a value of a single attribute, it can be an ordered pair such as the value for <Lot-size, Unit-cost>.

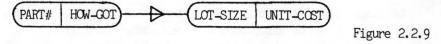

Figure 2.2.9

In general a simple association is a total function from a domain to a codomain. The essence of being simple is that <u>each</u> member of the domain maps to exactly one image which is in the codomain.

Conditional associations

An association is said to be <u>conditional</u> (i.e. <u>type C</u>) where each member in set A is associated with either one or none of B. Thus conditional associations correspond to partial functionality. They are another relation type of special interest to an analyst. We write

$$a: A \longrightarrow B$$

which reads 'a is a conditional association from A to B'. It is '... <u>to none or one</u>'. For example a man may be married either to one woman or unmarried.

Example 2.2.3

Let MEN = {Adam, Bob, Tom} and WOMEN = {Eve, Mary, Su} be associated as shown.

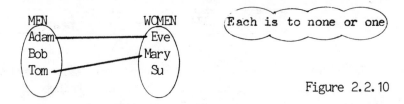

Figure 2.2.10

Then

$$\text{Husband-of: MEN} \longrightarrow \text{WOMEN}$$

is an example of a conditional association (i.e. a partial function).

Notice that

$$\text{HUSBAND-OF} \subset \text{MEN X WOMEN}$$

i.e. HUSBAND-OF represents a proper subset of the Cartesian product of MEN and WOMEN. The occurrences of Husband-of can be represented by a set of ordered pairs such as

$$\{<\text{Adam, Eve}>, <\text{Tom, Mary}>\}$$

Since a man may have at most one wife (possibly none) the association from Men to Women is conditional.

Complex Associations

An association is said to be <u>complex</u> (i.e. <u>type M</u> for <u>many</u>) where each member in set A can be associated with any number (including zero) of members in B. Thus complex associations correspond to relations.

A complex association from set A to set B is written

$$a: A \longrightarrow\!\!\!\rightarrow B$$

which reads 'a is a complex association from A to B'.

Example 2.2.4

Let STUDENTS = {Sally, Mary, Bob} and COURSES = {Phys, Math, Chem, English}. Suppose Sally attends physics and math, and Bob attends physics, math and chemistry.

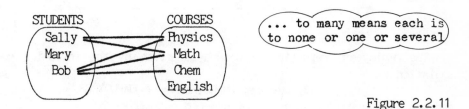

Figure 2.2.11

Thus Attends can be represented by a set of ordered pairs such as

ATTENDS = {<Sally, Phys>, <Sally, Math>,
<Bob, Phys>, <Bob, Math>, <Bob, Chem>}.

Then

Attends: STUDENTS $\longrightarrow\!\!\!\rightarrow$ COURSES

is an example of a complex association. It is a binary relation.

Notice that

ATTENDS $\subseteq$ STUDENTS x COURSES

i.e. the set ATTENDS represents a subset (not necessarily a proper subset) of the Cartesian product of STUDENTS and COURSES and may be written as a relation

ATTENDS (STUDENTS, COURSES).

Since a student may follow any number of courses (i.e. a student is usually associated with several courses) the association from Students to Courses is complex (is of type M).

Obviously if each student follows all courses this becomes

ATTENDS-ALL = STUDENTS x COURSES

i.e. ATTENDS-ALL is equal to the Cartesian product of STUDENTS and COURSES.

Association within one set

An association can be from members of a set to members of the same set.

Example 2.2.5

Let EMPLOYEES = {Atkins, Brown, Cohen, Jones, Smith, Watson}.

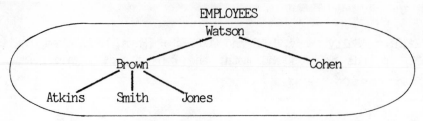

Figure 2.2.12

The employees' reporting structure is given by the following complex association
$$\text{Manager-of: EMPLOYEES} \longrightarrow\!\!\!\rightarrow \text{EMPLOYEES}$$
and can be represented by a set of ordered pairs such as
$$\text{MANAGER-OF} = \{\langle\text{Watson, Brown}\rangle, \langle\text{Watson, Cohen}\rangle,$$
$$\langle\text{Brown, Atkins}\rangle, \langle\text{Brown, Jones}\rangle, \langle\text{Brown, Smith}\rangle\}.$$
The interpretation of an ordered pair such as ⟨Watson, Brown⟩ is 'Watson is
the Manager-of Brown'. Fig. 2.2.12 shows the complex association Manager-of.

The above example has just one asociation. But it is possible to have
several associations from one set to another or within the same set.

Example 2.2.6

    Let
$$\text{EMPLOYEE\#} = \{E1, E2, E3, \ldots\}$$
$$\text{DATES} = \{6/2/38, 6/1/43, 22/6/67, 20/7/69, \ldots\}.$$
Three examples of associations involving these sets are
$$\text{Date-of-birth: EMPLOYEE\#} \longrightarrow \text{DATES}$$
$$\text{Marriage-date: EMPLOYEE\#} \longrightarrow \text{DATES}$$
$$\text{Start-date: EMPLOYEE\#} \longrightarrow \text{DATES}.$$

The concept of association can be generalized by postulating that both the
domain and the co-domain may each be subsets of a Cartesian product of any
number of sets, The notation
$$a: A \longrightarrow B$$
$$a: A \longrightarrow\!\!) \ B$$
$$a: A \longrightarrow\!\!\!\rightarrow B$$
used so far to represent a simple, a conditional and a complex association from
set A to set B is then replaced by
$$a: A_1, A_2, \ldots A_n \longrightarrow B_1, B_2, \ldots B_m$$
$$a: A_1 \ldots A_n \longrightarrow\!\!) \ B_1 \ldots B_m$$
$$a: A_1 \ldots A_n \longrightarrow\!\!\!\rightarrow B_1 \ldots B_m$$

where

$$A_1 \ldots A_n \subseteq A_1 \times A_2 \times \ldots A_n$$
$$B_1 \ldots B_m \subseteq B_1 \times b_2 \times \ldots B_m$$

Notice that an association with a domain $A_1 \ldots$ and a co-domain $B_1 \ldots$ still represents a subset of the Cartesian product of the domain and the co-domain both representing on their part subsets of a Cartesian product. Thus

$$a \subseteq A_1 \times \ldots A_n \times B_1 \times \ldots B_m$$

This expression denotes a relation with degree $m+n$.

Example 2.2.7

Let

SUPPLIER = {S1, S2, S3}
PRODUCT = {P1, P2, P3, P4}
STORE = {ST1, ST2}
QUANTITY = {8, 10, 15, 20}.

We first consider the complex association

Supplies-what: SUPPLIER $\longrightarrow\!\!\!\rightarrow$ PRODUCT.

Let Supplies-what be represented by the following set of ordered pairs

SUPPLIES-WHAT = {<S1, P1>, <S1, P3>, <S2, P4>}

i.e. by a subset of the Cartesian product of Supplier and Product.

We now associate the ordered pairs of Supplies-what with Store, i.e. we consider the complex association

Supplies-what-where: SUPPLIER, PRODUCT $\longrightarrow\!\!\!\rightarrow$ STORE.

Let Supplies-what-where be represented by the following set of ordered ternary tuples

SUPPLIES-WHAT-WHERE = {<S1, P1, ST1>, <S1, P1, ST2>,
<S1, P3, ST2>, <S2, P4, ST1>}

i.e. by a subset of the Cartesian product of Supplier, Product and Store.

We finally associate the ordered ternary tuples of Supplies-what-where with Quantity. Assuming that a given supplier supplies a given product to a given store only in a particular quantity we consider the simple association

Supplies-what-where-qty: SUPPLIER, PRODUCT, STORE $\longrightarrow$ QUANTITY.

Let Supplies-what-where-qty be represented by the following set of ordered quaternary tuples

SUPPLIES-WHAT-WHERE-QTY = {<S1, P1, ST1, 10>, <S1, P1, ST2, 20>,
<S1, P3, ST2, 15>, <S2, P4, ST1, 10>}.

Supplies-what-where-qty represents a subset of the Cartesian product of Supplier, Product, Store and Quantity. This means that the three associations Supplies-what, Supplies-what-where and Supplies-what-where-qty may be represented by a relation of degree 4.

SUPPLIES-WHAT-WHERE-QTY (SUPPLIER, PRODUCT, STORE, QUANTITY)

SUPPLIER	PRODUCT	STORE	QUANTITY
S1	P1	ST1	10
S1	P1	ST1	20
S1	P3	ST2	15
S2	P4	ST1	10

Figure 2.2.13

Mappings

Another term frequently used in the field of databases is mapping {2.5, 2.9, 2.10}. A mapping is always a rule of association between two sets, a domain and a codomain. They may or may not be the same set. It involves an association and its reverse. Each of the association and its reverse is either simple (type 1) or conditional (type C) or complex (type M). That gives 3 x 3 = 9 possible types of mapping.

We define the type of a mapping between two sets, say A and B, as

(Type-reverse : Type-forwards)

where Type-forwards represents the type (1, C, M) of the association from A to B and Type-reverse the type of the corresponding reverse association. For example

(1 : M)

indicates that the reverse association from set B to set A is simple and the A to B association is complex.

A (Tr:Tf)-mapping between A and B is symbolically denoted by

m: A Tr—Tf B

where Tr and Tf are represented by

$\leftarrow$ or $\rightarrow$ for type 1 associations
$\leftarrow$ or $\rightarrow$ for type C associations
$\twoheadleftarrow$ or $\twoheadrightarrow$ for type M associations.

For example the expression

m: A $\twoheadleftarrow\!\!\rightarrow$ B

denotes a (M:1)-mapping between A and B which reads 'm is a many to one mapping between A and B' i.e. the association from A to B is simple and the reverse is complex.

Example 2.2.8

Let STUDENTS = {S1, S2, S3} and COURSES = {C1, C2, C3, C4}. Furthermore, let the complex association

Attends: STUDENTS $\longrightarrow\!\!\!\rightarrow$ COURSES

define the students doing particular courses and let the complex association

Attended: COURSES $\longrightarrow\!\!\!\rightarrow$ STUDENTS define the courses done by particular students. Attended is the reverse of Attends. Thus the following (M:M)-mapping can be defined

Enrolment: STUDENTS $\ll\longrightarrow\gg$ COURSES.

Assume next that Attends is represented by the following set of ordered pairs

ATTENDS = {⟨S1, C1⟩, ⟨S1, C2⟩, ⟨S1, C3⟩, ⟨S2, C1⟩, ⟨S3, C2⟩, ⟨S3, C3⟩}

i.e. by a subset of the Cartesian product of STUDENTS and COURSES.

The set of ordered pairs representing the association Attended can be derived from Attends by simply inverting the order of the pairs appearing in Attends. Thus

ATTENDED = {⟨C1, S1⟩, ⟨C2, S1⟩, ⟨C3, S1⟩, ⟨C1, S2⟩, ⟨C2, S3⟩, ⟨C3, S3⟩}.

From the preceding example it follows that the representation of a mapping requires a <u>single</u> set of ordered pairs since, given such a set, say

$$S = \{⟨a, b⟩ \mid ...\}$$

the reverse can always be determined by

$$S^{-1} = \{⟨b, a⟩ \mid ⟨a, b⟩ \in S\}.$$

A mapping between two sets A and B is completely determined by a subset of the Cartesian product of A and B, i.e. by a single set of ordered pairs.

Since both the association from set A to set B and its reverse may be simple or conditional or complex we distinguish 3 x 3 = 9 different mapping types. Fig. 2.2.14 depicts these.

a	Reverse of a		
	Type 1	Type C	Type M
	$a^{-1}: B \rightarrow A$	$a^{-1}: B \rightarrow A$	$a^{-1}: B \twoheadrightarrow A$
Type 1 a: A→B	(1:1) m:A←→B	(C:1) m:A←→B	(M:1) m:A⟨⟨→B
Type C a: A→) B	(1:C) m:A←→B	(C:C) m:A⟨—)B	(M:C) m:A⟨⟨—)B
Type M a: A↠B	(1:M) m:a←→→B	(C:M) m:A⟨—↠B	(M:M) m:A⟨⟨—↠B

Figure 2.2.14

Mapping types are symmetric. This means that the mappings (C:1), (M:1) and (M:C) may be obtained by reversing the sets involved in respectively (1:C), (1:M) and (C:M) mappings. Thus of the 9 mapping types only 6 are really different.

Example 2.2.9

Let

$$MEN = \{Adam, Bob, Max, Eric, Paul, Charles, Tom\}$$
$$WOMEN = \{Eve, Mary, Su, Ann, Sally, Nancy\}$$
$$HUSBANDS = \{Adam, Max, Eric, Bob\}$$
$$WIVES = \{Eve, Su, Sally, Nancy\}.$$

So HUSBANDS ⊂ MEN and WIVES ⊂ WOMEN, i.e. HUSBANDS and WIVES represent proper subsets of MEN and WOMEN.

The mapping

$$Marriage\text{-}1: HUSBANDS \longleftrightarrow WIVES$$

represents a (1:1)-mapping since every husband has exactly one wife and every wife has exactly one husband (Fig. 2.2.15).

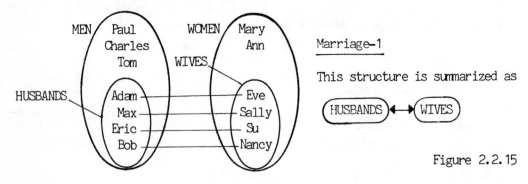

Figure 2.2.15

The mapping

$$Marriage\text{-}c: HUSBANDS \longleftrightarrow WOMEN$$

represents a (C:1)-mapping since every husband has exactly one wife but a woman may have one or no husband (Fig. 2.2.16).

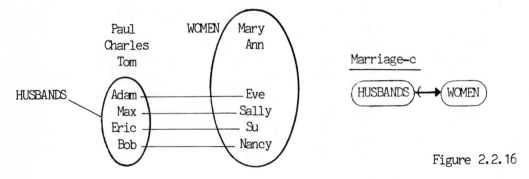

Figure 2.2.16

If a woman may have any number of husbands and a husband has exactly one wife then

$$Polyandry: HUSBANDS \longleftrightarrow WOMEN$$

is an example of a (M:1)-mapping (Fig. 2.2.17).

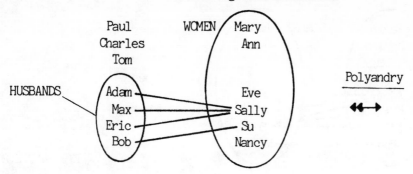

Polyandry

Figure 2.2.17

The mapping

$$\text{Marriage-cc: MEN} \longleftrightarrow \text{WOMEN}$$

represents a (C:C)-mapping since a man may have one or no wife and a woman may have at most one husband (Fig. 2.2.18).

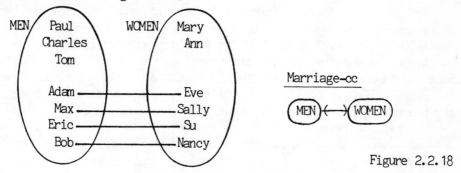

Marriage-cc

Figure 2.2.18

If a man may have any number of wives and a woman has at most one husband then

$$\text{Polygyny: WOMEN} \ll\!\longrightarrow \text{MEN}$$

is a (M:C)-mapping (Fig. 2.2.19).

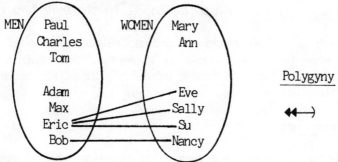

Polygyny

Figure 2.2.19

If a man can have any number of wives and a woman have any number of husbands then

$$\text{Chaos: MEN} \ll\!\longrightarrow\!\!\gg \text{WOMEN}$$

is a (M:M)-mapping (Fig. 2.2.20).

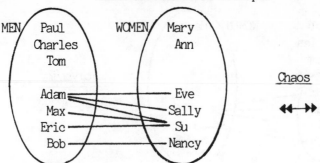

Figure 2.2.20

Time development of associations

The above are types of mapping that could exist at a particular instant. There may also be integrity rules about the creation and continuation of associations. When each element in the domain is created either

- it must be associated, i.e. its association to one of the codomain elements must be created at the same time. In CODASYL this is called insertion is automatic, i.e. the DBMS will create the representation of an association when the record corresponding to the element is first stored; or

- it need not have an associated element of the codomain, i.e. it can be created without an association. Then the association can be created later. This is called insertion is manual because an application program run does it.

There may also be a rule about retention or modification of any existing association. This rule would apply to each element of the domain after it has been associated to one of the codomain. The rule can be one of

- retention is fixed, i.e. the element cannot change its association, e.g. once married no change of partner is allowed.

- retention is optional, i.e. the association can be terminated, e.g. divorce; or

- retention is mandatory, i.e. change to become instead associated to another element of the codomain is allowed. Once the element of the domain has been associated it is always associated to some element or other of the codomain.

Role names with mappings

The interpretation of a mapping causes no problems where the sets participating are different. Interpretation problems may occur where a mapping is defined on a single set only. Role names are then needed.

Example 2.2.10

Let

COURSES = {Math, Physics, English, Chem, ...}

be the set of courses offered at a university. Furthermore, let the complex association

Prerequisites: COURSES $\longrightarrow\!\!\!\rightarrow$ COURSES

represent the rules about the sequence in which the courses have to be followed. Assume that Prerequisites is determined by the following set of ordered pairs

PREREQUISITES = {<Math, Physics>, <Math, English>,
<Physics, Chem>, ...}.

The reverse of Prerequisites is an association named say Needs. For example

NEEDS = {<Physics,Math>, ...}.

The following (M:M)-mapping can be defined

Courses-structure: COURSES $\ll\!\!\longleftrightarrow\!\!\gg$ COURSES.

For example

COURSES-STRUCTURE = {<Math, Physics>, <Math, English>,
<Physics, Chem>, ...}.

The problem is that there is no way to deduce from an ordered pair which course represents the predecessor and which the successor.

So we introduce the concept of role-names.

A role-name allows one to determine the meaning of a set in a mapping. The notation

m: A Tr─Tf B

used so far to represent a (T-reverse :T-forward) mapping between A and B is then extended to

m: R1.A Tr─Tf R2.B

where R1 and R2 denote the roles the sets A and B play within the mapping.

Example 2.2.11

For example

Courses-structure: Before.COURSES $\ll\!\!\longleftrightarrow\!\!\gg$ After.COURSES

has the elements of an ordered pair qualified by the role-names. Courses-structure is then determined by

COURSES-STRUCTURE = {<Before.Math, After.Physics>,
<Before.Math, After.English>,
<Before.Physics, After.Chem>, ...}

With role names the meaning is not carried by the order of the elements. Changing the order of a pair causes no interpretation problems since the roles are stated.

Role-names usually do not have to be specified explicitly since the roles played by the sets involved in a mapping are immediately apparent from the names of these sets. This means that set names may act as role-names as well.

Mappings between Subsets of two Cartesian Products

So far we have only discussed mappings between two sets or within a single set. The concept of mapping can however be generalized by postulating that mappings may also be defined between two subsets of Cartesian products applied on any number of sets. The notation

$$m: A \quad Tr\!\!-\!\!\!Tf \quad B$$

used so far to represent a mapping between A and B is then replaced by

$$m: A_1 \ldots \quad Tr\!\!-\!\!\!Tf \quad B_1 \ldots$$

where

$$A_1, \ldots \subseteq A_1 \times \ldots$$
$$B_1, \ldots \subseteq B_1 \times \ldots$$

A mapping between the Cartesian products on several sets is a subset of the Cartesian product of all the sets i.e.

$$M \subseteq A_i \times A_2 \times \ldots A_n \times B_1 \times B_2 \times \ldots B_p$$

where M is the name of the relation corresponding to the mapping.

Representing Associations and Mappings by Relations

From the preceding discussion it follows that an association as well as a mapping is determined by a relation as defined in Section 2.1. In the field of databases it is common practice to depict a relation in the form of a table {2.4}. In doing so, all the values appearing in a table column correspond to the values of members of a single set (usually called the domain) and all the values appearing in a single row represent a n-tuple. For a particular relation each table column has a distinct name called the <u>attribute name.</u> The values in a table column are called <u>attribute values.</u> The attribute name usually corresponds to the domain name provided no ambiguities occur. To avoid ambiguity the attribute name may consist of the domain name qualified by an appropriate role name. The distinct attribute names obtained thereby allow one to drop the imposition of an ordering (as is common in mathematics) on the domains appearing in a relation.

Such attribute and role names may be in lower case with an initial capital, which makes reading easier.

Example 2.2.12

Suppose the first tuple of the following means that ten of part P1 were supplied by S1 to Store ST1 ...

SUPPLIES-WHAT-WHERE-QTY (SUPPLIER, PRODUCT, STORE, QTY)

SUPPLIER	PRODUCT	STORE	QTY
S1	P1	ST1	10
S1	P1	ST2	20
S1	P3	ST2	15
S2	P4	ST1	10

— Values from domains

Figure 2.2.21

Supplies-what-where-qty is a relation of degree 4 defined on the domains
Supplier, Product, Store and Qty (quantity). The domain Supplier, for example,
represents the set of all suppliers. By contrast the attribute Supplier in the
relation Supplies-what-where-qty represents a list of suppliers taken from the
domain Supplier. A particular supplier may occur several times in the column of
attribute values though only once in the set.

Project Operation

The project operation takes one relation as operand and forms a 'vertical'
subset by extracting specified columns and removing any redundant rows in the
set of columns extracted.

The project operation can formally be defined as follows {2.12}. Suppose r
is a tuple of a n-ary relation R and A is an attribute of R. The notation

$$r[A]$$

then designates the A-component of r. Now suppose A is instead a list $(A_1 \ldots)$
of attributes of R. The notation

$$r[A]$$

then designates the corresponding components of r.

$$r[A] = \langle r[A_1], r[A_2], \ldots r[A_k] \rangle$$

For example in Fig. 2.2.21 if A is Supplier and Product, and r is the third
tuple then $r[A] = \langle S1, P3 \rangle$.

The projection of R on the attribute list A, denoted by

$$R[A]$$

is then defined by

$$R[A] = \{r[A] \mid r \text{ belongs to } R\}.$$

In the same example R[A] is

SUPPLIER	PRODUCT
S1	P1
S1	P3
S2	P4

—— This tuple only occurs once here

Example 2.2.13

Suppose we are given the following relation.
SUPPLIES-WHAT-WHERE-QTY (SUPPLIER, PRODUCT, STORE, QTY)

SUPPLIER	PRODUCT	STORE	QTY
S1	P1	ST1	10
S1	P1	ST2	20
S1	P3	ST2	15
S2	P4	ST1	10
S3	P2	ST1	12
S3	P3	ST1	15
S3	P3	ST2	17
S3	P4	ST2	25

Figure 2.2.22

The interpretation of
<S1, P1, ST1, 10>
as a tuple is that supplier S1 supplies product P1 to store ST1 in a quantity of 10.

Suppose we are asked to form a table of all the suppliers supplying any product.

The answer may be obtained by extracting (i.e. copying) from the Supplies-what-where-qty relation the Supplier column and removing from the resulting list redundant values where there is duplication of supplier names. Thus the answer is given by the 'vertical' subset
{S1, S2, S3}.

The problem can be solved by the project operation formally written as
SUPPLIES ← SUPPLIES-WHAT-WHERE-QTY [SUPPLIER].

The backwards arrow means assignment, i.e. the right side expression is evaluated and the result is assigned to a structure whose location is referred to by the name on the left side.

The action of the project operation is to take all the distinct occurrences of rows of values for the attribute or attributes listed in the square brackets. The square brackets only contain Supplier, so all other columns of Supplies-what-where-qty are ignored. The value S1 occurs in the first three rows of Supplies-what-where-qty but only one copy of this is included in the result.

The result is a unary relation called Supplies.

SUPPLIES (SUPPLIER)

SUPPLIER
S1
S2
S3

Figure 2.2.23

Next suppose the user wishes to determine all the suppliers together with the parts they supply.

The problem can be solved by the following project operation

SUPPLIES-WHAT ← SUPPLIES-WHAT-WHERE-QTY [SUPPLIER, PRODUCT].

The result is a binary relation called, as the left side specifies, Supplies-what.

SUPPLIES-WHAT (SUPPLIER, PRODUCT)

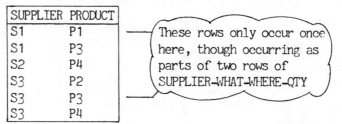

SUPPLIER	PRODUCT
S1	P1
S1	P3
S2	P4
S3	P2
S3	P3
S3	P4

These rows only occur once here, though occurring as parts of two rows of SUPPLIER-WHAT-WHERE-QTY

Figure 2.2.24

Join Operation

The join operation takes two relations as operands and forms a new, wider relation in which each tuple is formed by joining (i.e. concatenating) two tuples - one from each of the original relations - wherever there are two tuples that satisfy a certain condition.

The join operation can formally be defined as follows {2.12}. Suppose r and s are tuples containing respectively the elements $r_1 \ldots r_m$ and $s_1 \ldots s_n$.

The concatenation (denoted by the $\|$ sign) of r with s yields a $(m+n)$-tuple

$$r \| s = \langle r_1, \ldots r_m, s_1, \ldots s_n \rangle.$$

Let θ denote any one of the operations

$$= \quad \neq \quad < \quad \leqslant \quad > \quad \geqslant$$

such as equals. The θ join is a new relation in which values in attribute column A of R and values in column B of S have been compared, and a new concatenated tuple put in the new relation if

$$r[A] \; \theta \; r[B].$$

In this join every row of R is compared with every row of S by testing the values in column A of R with those in column B of S.

The result in symbols is written

R[A $\ominus$ B]S = {<r||s> | r belongs to A, s belongs to B and r[A] $\ominus$ s[B]}

The join operation can only be done if the two attributes A and B are compatible for testing using $\ominus$. For example if values of attribute A are numbers and values of B are strings of letters then join using equals cannot be done with those attributes. But join using less than could be done if every character was regarded as having a value as in a code like ASCII, so less than means earlier when put in ASCII alphabetical order.

Example 2.2.14

Suppose we are given the following two relations.
S(SUPPLIER, LOCATION)

SUPPLIER	LOCATION
S1	London
S1	Zurich
S2	Paris
S2	Rome

SP(SUPPLIER, PRODUCT, STORE)

SUPPLIER	PRODUCT	STORE
S1	P1	ST1
S1	P1	ST2
S1	P3	ST2
S2	P4	ST1
S3	P2	ST1
S3	P3	ST1
S3	P3	ST2
S3	P4	ST2

Figure 2.2.25

Suppose the user wants a wider relation which includes Supplier, Location, Product and Store.

The problem can be solved by means of the following join operation which creates a row in the result for each pair of rows from S and SP that have the same value of Supplier

S-SP $\leftarrow$ S [SUPPLIER = SUPPLIER] SP.

The result is a relation of degree 5 (2 attributes from the relation S plus 3 attributes from the relation SP). The resulting relation is S-SP.

S–SP(S.SUPPLIER, LOCATION, SP.SUPPLIER, PRODUCT, STORE)

S.SUPPLIER	LOCATION	SP.SUPPLIER	PRODUCT	STORE
S1	London	S1	P1	ST1
S1	London	S1	P1	ST2
S1	London	S1	P3	ST2
S1	Zurich	S1	P1	ST1
S1	Zurich	S1	P1	ST2
S1	Zurich	S1	P3	ST2
S2	Paris	S2	P4	ST1
S2	Rome	S2	P4	ST1

Figure 2.2.26

Note that - in order to avoid ambiguity - we have qualified the two Supplier columns by the name of the relations these columns originally came from. Also note that for the join on = (called the equi-join) two of the attributes of the resulting relation are identical in content (i.e. S.Supplier and SP.Supplier). If one of the redundant attributes is removed by a project operation then the result is the natural join {2.11} of the given relations.

Next suppose we want a relation listing all suppliers supplying part P3. This is done by the join

SP [Product = Product] R

where R represents a unary relation containing a single tuple for part P3.

R (PRODUCT)

Product
P3

Figure 2.2.27

The result represents - as illustrated below - a relation of degree 4. If we call the resulting relation SP-R we obtain

SP-R (Supplier, SP.Product, Store, R.Product)

Supplier	SP.Product	Store	R.Product
S1	P3	ST2	P3
S3	P3	ST1	P3
S3	P3	ST2	P3

Figure 2.2.28

We have already pointed out that for the equi-join two of the attributes of the resulting relation are identical. A definition for an operation which automatically removes one of the redundant attributes, called the natural join operation is as follows.

Let X, Y, Z be disjoint collections of attributes, Y being common to the relations R{X,Y} and S{Y,Z}. The natural join of relations R and S

$$R * S$$

is the relation T(X, Y, Z)

$$T(X, Y, Z) = \{\langle x, y, z\rangle \mid \langle x, y\rangle \in R \text{ and } \langle y, z\rangle \in S\}.$$

The natural join glues together tuples of R with tuples of S that have identical values for all attributes that are common to the two relations {4.4}.

Example 2.2.15

Consider the following relations.

STUDENT-NAME (S#, NAME)   OPINION(S#, C#, RATING)

S#	NAME
S1	Brown
S2	Smith
S3	Brown

S#	C#	RATING
S1	C1	Good
S1	C2	Poor
S1	C3	Good
S2	C2	Satisfactory
S2	C3	Satisfactory
S2	C4	Good

Figure 2.2.29

The natural join of Student-name and Opinion

R ← STUDENT-NAME * OPINION

yields the following quaternary relation

R (S#, NAME, C#, RATING)

S#	NAME	C#	RATING
S1	Brown	C1	Good
S1	Brown	C2	Poor
S1	Brown	C3	Good
S2	Smith	C2	Satisfactory
S2	Smith	C3	Satisfactory
S2	Smith	C4	Good

Figure 2.2.30

A tuple such as

⟨S1, Brown, C1, Good⟩

indicates that the student with student number S1 and named Brown attends a course with course number C1 and rates its usefulness as good.

Properties of relations

1 Column homogeneity: the elements within a column are all of the same type (i.e. all numeric values or all character strings).

2 Each element in the relation (i.e. each attribute value in each tuple) is atomic (not decomposable). An element is considered to be atomic if a decomposition would change its meaning. Thus a single character string or a numeric value are considered to be not decomposable.

3 Tuples are distinct: a relation never contains identical tuples.

4 The ordering of tuples is immaterial since tuples are identified by content and not by position.

5 The ordering of attributes (columns) is immaterial since attributes are always identified by name and not by position.

From here on we shall always depict the tuples of a relation in the form of a table.

Summary

1 Associations are 'from-to' relationships between the elements of two single sets or between the n-tuples of two subsets of Cartesian products applied on any number of sets. The two sets (subsets) are called respectively the domain and the co-domain of the association.

2 Depending on the number of elements (n-tuples) within the co-domain that each element (n-tuple) within the domain is associated with, we distinguish between simple (synonym: type 1), conditional (type C) and complex (type M) associations.

3 Generally speaking, an association is determined by a relation, i.e. by a subset of the Cartesian product applied on the domain and the co-domain of the association. The degree of this relation is binary if the association involves two single sets. Otherwise, the degree is equal to the sum of the degrees of the relations representing respectively the domain and the co-domain.

4 Simple and conditional associations respectively correspond to total and partial functionality.

5 A mapping always involves an association and its reverse, both being either simple, conditional or complex. A mapping is determined by listing ordered pairs (ordered n-tuples).

6 The purpose of role-names is two fold
 role names allow one to overcome interpretation problems which may occur for mappings defined on single sets
 role names allow one to drop the imposition of an ordering on the elements appearing in a pair or a n-tuple, provided that these elements are qualified by the role-names of the sets they belong to.

7 Role-names are usually not required because the functions played by the sets involved in a mapping are already apparent from the names of these sets. In many cases set names may act as role names.

8 In the field of databases it is common practice to depict a relation in the form of a table in which all the values appearing in a column correspond to values from a single set and in which all the values appearing in a single row denote a n-tuple. For some kinds of information such tables are convenient for people - though for other information sometimes forms or other layouts are preferred.

9 From a relation new relations can be obtained by operations such as project and join. Sometimes a relation can be split into projections without loss of information. In such cases the original relation can be recreated by joining. This is applied in later chapters.

10 From here on we shall always implicitly assume that the elements of a tuple are qualified by attribute names which correspond either to single domain names or to domain names qualified by appropriate role names, even in cases where these names do not appear explicitly.

   This section covered
 - Associations and mappings
 - Role names
 - Representation by relations
 - Project and join operations.

EXERCISES

    1. Let A = {a, b, c}
(i) List all the subsets of A
(ii) List all the proper subsets of A.

    2. Let A = {a, b, c} and B = {b, c}. Are the following statements correct?
(a)   b ∈ A
(b)   b ⊂ A
(c)   B ⊂ A
(d)   B ⊆ A
(e)   {b} ⊂ A
(f)   {b} ⊆ A

    3. Let
A = {Tom, Su, Ann, Mary}
B = {Su, Mary, Pam}
C = {Ann, Mary, Bob, Pam}.
    Determine
(a)   A ∪ A
(b)   A ∪ B
(c)   A ∪ C
(d)   B ∪ C
(e)   (A ∪ B) ∪ C
(f)   A ∪ (B ∪ C)
(g)   A ∩ B
(h)   (A ∩ B) ∩ C
(i)   A ∩ (B ∩ C)
(j)   (A ∪ B ∩ C)
(k)   A – C
(l)   C – A
(m)   B – B.

    4. Given appropriate total functions

$$f: A \rightarrow B$$
$$g: A \rightarrow C$$
$$h: B \rightarrow C$$
$$i: C \rightarrow B$$

state whether the following statements are true or false.
(a)   f = i o g
(b)   g = h o f
(c)   h = g o f

5. (i) Determine the sets and the mapping types underlying the following sets of ordered pairs

(a) {<Ann, Bob>, <Mary, Bob>, <Su, Tom>, <Sally, Max>}

(b) {<Ann, Bob>, <Ann, Eric>, <Su, Tom>, <Sally, Dick>}

(c) {<Mary, Harry>, <Su, Paul>, <Liz, Tom>, <Ann, Edward>}

(d) {<Ann, Bob>, <Ann, Tom>, <Su, Tom>, <Sally, Bob>}

(ii) Which of the above sets represents a function from GIRLS to BOYS?

6. Let Suppliers = {S1, S2, S3, ...}, Products = {P1, P2, P3, ...}, Machines = {M1, M2, M3, ...}, Employees = {E1, E2, E3, ...} and Departments = {D1, D2, D3, ...}.

(i) Make reasonable assumptions concerning possible associations between the above sets and define mappings between the following sets

(a) Suppliers, Products

(b) Products, Machines

(c) Machines, Employees

(d) Employees, Departments.

(ii) Could the same two sets be associated by two different mappings with different meanings?

7. Let Products = {Chair, Leg, Back, Seat, Stool}. A chair is made from some of each of Leg, Back, Seat; how many of each are used as components is for simplicity omitted. A Stool is made similarly from Leg, Seat. Thus Leg is used in making both.

(a) Define an association Made-from which determines the product assemblies.

(b) Represent Made-from by a set of ordered pairs.

(c) Define an association Where-used which determines the product usage.

(d) Represent Where-used by a set of ordered pairs.

(e) Define a mapping named Structure whose underlying associations are Made-from and Where-used.

8. Let STUDENTS = {S1, S2, S3, ...} and PROFESSORS = {P1, P2, P3, ...}.

Define the following associations and give examples of them by sets of ordered pairs

(a) TAUGHT-BY

(b) ADVISED-BY (assume that each student is advised by one professor)

(c) EXAMINED-BY

(d) Reverse of TAUGHT-BY

(e) Reverse of ADVISED-BY

(f) Reverse of EXAMINED-BY.

REFERENCES AND BIBLIOGRAPHY

2.1 ANSI/X3/SPARC: Interim Report: Study Group on Data Base Management Systems. FDT ... Bulletin of ACM - SIGMOD the Special Interest Group on Management of Data, Volume 7, Number 2, 1975

2.2 ANSI/X3/SPARC DBMS Framework, 'Report of the Study Group on Database Management Systems', Tsichritzis, D.; Klug, A.: Eds., AFIPS PRESS, 210 Summit Avenue, Montvale, New Jersey 07645, 1978

2.3 Berztiss, A.T.: 'Data Structures, Theory and Practice', Academic Press, 1975

2.4 Codd, E.F.: 'A Relational Model of Data for Large Shared Data Banks', CACM 13, 6, June 1970, Pages 377-387

2.5 DBDA (Data Base Design Aid), Designer's Guide, IBM Form Number: GH20-1627

2.6 Date, C.J.: 'An Introduction to Database Systems', Addison-Wesley Publishing Company, 1977 2nd edition

2.7 Jackowski, A.J.; Sbrega, J.B.: 'Fundamentals of Modern Mathematics', Prentice-Hall, Inc., Englewood Cliffs, New Jersey, 1970

2.8 Lipschutz, S.: 'Theory and Problems of Set Theory and Related Topics', Schaum's Outline Series, McGraw-Hill Book Company, 1964

2.9 Vetter, M.: 'Hierarchische, Netzwerkfoermige und Relationalartige Datenbankstrukturen (mit ausgewaehlten Beispielen aus einem Fertigungsunternehmen)', Ph.D. Dissertation, ETH Zurich (Swiss Institute of Technology), Juris-Verlag, 1976

2.10 Vetter, M.: 'Principles of Data Base Systems', Proceedings of the International Computing Symposium (ICS77/ACM), Liege, Belgium, April 4th to 7th, 1977, Pages 555-580

2.11 Codd, E.F.: 'Further Normalization of the Relational Model', in 'Data Base Systems', Courant Computer Science Symposium 6, 1971, Rustin, R.: Ed., Prentice-Hall Inc., Englewood Cliffs, New Jersey, 1972, Pages 33-64

2.12 Codd, E. F.: 'Relational Completeness of Data Base Sublanguages', in 'Data Base Systems', Courant Computer Science Symposium 6, 1971, Rustin R.: Ed., Prentice-Hall Inc., Englewood Cliffs, New Jersey, 1972, Pages 65-98.

3

Modelling the Real World

In traditional systems analysis for a file based computer system the aim is
to
- define the input, i.e. the data that flows from the user to the computer
system
- define the output needed, including its format and sequence
- define the record and file structures.

The resulting file structures may be unsuitable for some new requirement involving using the same information in a new way that evolves months or years
later. This is not solely because file structures have been used. It is a consequence of thinking in terms of the input, output and stored data for a particular application or for several closely related applications. It is not so
much the structuring of the file for efficient computer performance, but it
comes from having only the types of pointers needed for the applications. Other
possible pointers may be missing.

The essence of analysis for successful databases is to devise data structures that can support any applications. This includes applications devised
later that use the same types of data as exist. The structure must also be such
that further data types can easily be added. In the analysis the information in
use or needed is identified and classified in ways that transend current
policies, practice, priorities, pressures and applications. The aim is to document and model the type of things that the organization deals with, always has
and always will. This gives a single common reference point, the conceptual
data model for the whole organization.

In different departments or functional areas different names may be used for
the same thing, but such inconsistency must be avoided in the global conceptual
data model. The variations should also be documented so that correct terms are

used both when talking to the various staff and in the eventual implemented displays to users of applications.

The various departmental models giving the types of information in use in the departments are called <u>local</u> conceptual data models. Each corresponds to a mapping from a part of the global conceptual data model. In these mappings there may be changes of names but not of underlying structure of the associations between information types. For example each area in their own terminology should agree that larger parts (or assemblies, products, items) are made from smaller ones, that parts are sold to customers and that (small or intermediate sized) parts are purchased as raw materials from suppliers. Each should agree that parts are identified by a part-number (or item-number ...) and that customers and suppliers have identifying numbers, names and addresses. The task for the analyst is to create the global conceptual data model from the fragments gleaned from documents and interviews.

There may be a few thousand named types of information in the eventual global conceptual data model. There will be millions of occurrences of corresponding actual information. All should conform exactly to the model. The conceptual data model includes all the types of information, including associations, that can occur. Each type of information, including each type of association, is named.

The aim of this chapter and the next is to describe how to discover the correct conceptual data model for an organization.

Two main stages

The method is such that the analyst can choose to start in any department or any functional area, gradually merging local models into tentative global conceptual data models. The analyst's later activities are such that essentially the same global conceptual data model should be produced irrespective of the choices made at the start. Later activities include checks to ensure self-consistency of eventual data occurrences.

We suggest the analyst develops the full conceptual data model in two main stages. The first produces a skeleton conceptual data model. In the second all details are filled in and checks made. This chapter discusses the first stage. The next chapter covers extras needed for the second. The analyst should however be familiar with both stages before starting on a real analysis, since in interviews people may give the analyst explanations that are relevant to either stage.

The first main stage can be divided into
- deciding what are the relevant <u>information subject areas</u> within the organization i.e. what overall kinds of subjects should be analysed
- documenting what <u>types of information</u> can occur.

For a school or college the information subjects would probably include staff, students, courses, admissions, buildings, fees, grants, suppliers, invoices, departments ... This is a list of topics. Some of them are names of types of entities, e.g. student, course. For each named entity type there will be many occurrences, e.g. P.M.Adams, French-2. Each person and each course is an entity. Many means none, one or more. The number of occurrences will vary with time.

An entity is anything that has reality and distinctness. It can really exist - as a person, or be abstract - as a course.

The analyst's second activity within the first stage is to document what kinds of information can occur. This includes the types of entities and associations and their meaning. At this stage the aim is to form the essentials of the global conceptual data model, leaving some details till later.

The activity is covered in two ways
- studying documents that describe existing systems
- discussion with people who use the information in their jobs. Such interviews are usually more important than documents of previous computer systems.

The procedure is iterative - see Mr A then Mrs B then check with Mr A again for further explanation of a point raised by Mrs B.

Documents give some background. But they may be incomplete. Names of record types in them may be misunderstood. Only by proper interviewing of staff at all relevant levels in all the relevant areas of the organization can a complete picture be built up.

In particular the analyst aims to identify and record
- the situations in which occurrences of each type of entity come into being and cease to exist from the viewpoint of the organization
- the types of information about each type of entity
- the situations in which each type of information about each type of entity can be created, modified, deleted. In general each business activity involves the retrieval of certain information and possibly the creation, modification or deletion of other information that corresponds to the business transacted. Some business actions and transactions are triggered by an event. An event is either a particular time e.g. noon every Thursday, or a situation such as receipt of an order from a customer.

This activity of interviewing must be wide enough to discover the originating sources where information is created. For example lots of people will have told the analyst about Part-numbers, Order-numbers or Student-numbers. But the analyst must find out how each is created and allocated, and hence whether they are unique within the factory site, the campus, the organization, the country or the whole world.

The analyst needs to be able to classify the various types of information as in the following example.

To build up an explanation of the classifications our approach is to start

Information	Statement about type of information	Classification
1045 is B. Jones	Each employee has a unique number	The entity type Employee has an attribute that is a unique identifier
F.Dunn got 70 for chemistry	Each student enrolled for a course gets a final grade	The two entity types student and course are associated and that association has an attribute named Grade
Dr Bull takes Chemistry-1 in room R2.3 at 1000 Tuesdays	A teacher takes a class in a room at a time given in the timetable	Four entity types are associated

Figure 3.0.1

with primitives that cannot be meaningfully divided into even simpler classes, then to build up from the primitives. After you can classify information types our theoretical distinction between primitives and other classes will become unimportant. The analyst needs to be able to spot occurrences of the various classes and to decide the classification of any information that is met.

Chapter 3 consists of 3 sections. In Section 3.1 we introduce what we consider as primitives of the real world.

In this book a primitive has the same meaning as in mathematics, it represents an element which is not derived from another or an element from which some construction begins {3.10}.

Section 3.2 then discusses some constructions that are entirely based on the primitives introduced in Section 3.1. These constructions represent so called conceptual objects {3.5} existing solely in our minds. They allow us to classify our ideas about the real world and to base the database design process on a firm theory.

In Section 3.3 we are concerned with how to represent the conceptual objects existing in our minds by means of data.

Chapter 3 deals with the three realms of interest in the philosophy of information
- the real world
- ideas about the real world existing in people's minds
- symbols on paper or some other storage medium representing these ideas.

3.1 PRIMITIVES OF THE REAL WORLD

An entity may be 'anything that has reality and distinctness of being in fact or in thought' {3.13}. It has 'an existence of its own and it forms a whole which can be distinguished from its environment; in particular from all other entities of interest' {3.12}.

An entity may be
- a real object (i.e. a thing) like a place, a machine, a building, e.g. The White House
- an individual (i.e. a person) like a student, an employee, a citizen
- an abstract concept like a color, a skill, a course, a time period, a time point, an organization, e.g. Denver University
- an event i.e. a situation that something is happening, is planned or has happened, such as receipt of an order from a customer
- a relationship, e.g. a marriage.

Entities of the same type are regarded as in sets. The analyst must invent a name for each entity type, e.g. Building, Employee. The names of the entity types may eventually seem like names of record types. Usually - because early computer equipment did not have available lower case letters, record types have names in upper case. Hence some people also use upper case names for entity types, but that is not necessary. Usually an initial capital letter is enough.

Each entity type is something about which users may wish to store information. Designating something as an entity type means that users would like to collect and to store information about corresponding entities.

From the preceding discussion it follows that essentially anything can be considered as an entity.

The analyst restricts consideration to the entities relevant to subject areas agreed with the project management. The decision as to whether or not an entity is relevant to an organization depends on what the organization aims to achieve. For example a paint manufacturer must hold information about colors produced. Hence the paint manufacturer will certainly consider these colors as entities. On the other hand a car manufacturer may just want to associate the cars with their colors: the car manufacturer will most likely consider colors not as entities but as properties of its products.

A property is a named characteristic of an entity {3.2}. Examples are: Name, Weight, Color. Properties allow one to identify, to characterize, to classify and to relate entities.

A property value is an occurrence of a property of an entity {3.2}. A property value by itself has no meaning. People work with property/property-value pairs such as Color/red, Name/Brown, Age/14.

A <u>fact</u> is an assertion that a particular entity has a particular value for a property. This is associated in a particular meaning, e.g. this particular left shoe is size 9.

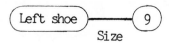

                                                                    Figure 3.1.1

A fact can also be an assertion associating several property values in a particular meaning. E.g. Big Ben and the Tower of London are in the same city.

Sue Allen has brown eyes and brown hair can be analysed as two facts. The properties are eye color and hair color. But they both use the same value, giving two occurrences of the property value Brown.

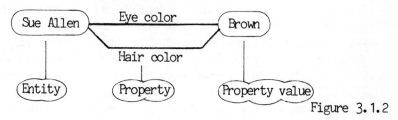

                                                                    Figure 3.1.2

A <u>fact</u> involves (either explicitly or implicitly)
- the entity and the property values e.g. Sue, Brown
- the name of the property, e.g. Shoe size
- the direction of the association i.e. which is the entity and which is the property value.

A <u>relationship</u> is an association among entities.

<u>Example 3.1.1</u>

The following statements designate relationships
1 Bob (entity) is the husband of (association) Ann (entity).
2 Sally (entity) attends (association) courses in Physics and Mathematics (entities).
3 Eric (entity) manages (association) Albert, Karl and Max (entities).
4 Part P1 (entity) consists of (association) parts Nut, Bolt, Washer (entities).

A relationship involves (either explicitly or implicitly)
- the individual entities associated, e.g. Bob and Ann
- the name of the association, e.g. Husband-of
- the direction of the association, e.g. who is the manager.

The concepts above are <u>primitives</u>. The primitives that occur in the real world include
- entities
- entity properties
- property values
- relationships.

Facts and relationships are based on the same idea. So relating an entity to another means that the two entities mutually appear as entity properties. This means that entities and entity properties may quite well interchange their roles. The choice depends on one's point of view.

Example 3.1.2

Consider a particular student, say Bob, as an entity. Obviously the courses attended by Bob (e.g. Physics, Math, Chem) characterize the entity Bob somehow. These courses act as occurrences of the entity property Attended-courses.

Consider now a particular course, say Math, as an entity. In this case, the students attending this course (e.g. Bob, Sally, Tom) are characterizing the entity Math; hence these students are acting as occurrences for the entity property Attending-students.

A relationship can sometimes be considered as an entity. For example consider 'Bob is married to Ann'. To many people the model is that Bob and Ann are entities and there is an association, Marriage. But to some people the Marriage certificate is an entity and it has their names and the date as values of some of its attributes.

Summary

1 Fundamentally, anything can be considered as an entity. However designating something as an entity type means that users would like to collect and to store information about it.

2 Each entity is characterized by properties having particular property values.

3 What one considers as entities and entity properties depends on one's viewpoint. In some sense the viewpoint should reflect the organization's aims. The initial choice made by an analyst may be wrong - procedures in later chapters cover this.

4 The distinctions between entities and entity properties usually come into being only when one adopts a particular point of view. This means particularly that entities and properties may reverse their roles.

5 Only relevant properties are used to characterize entities. The decision as to whether or not a property is relevant depends on aims.

3.2 CONCEPTUAL OBJECTS

The analyst needs to be able to classify and model constructions that people explain to him or her. E.g.
- raw materials are bought from suppliers and used as components
- the timetable gives who teaches which course in which room when
- Peter Roberts got a Good for French last year.

Various constructions can be created from the primitives. Familiarity with these enables analysts to correctly classify the kinds of information about the real world and thus devise appropriate models based on firm theory.

Some conceptual data model constructions are
- entity sets
- relationship sets
- domains
- entity attributes
- relationship attributes.

Entity set

Entities having the same kind of properties are said to be entities of the same type. We call it an entity type or a type of entity and use upper case for its name in expressions and diagrams usually. An entity set is the collection of entities of the same type that exist at a particular instant. Examples are
- set of employees (called for example EMPLOYEE)
- set of members of a health insurance scheme (SUBSCRIBERS)
- set of products (PRODUCT)
- set of machines (MACHINE).

In the case of manufacturing parts, each resistor or screw is not necessarily individually identified. The analyst may find that a particular size of screw has a Part-number that is unique within the organization. The analyst may decide to model Part as an entity type, with Part-number or Part# as identifying attribute. Entity sets are not necessarily mutually disjoint, i.e. an entity may be a member of more than one entity set at a time. For example a person (entity) may belong to the set of employees, the set of residents and the set of members of a health insurance.

Formally the analyst may define each entity set as the collection of entity occurrences that have the properties chosen as predicate. Each entity set has some rule that determines whether an entity belongs to the set i.e.

$$E_i = \{e_i \mid P_i\}$$

i.e. the entity set E_i has as members those e_i that satisfy the predicate P_i.

Relationship Set

A relationship set is a n-ary relation on n entity sets: these entity sets need not be distinct. It is a way of representing a type of relationship between entities.

Example 3.2.1

Fig. 3.2.1 illustrates a relationship set Sequence representing relationships between the entities of the entity set Course, i.e. between one course and another.

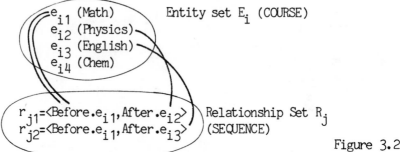

Figure 3.2.1

Sequence may be defined either by an expression denoting a set such as

$$\text{SEQUENCE} = \{\langle e_1, e_2 \rangle \mid e_1 \in \text{Before.COURSE and}$$
$$e_2 \in \text{After.COURSE}\}$$

or by a mapping expression such as

Sequence: Before.COURSE $\ll\longleftrightarrow\gg$ After.COURSE

which represents a subset of the Cartesian product of Course with itself. Thus

SEQUENCE $\subset$ Before.COURSE x After.COURSE

The general situation is as follows. A relationship set R is a named collection of relationships among entities belonging to designated entity sets. It represents basically a n-ary relation ($n \geq 2$) on n not necessarily distinct entity sets E_1, E_2, ... E_n. Let R denote such a relationship set. It is formally defined by

$$R = \{\langle e_1, \dots e_n \rangle \mid e_1 \in R_1.E_1, \dots e_n \in R_n.E_n\}$$

where (for k = 1 ... n) each e_k represents an entity taken from an entity set

E_k. The role of the entity e_k within the relationship is defined by R_k. (Remember that role-names allow one (1st) to avoid possible interpretation problems and (2nd) to drop the imposition of an ordering on the elements appearing in a pair or in a n-tuple.)

Example 3.2.2

Fig. 3.2.2 illustrates a relationship set Enrolment representing possible relationships between the entities of the entity sets Student and Course (i.e. between students and courses).

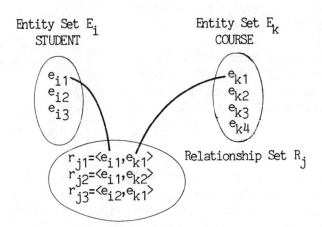

Figure 3.2.2

Enrolment may be either defined by an expression denoting a set such as

ENROLMENT = {<e_1,e_2> | $e_1 \in$ Attending.STUDENT and $e_2 \in$ Attended.COURSE}

or by a mapping expression such as

Enrolment: Attending.STUDENT $\longleftrightarrow\!\!\!\!\longrightarrow$ Attended.COURSE

which represents a subset of the Cartesian product of Student and Course. Thus

ENROLMENT $\subseteq$ Attending.STUDENT x Attended.COURSE

Role-names are not needed in this example since the functions played by the sets involved in the relation Enrolment are already apparent from the names of these sets.

Example 3.2.3

Fig. 3.2.3 illustrates a relationship set Taught-by-where representing possible relationships between the entities of the entity sets Course, Professor and Room (i.e. between courses, professors and classrooms).

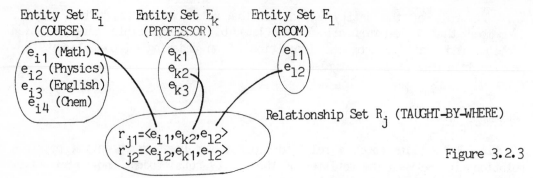

Figure 3.2.3

Taught-by-where may be defined either by an expression denoting a set such as

$$\text{TAUGHT-BY-WHERE} = \{<e_1,e_2,e_3> \mid e_1 \in \text{COURSE},$$
$$e_2 \in \text{PROFESSOR and } e_3 \in \text{ROOM}\}$$

or by the mapping expressions

Taught-by: COURSE $\longleftrightarrow\hspace{-0.6em}\rightarrow$ PROFESSOR

Taught-by-where: COURSE, PROFESSOR $\longleftrightarrow$ ROOM

which represent a subset of the Cartesian product of Course, Professor and Room.

$$\text{TAUGHT-BY-WHERE} \subseteq \text{COURSE x PROFESSOR x ROOM}.$$

Domains

A <u>domain</u> is the set of eligible values for a property {3.2}. A domain has the same characteristics as a set, i.e. the values belonging to a domain are distinct and their order is immaterial. A domain is defined either by listing all its members (tabular form as illustrated by the Examples 3.2.4 (a) and (b) below) or by stating the properties the members have to satisfy (set builder form as illustrated by Example 3.2.4 (c) below). A predicate is associated with each domain allowing one to determine whether a given value belongs to the domain in question.

Thus the formal definition for a domain D_i is

$$D_i = \{v_i \mid P_i\}$$

where v_i represents a value satisfying the predicate P_i. Domain names may be lower or upper case. We usually use the term domain for the values that occur at a particular instant of time, rather than for the set of all theoretically possible values.

Example 3.2.4

The following expressions are examples of domains
(a) NAME   = {Brown, Evans, Smith, ...}
(b) COLOUR = {blue, brown, green, red, ...}
(c) AGE   = {x | x $\geq$ 0 and x $\leq$ 130}.

Entity or Relationship Attribute

The entity attribute or relationship attribute A_i can be formally defined as an association from an entity set E_i or a relationship set R_i to a domain D_i or to the Cartesian product of several domains $D_1 \ldots D_n$. Thus the expressions

$$A_i : E_i \xrightarrow{T} D_i$$
$$A_i : E_i \xrightarrow{T} D_1 \times \ldots D_n$$

denote entity attributes whose underlying associations are of type T (i.e. simple, complex or conditional) whereas the expressions

$$A_i : R_i \xrightarrow{T} D_i$$
$$A_i : R_i \xrightarrow{T} D_1 \times \ldots D_n$$

denote relationship attributes.

P.P.-S. Chen, whose paper {3.5} has influenced the content of this chapter, defines an attribute as a function (i.e. a simple association) that maps from an entity set or relationship set into a domain or a Cartesian product of domains. (In {3.5} a domain is called a 'value set'.) However Chen's definition leads to implications that are not desirable at the level of abstraction we are concerned with.

Example 3.2.5

Fig. 3.2.4 shows some student attributes.

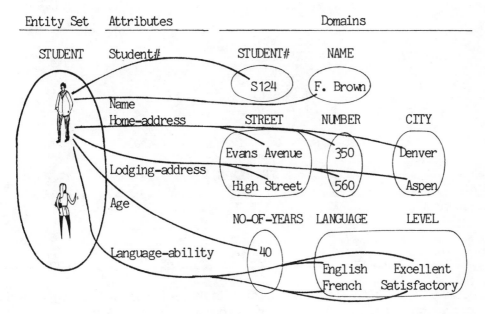

Figure 3.2.4

The figure shows the following points about attributes.

1 An attribute usually associates an entity set to a single domain. The attribute name corresponds to the domain name. For example the attributes Stu-
dent# and Name associate the entity set Student with respectively the domains
Student# and Name.

2 The name of an attribute does not have to correspond to the domain name. For
example the attribute Age associates the entity set Student with the domain No-
of-years.

3 An attribute may associate an entity set with the Cartesian product of
several domains. For example the attributes Home-address and Lodging-address
associate the entity set Student with the Cartesian product of Street, Number
and City. The attribute Language associates the entity set Student with the
Cartesian product of Language and Level.

4 Several attributes may associate an entity set with the same domain or a
single Cartesian product of several domains – but with different meanings. E.g.
Home-address and Lodging-address both associate Student with the Cartesian
product of Street, Number and City.

5 The association type of an attribute can be simple, conditional or complex.
For example Student#, Age, Name and Home-address are simple. Lodging-address is
conditional since a student may or may not have a lodging address. Language is
complex.

Example 3.2.6

Fig. 3.2.5 illustrates an attribute defined on the relationship set Enrolment.

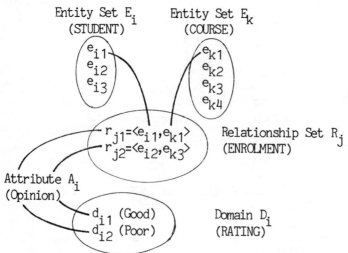

Figure 3.2.5

The association type of the attribute Opinion is simple, meaning that there is a
rating of the quality and usefulness of each course by each student enrolled for
it.

In developing the conceptual schema the analyst and designer must be able to model time appropriately. Broadly there will be real mini world events and activities. These will usually be reported into the computer system soon afterwards. Occasionally there will be delays and errors. There will also be genuine changes to the information corresponding to real changes.

Real world event	Computer system operation corresponding to recent event	Computer system operation not corresponding to recent event
Mrs. Peel moves to 300 Park St.	None	
Starts insurance at XYZ	Name and address stored	
Moves to 500 Park Av.	Address data changed	Old address retained
Discontinues insurance	Flagged as not current, but retained	
Year later		Data deleted

Figure 3.2.6

There are static elements, i.e. occurrences of primatives corresponding to the state of the mini world, e.g. that Mrs. Peel lives at 300 Park Street is a static mini world fact. A conceptual data model should specify all the rules about the existence of such types of information. The state of the mini world is continually changing and the conceptual functional model should specify all the rules about the existence of allowable changes, called dynamic elements. These dynamic elements may be

- discrete events, i.e. regarded as happening instantaneously
- gradual, i.e.continuously happening over a period of time, in which case they have to be modelled as discrete because computer systems can only hold digital representations that are discrete and also because the input and output involve discrete operations.

Thus every event is an instantaneous mini world transition from one state to another. Some of these have corresponding computer operations. Others may not. Some computer operations do not correspond to mini world events. The input of the change of address to 500 Park Avenue may be either reflecting a real move by Mrs. Peel or may be a correction of an earlier error. The deletion of the record in the database about Mrs. Peel does not correspond to her death. Creation and removal of a record does not correspond to the corresponding entity being created or ceasing to exist.

Summary

1 Conceptual objects such as   – domains
 – entity sets   – entity attributes
 – relationship sets   – relationship attributes
are subsidiary constructions that exist solely in people's minds. Database
design is based on their application.

2 An entity attribute and a relationship attribute are strictly different
structures from a domain.

3 A fact can be considered as an occurrence of an entity attribute.

3.3 REPRESENTATION OF CONCEPTUAL OBJECTS BY DATA

This section describes how to represent entity sets, relationship sets and
attributes as data.

Entity key

An entity key is an attribute that has different values for each occurring
entity. I.e. it is an attribute such that the mapping between the entity set
and the domain underlying this attribute is (1:1).

An entity key represents a compound key if it corresponds to a group of attributes such that the mapping between the entity set and the subset of the
Cartesian product applied on the domains underlying the group of attributes is
(1:1).

Sometimes it is necessary to define an artificial attribute since it may not
be possible to find a (1:1)-mapping on available data. An artificial attribute
may also be appropriate if one intends to simplify the identification of entities. If several entity keys exist for a given entity set then one of them is
arbitrarily chosen as the primary entity key (or simply primary key). Some
people use the term identifier instead of primary key.

Example 3.3.1

In Fig. 3.2.4 the attribute Student# is such that the mapping between the
entity set Student and the domain Student# is (1:1). Hence, the attribute Stu-
dent# represents an entity key. This means that each value within the domain
Student# acts as a token for an entity, i.e. for a student. If Student# is the
only attribute meeting the entity key criterion then it must be chosen as the
primary key.

Representation of entity and relationship sets

The first step is for the analyst to determine a primary key for each entity set. Each entity set is then replaced by the domain underlying its primary key. Where the primary key is compound the entity set is replaced by a set of n-tuples representing a subset of the Cartesian product of the domains underlying the primary key. Each n-tuple is a token for an entity.

From here on we call the domain which replaces the entity set the primary key domain or primary identifier.

Similarly for a relationship set the analyst replaces the entity sets involved in the relation by corresponding primary key domains. Note that the primary key of a relationship set is compound, being composed of the primary keys of the entity sets participating in the relation.

An attribute A_i is now defined as an association from a domain corresponding to the primary key of an entity set E_i or a relationship set R_i to a domain D_i or the Cartesian product of several domains D_1, D_2 ... D_n.

Example 3.3.2

Fig. 3.3.1 has been derived from Fig. 3.2.4 by replacing the entity set Student by the domain Student#.

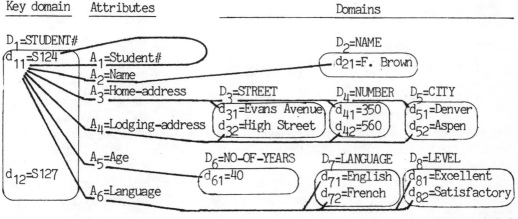

Figure 3.3.1

Note that attributes are now associating the domain Student# with other domains (e.g. Age, Name now do so) or with the Cartesian product applied on several domains (e.g. Home-address, Lodging-address, Language). Also note that the attribute Student# did not disappear by this replacing operation; it simply associates the domain Student# with itself.

The attributes in Fig. 3.3.1 can be defined by the associations

      Age: STUDENT# $\longrightarrow$ NO-OF-YEARS
      Name: STUDENT# $\longrightarrow$ NAME

```
      Home-address:     STUDENT# —→    STREET, NUMBER, CITY
      Lodging-address:  STUDENT# —)    STREET, NUMBER, CITY
      Language:         STUDENT# —→→ LANGUAGE, LEVEL
```
or by the relations
```
      AGE (STUDENT#, NO-OF-YEARS)
      NAME (STUDENT#, NAME)
      HOME-ADDRESS (STUDENT#, STREET, NUMBER, CITY)
      LODGING-ADDRESS (STUDENT#, STREET, NUMBER, CITY)
      LANGUAGE (STUDENT#, LANGUAGE, LEVEL).
```

Example 3.3.3

Fig. 3.3.2 has been derived from Fig. 3.2.5 by replacing respectively the entity sets Student and Course by the domains Student# and Course#.

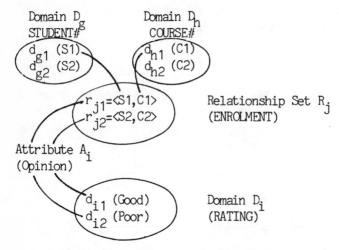

Figure 3.3.2

The relationship set Enrolment represents a collection of relationships defined by the primary keys of the entity sets involved in the relation, Student# and Course#.

The attribute Opinion associates the relationship set Enrolment (representing a subset of the Cartesian product on Student# and Course#) with the domain Quality.

The attribute Opinion depicted in Fig. 3.3.2 can formally be defined by the association

Opinion: Attending.STUDENT#, Attended.COURSE# —→ RATING
or by the relation

OPINION(Attending.STUDENT#, Attended.COURSE#, RATING).

The diagrammatical representation of information about entities in an entity set as in Fig. 3.3.1 is not very convenient and is usually replaced by a table as illustrated by Table 3.3.1.

Primary
Key

Attri-bute	Student#	Name	Age	Home-address			Lodging-address			Language	
Domain	STUDENT#	NAME	NO-OF-YEARS	STREET	NUMBER	CITY	STREET	NUMBER	CITY	LANG.	LEVEL
Entity Tuple 1	S124	Brown	40	Evans Av	350	Denver	High St	560	Aspen	Engl French	Excel Satis
	S127	Smith	35	Louise	5	Brussels	-	-	-	French	Excel

How to represent information about entities by a table   Table 3.3.1

1 Each row in Table 3.3.1 is called an <u>entity tuple</u>. It represents facts about a single entity. The entity itself is represented by the occurrence of a primary key value. A fact is represented by the value(s) located at the inter-section of an entity tuple and a column. Note that
- a single value occurs at the intersection if the association type of the cor-responding attribute is simple (e.g. facts for Name, Age, Home-address (i.e. Street, Number and City) are always represented by single values)
- a single value optionally may or may not occur at the intersection if the as-sociation type of the corresponding attribute is conditional (e.g. facts for Lodging-address (i.e. Street, Number and City) may or may not be represented by single values)
- multiple values (including zero) may occur at the intersection if the as-sociation type of the corresponding attribute is complex (e.g. facts for Language (i.e. Language and Level) are usually represented by multiple values).

2 The values in a column are taken from a single domain.

3 Fig. 3.3.1 and Table 3.3.1 represent different forms of the same informa-tion.
The description can be written either using domain names
STUDENT-DESCR (STUDENT#, NAME, NO-OF-YEARS, Home-address.STREET
Home-address.NUMBER, Home-address.CITY, Lodging-address.STREET,
Lodging-address.NUMBER, Lodging-address.CITY, LANGUAGE, LEVEL)
or by the following which is regarded as equivalent
STUDENT-DESCR (Student#, Name, Age, Home-address, Lodging-address, Language)
where an attribute name may stand for more than one domain. (Some real world addresses do not fit the domains above, e.g. house and building names, numbering of flats and so on.)

Similarly the diagrammatical representation of information about relationships in a relationship set like Fig. 3.3.2 is usually replaced by a table like
Table 3.3.2.

	Primary key		Relationship Attribute
Role.Attribute ————————	Attending. Student#	Attended. Course#	Opinion
Domain ————————————	STUDENT#	COURSE#	RATING
Relationship tuple 1 ———	S1	C1	Good
	S1	C2	Poor
Relationship tuple 3 ————	S1	C3	Satisfactory
	S2	C2	Satisfactory
	S2	C3	Satisfactory
Relationship tuple 6 ———	S2	C4	Good

Table 3.3.2

1 Each row in Table 3.3.2 is called a <u>relationship tuple</u>. It represents one
relationship among the entities determined by primary key values.

For example a relationship between a particular student and a particular
course is determined by a Student#–Course# value pair. Note that Student# and
Course# are primary keys for the entities involved in the relationship; they
both determine the relationship and do not act as relationship attributes.

2 A relationship tuple contains facts describing one relationship. For example Opinion determines the quality of a single course as seen by a single student. Hence Opinion is a relationship attribute.

3 The primary key of the relationship set is a compound key consisting of
the primary keys of the entity sets involved.

4 A role name may be used where the meaning of an attribute is not immediately apparent from its name.

5 Fig. 3.3.2 and Table 3.3.2 represent different forms of the same information.

Combining tables

A table representing information about entities can be merged with a table representing information about relationships. E.g. Table 3.3.3 is the result of merging Tables 3.3.1 and 3.3.2.

Role. Attribute	Primary Key Attending. Student#	Name	Age	Home-address			Language		Attended. Course#	Opinion
Domain	STUDENT#	NAME	NO-OF- YEARS	STREET	NUMBER	CITY	LANG.	LEVEL	COURSE#	RATING
Entity Tuple 1	S124	Brown	40	Evans Av	350	Denver	Engl French	Excel Satis	C1 C2	Good Poor
Entity Tuple 2	S127	Smith	35	Louise	5	Brussels	French	Excel	C2 C3 C4	Satis Satis Good

Table 3.3.3

In Section 3.1 we pointed out that facts and relationships are based on the same principles. Relating an entity to another entity has the consequence that the two entities appear mutually as entity properties. The conclusion was that entities and entity properties may quite well reverse their roles {3.17}. The distinction between entities and entity properties comes into being only when one adopts a particular point of view {3.15}.

The conclusions of Section 3.1 become apparent if one analyses Table 3.3.3. Each row in Table 3.3.3 is still an entity tuple representing facts for a par- ticular student i.e. a particular entity.

For example one of these facts is that the student represented by the Stu- dent# value S1 is associated with the courses (entities) represented by the Course# values C1, C2 and C3. These Course# values represent courses (i.e. en- tities), and they now also represent property values for the student property Attended.Course#. Hence courses are now considered as properties for the entity Student.

Similarly when merging a table containing information about courses in an entity set with a table containing information about student-course relation- ships in a relationship set (e.g. Table 3.3.2) then students (represented by Student# values) will act as property values for the course property At- tending.Student#.

We can now restate the definition of an entity taking the concept of primary keys into consideration.

Restating the definition of an entity

Fundamentally, anything can be considered as an entity. However by designating something as an entity one establishes a statement of intention whereupon
1 users would like to collect and to store information about it
2 users would like to start with the storage of information as soon as at least the primary key value of the entity in question is known.
Note that point 2 requires that the available storage structure is such that it allows consideration of an entity on its own; that is to say by means of its primary key value only. From now on we shall always use this restated entity definition.

Summary

1 The representation of conceptual objects (i.e. entity sets and relationship sets together with their attributes) requires that one determines a primary key for each entity set. Each occurring primary key value represents a token for a particular entity. The purpose of a primary key is to identify and not to describe entities. Therefore a primary key should be chosen such that it is as simple as possible.

2 Replacing entities within entity sets and relationship sets by primary key values allows one to represent these sets - together with the domains they are associated with (i.e. their attributes) - either in diagrammatical form or in table form.

3 At the level of abstraction we are concerned with there is no intrinsic reason not to merge the content of a table containing information about entities in an entity set with a table containing information about relationships in a relationship set. Such a merge operation allows one to illustrate that entities and entity properties may reverse their roles.

EXERCISES

1 What is the main difference between analysis to derive a conceptual data model and earlier analysis methods for developing computer applications using file-based data structures?

2 Why should the analyst distinguish the following
(a) information subject areas, i.e. project identification
(b) situations in which entities are created or cease to exist
(c) types of information about each entity set and relationship set
(d) situations in which such types of information are updated?

3 (i) Analyse the following statements, indentifying entities, entity properties, property values and relationships. Give an example of a fact.
'The automobile's number is ABC 123. The grey case and the brown box are in it. It was rented for a week starting at 18.30 on 1 July from Rentout Inc.
(ii) Make statements about conceptual objects to fit cars being loaded and so on.

4 Give some alternative attributes of a person that could be used as a primary identifier. Specify the domains of each. Discuss the advantages and disadvantages of each alternative for use as primary key in a computer-based information system for
(i) employee data
(ii) airline reservations
(iii) owners or inhabitants of buildings.

5 (i) Identify all the types of relationships that are implied in the following. Ships make stops at ports. Each stop has an arrival date and a departure date. Each ship can be loaded with many containers. Each container is on a voyage from an origin port to a destination port. Several containers together may form a consignment, but some containers are individual loads.
(ii) Represent the entity types and relationship types as a simple model of that portion of the real world. State any assumptions made.

6 Are facts and relationships based on the same principles?

7 What is the purpose of analysts learning about conceptual objects?

8 This question tests your ability to identify relationships.
The context is a hypothetical university, which may be not exactly the same as an actual university. You are asked to analyse the information here, as though it had been obtained from interviews and documents.
1 Using the word professor to mean any member of the teaching staff, a professor may teach several courses.
2 A professor may be advisor of studies to several students or none. Each student only has one advisor at most.
3 A professor has a room as his or her office. Occasionally a professor may have more than one room and two or more professors may share the same room.
4 A student or several students may occupy a room.

5 A student may be enrolled for several courses.

6 A course is always taught in a single classroom. Several courses may take place in the same room.

7 For some courses students must have successfully completed other prerequisite courses.

(ii) Suggest some attributes for these entity types and relationship types.

(iii) Draw a diagram of the entity types Student, Course, Room and Professor showing the seven relationships by appropriate arrows.

(iv) Make a list of entity types writing each as a relation giving the attributes in round brackets like a specification of a relation.

REFERENCES AND BIBLIOGRAPHY

3.1 Abrial, J.R.: 'Data Semantics', Proceedings of the IFIP Working Conference on Data Base Management, Cargese, Corsica, France, 1974, Klimbie, J.W. and Koffeman, K.L.: Eds., North-Holland Pub. Co., Amsterdam, Pages 1-59

3.2 ANSI/X3/SPARC: Interim Report: Study Group on Data Base Management Systems. FDT ... Bulletin of ACM - SIGMOD the Special Interest Group on Management of Data, Volume 7, Number 2, 1975

3.3 ANSI/X3/SPARC DBMS Framework, 'Report of the Study Group on Database Management Systems', Tsichritzis, D; Klug, A.: Eds., AFIPS PRESS, 210 Summit Avenue, Montvale, New Jersey 07645, 1978

3.4 Bubenko, J.A.: 'IAM: An Inferential Abstract Modelling Approach to Design of Conceptual Schema', ACM SIGMOD, Proc. of the International Conference on Management of Data, Toronto, Canada, 1977, Smith, D.C.P.: Ed., Pages 62-74

3.5 Chen, P. Pin-Shan: 'The Entity-Relationship Model - Toward a Unified View of Data', ACM Transactions on Database Systems, Vol. 1, No. 1, March 1976, Pages 9-36

3.6 Chen, P.P.: 'Design and Performance Tools for Data Base Systems', Proc. of the Third International Conference on Very Large Data Bases, Tokyo, Japan, Oct., 1977, Pages 3-15

3.7 Hall P.; Owlett, J.; Todd, S.: 'Relations and Entities', Proc. of the IFIP Working Conference on Modelling in Data Base Management Systems, Freudenstadt, Germany, 1976, Nijssen, G.M.: Ed., North-Holland Pub. Co., Amsterdam, Pages 201-220

3.8 Kent, W.: 'Describing Information (Not Data, Reality?)', IBM General Products Division, Palo Alto, California, Technical Report TR03.012, 1976

3.9 Kent, W.: 'Entities and Relationships in Information', Proc. of the IFIP-TC-2-Working Conference, Nice, 1977

3.10 Little, W.; Fowler, H.W.; Coulson, J.: 'The Shorter Oxford English Dictionary on Historical Principles', Oxford University Press, Ely House, London W.I., 1966

3.11 Mealy, G.H.: 'Another Look at Data', Proceedings of the AFIPS Fall Joint Computer Conference, 1967, Vol. 31, AFIPS Press, Montvale, N.J., Pages 525-534

3.12 Pirotte, A.: 'The Entity - Association Model: An Information - Oriented Data Base Model', Proc. of the International Computing Symposium, Liege, Belgium, 1977, Morlet, E. and Ribbens, D.: Eds., North-Holland Pub. Co., Amsterdam, Pages 581-597

3.13 Senko, M.E.; Altman, E.B.; Astrahan, M.M.; Fehder, P.L.: 'Data Structures and Accessing in Data Base Systems', IBM Systems Journal, Vol. 12, No. 1, 1973, Pages 30-93

3.14 Senko, M.E.: 'Data Description Language in the Concept of Multilevel Structured Description: DIAM II with FORAL', in 'Data Base Description', Dougue, B.C.M. and Nijssen, G.M.: Eds., North-Holland Pub. Co., Amsterdam, Pages 239-258

3.15 Senko, M.E.: 'DIAM as a Detailed Example of the ANSI SPARC Architecture', Proc. of the IFIP Working Conference on Modelling in Data Base Management Systems, Freudenstadt, Germany, 1976, Nijssen, G.M.: Ed., North- Holland Pub. Co.,Amsterdam, Pages 73-94

3.16 Senko, M.E.: 'DIAM II: The Binary Infological Level and its Database Language - FORAL', ACM Sigplan / Sigmod Conference, Salt Lake City, Utah, 1976

3.17 Vetter, M.: 'Principles of Data Base Systems', Proceedings of the International Computing Symposium (ICS77/ACM), Liege, Belgium, April 4th to 7th, 1977, Pages 555-580.

4

The Conceptual Realm

Completion of the conceptual data model

In developing the skeleton conceptual data model the only attributes that needed detailed discussion at interviews were those used for identifying individual entity occurrences and those involved in relationships. Details of the other attributes are not necessarily recorded at the skeleton stage. For example the structure of customer names and addresses is initially unimportant by comparison with the fact that each customer has a unique customer number.

To complete the conceptual data model involves several activities. There is a choice of strategy about which sequence to do these in, or even to do them in parallel.

From any partial skeleton, e.g. the local conceptual data model for a functional area, the following are possible.

(a) Further analyse the areas covered thus developing the full conceptual data model for those areas.

(b) Extend gradually into adjacent areas of the organization.

(c) Analyse a separate area of the organization to develop its skeleton local conceptual data model. Then merge the local data model with the existing partial data model to form a larger part of the eventual global conceptual data model.

(d) If the initial analysis was mainly data analysis, i.e. oriented to the types of data needed to represent the information that exists, then concentrate on functional analysis, i.e. what activities are done and what information is used how for each.

(e) If the initial analysis was mainly functionally oriented, e.g. interviewing people about their activities and what information they use, then concentrate on data analysis i.e. identify the types of information and their structure.

(f) Normalize the conceptual data model. This means do checking to ensure eventual self-consistency as in Chapter 5. For example the conceptual data model cannot allow an order with no corresponding customer. It also cannot allow in some roundabout way two occurrences of the same fact. For example if each teacher only teaches one subject, student James cannot have Mr Brown for French while Jones has him for English. Equivalently the conceptual data model cannot allow a relationship such as the following table.

Student	Teacher	Course
James	Mr Brown	French
Jones	Mr Brown	French
Judd	Mr Cass	German

Figure 4.0.1

This table could become inconsistent if a user altered one of the items in it - e.g. changed Jones's French to English. A correctly normalized conceptual data model does not contain any structure that could allow stored data to be inconsistent.

To complete the conceptual data model for the whole organization usually needs activities of all the above kinds. Analysts in different organizations may find it convenient to do them in different orders.

The further analysis of areas for which a skeleton exists, i.e. (a) above, includes the following.

(i) Identify all attributes of each entity type and relationship type. That means knowing
- each attribute name
- corresponding domain names
- what are allowable property values
- how to represent the property values when displaying to users, i.e. formats.

(ii) Ensure that the model is complete in the sense of including every type of information that is created, retrieved, updated, deleted, or used in any way (e.g. statistical averaging) and that may be computerized.

(iii) Identify all the different ways that information can be specified when selecting for retrieval or any other manipulation. E.g. in dealing with a telephone enquiry about an order the Order-number and the Customer-number may be unknown, so the retrieval may need to be by first matching on names and addresses of customers, then by a path from the customer to the orders for that customer, then selecting the relevant order after displaying some details of each possible order to the user on-line. However for entities with a unique identifying key the entry point is usually directly from the user quoting the value of the primary key.

(iv) Decide the authorization rules specifying the type of access allowed for each user to each data item and to each fact. The type of access may be any sensible combination of

- not know of the existence
- use in specified procedures such as averaging
- retrieval i.e. find and read only
- modify (but not create or delete occurrences) e.g. modify data items that are not the primary key
- update, i.e. create, delete and modify
- append, i.e. add to the end of the existing data but not read the existing.

Note that different occurrences of the same type of data or fact can be treated differently for access authorization. E.g. a manager may be able to access facts relating to his or her section but not to other sections. For some particular types of information one user may be regarded as the owner i.e. responsible for the accuracy of the information. The owner is authorized to create, update and delete occurrences to keep them in agreement with reality. Some other users may have access to retrieve, others to use in anonymous procedures.

At this stage of data analysis the analyst is not concerned with how security will eventually be ensured in the computer system and environment. For example it may later be decided either to prevent an application program from retrieving particular data or to allow the program to read the data but the program is trusted not to display it to unauthorized users.

Authorization may require two or more people each to quote their secret password or produce their badge or key. With such arrangements collusion of at least two people is required to produce deliberate security violation. The analyst or someone must decide whether such a two-person access is needed in the design. For audit and recovery the system can log every action, including passwords and which terminals were used, and keep copies of stored data before or after each change. In general the procedures to ensure integrity are different from those for security. While developing the conceptual data model the analyst need not be concerned with these procedures.

Thus the purpose of the conceptual realm is to derive a consistent model of the real world valid for all applications.

There are few database management systems with facilities to support properly a conceptual data model. Its coded description is usually called the conceptual schema.

However, many authors {4.2}, {4.13}, {4.25} have recognized the importance of a conceptual model. So the analyst's aim is to construct a conceptual data model at a suitable level of abstraction regardless of whether or not the database management system available supports the conceptual design directly. This chapter provides some hints that may be useful when constructing such a model regardless of whether this will be held as a conceptual schema by an appropriate DBMS or held in manuscript or typescript form.

A conceptual data model not only represents all the entity types, attributes and relationships but should include the data aspects of the appropriate authorization and integrity constraints. This chapter is concerned with the modelling of conceptual objects (i.e. entity sets, relationship sets, entity attributes and relationship attributes). The conceptual data model represents a central reference point for all user's views. From it the actual data structures within the computer system are derived as in later chapters. The conceptual data model is stable in the sense that it should only have to be changed if a change occurs in the mini world covered by the conceptual data model or - more usually - when there is an extension of this real world portion. The conceptual data model should not be affected by modifications to the database software or application programs.

Moreover, the conceptual model should possess the following properties

1 It should correspond only to basic facts (e.g. a person has an age and a salary are two different facts and should be considered separately). This guarantees a smoother adaptation of the conceptual model to real world changes {4.20}. Other authors express the same idea by saying that <u>canonical</u> structures should be used for the conceptual model i.e. each fact should only occur once.

2 The model must behave in a totally predictable fashion {4.13}. This is achieved by conforming to a structure that ensures the desired properties.

3 The conceptual data model should not depend on the peculiarities of specific hardware or software. We use the term <u>global logical model</u> to mean the corresponding overall model that is implemented on a particular computer system.

4 The corresponding global logical model should provide logical data independence, growth independence and physical data independence. I.e. no maintenance should be needed to applications whose specifications are unchanged when there are mini-world changes.

Through the 1970s experts argued about how to satisfy these objectives{4.25}. The methods discussed in this chapter are not the only way. But they mostly satisfy the above requirements and represent a sound consensus of various approaches in the literature.

Chapter 4 has five Sections. In section 4.1 we discuss how to model part of the real world. The analyst works with conceptual objects i.e. entity types, relationship types, entity attributes and relationship attributes. One needs to be aware that the analyst's mini world is restricted to an abstraction that has suppressed all details except the relevant.

Section 4.2 discusses how the analyst may transform the first rough set of conceptual objects representing the mini world into a list of irreducible units which we call elementary relations. The list of elementary relations represents all relevant types of information of the mini world.

The transformation of conceptual objects into a list of elementary relations is justified because

1 The transformation allows the analyst to refine the rough mini world model

2 additional elementary relations may thus be derived by an appropriate procedure. Thus relationships which might have been overlooked while specifying conceptual objects may now become apparent.

The maximal set of all elementary relations (i.e. derivable and not derivable elementary relations) is called the transitive closure {4.14}. For a given list of elementary relations the transitive closure is unique.

The methods of this chapter are analysing the dependencies. (Elementary) relations are only a method of representing the dependencies and grouping together attributes according to what they depend on.

Section 4.3 explains the procedure for deriving the transitive closure from a given list of elementary relations.

3 Removing from a transitive closure all redundant elementary relations yields a new collection that contains as few as possible, called a minimal cover {4.14}. A minimal cover is a minimal set of elementary relations from which the transitive closure and all information-bearing relationships and attributes can be derived {4.1}. In general there can be many alternative minimal covers. Each minimal cover represents a possible logical choice for a non-redundant representation of the real world. The determination of minimal covers is valuable for the design of optimum global logical and physical models. Section 4.4 discusses how to remove redundant elementary relations from a closure in order to obtain all the minimal covers. In general there will be several of these minimal covers, each minimal cover being a set of elementary relations. The most appropriate should be chosen as global conceptual data model.

Section 4.5 explains a procedure for grouping attributes according to like dependencies. This reduces the number of elementary relations to be handled. It gives the model in a form with as few relations as possible.

4.1 DETERMINING CONCEPTUAL OBJECTS

The following steps may be used to identify the conceptual objects. In practice the steps are quite easy when understood.

Step 1: Determine each type of entity and assign a unique name to each.

Step 2: Determine the domains and assign a unique name to each. This gives a collection of types of information which will appear somewhere in the eventual model, e.g. perhaps as attributes.

Although this suggestion is oriented to current applications it may be convenient at the same stage to determine the minimum, average and maximum number of or rate of occurrence if it is possible to estimate such.

Step 3: Determine the primary key for each type of entity. The choice of primary key depends on meaning and use. Usually it is an attribute that has unique values and that is assigned as soon as it is known that the entity exists - possibly before values of other attributes are known.

Step 4: Replace each entity set by its primary key domain(s) and determine and name relations corresponding to entity attributes.

Remember that an entity attribute is formally defined as an association. It is from a domain (or from a subset of the Cartesian product of several domains) representing the primary key of an entity set to another domain (or to the Cartesian product of several other domains). Since an association is completely specified by an equivalent relation, this Step 4 can be achieved by specifying an adequate collection of relations.

Step 5: Determine all the types of relationships and uniquely name each.

Step 6: Replace the entity types mentioned in relationships by appropriate primary keys and represent relationship attributes by appropriate relations. E.g. if initially the analyst had thought in terms of a relationship between books and shelves, by this step it will become a relation between acquisition numbers and shelf numbers.

Example 4.1.1

Suppose that the mini world appears to consist of entity sets and entity attributes as in Fig. 4.1.1 and of relationship sets and relationship attributes as in Fig. 4.1.2. This represents how far the analyst has reached in developing the conceptual model just before doing these steps.

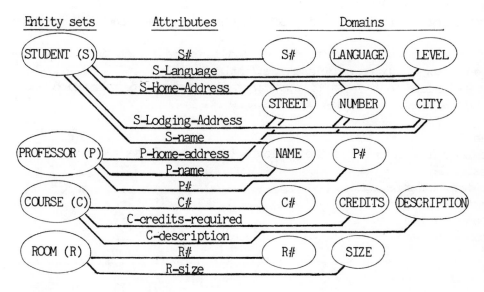

Figure 4.1.1

Domains	Relationship sets and relationship attributes	Entity sets	Relationship sets

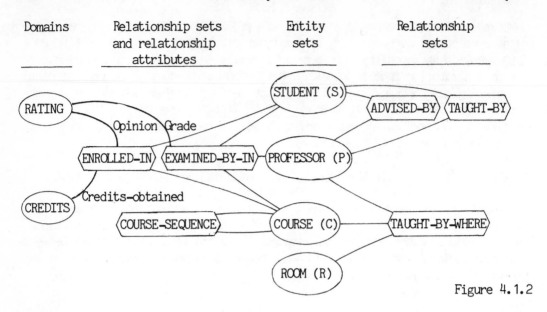

Figure 4.1.2

Step 1

The analyst thinks the mini-world consists of the following entity sets

STUDENT (S)
PROFESSOR (P) (i.e. university teacher)
COURSE (C)
ROOM (R).

By choosing the above as entity sets the analyst establishes an intention that

1 the organization would like to collect and to store information about students, professors, courses and classrooms (entity types)

2 they would like to be able to start with the storage of information about such entities as soon as the key value is known.

Step 2

The analyst distinguishes the following domains. These are not yet attributes.

S# (student number)
P# (professor number)
C# (course number)
R# (room number)
CITY
CREDIT
RATING
DESCRIPTION
NAME

NUMBER
SIZE
STREET.

Step 3
The following are entity keys
S# (for the entity set Student)
P# (for the entity set Professor)
C# (for the entity set Course)
R# (for the entity set Room).

Step 4
In the associations between entity sets and domains the entity sets from
Step 1 are replaced by their primary keys.
Each attribute is named and is a relation between the primary key
(representing the entity set) and the associated domain or domains.
For the entity set Student
S-HOME-ADDRESS (S#, STREET, NUMBER, CITY)
S-LANGUAGE (S#, LANGUAGE, LEVEL)
S-LODGING-ADDRESS (S#, STREET, NUMBER, CITY)
STUDENT-NAME (S#, NAME)
For the entity set Professor
P-HOME-ADDRESS (P#, STREET, NUMBER, CITY)
P-NAME (P#, NAME)
For the entity set Course
C-CREDITS-REQUIRED (C#, CREDIT)
C-DESCRIPTION (C#, DESCRIPTION)
For the entity set Room
R-SIZE (R#, SIZE).

Step 5
The analyst distinguishes the following relationship sets, having already
replaced the entity sets by their primary key domains
ADVISED-BY (S#, P#)
ENROLLED-IN (S#, C#)
EXAMINED-BY-IN (S#, P#, C#)
COURSE-SEQUENCE (Before.C#, After.C#)
TAUGHT-BY (S#, P#)
TAUGHT-BY-WHERE (C#, P#, R#).

The analyst has noted the following.
- Advised-by indicates the advising professor for a particular student, so
$$S\# \longleftrightarrow P\#.$$
A student is advised by one professor only but a professor can advise several
students.

- Enrolled-in indicates the courses a student is enrolled in, so

$$S\# \Longleftarrow \Longrightarrow C\#.$$

A student can attend several courses and a course can be followed by several students.

- Examined-by-in indicates the professor examining a student in a particular course subject.
- Course-sequence corresponds to prerequisite requirements.
- Taught-by indicates the professors and others that teach a particular student, so

$$S\# \Longleftarrow \Longrightarrow P\#.$$

A student can be taught by several professors and a professor can teach several students.

- Taught-by-where indicates the classroom in which a course is taught by its professor.

Step 6

For the relationship sets defined in Step 5 the analyst distinguishes the following relationship attributes (defined by means of relations)

For the relationship set Enrolled-in

CREDITS-OBTAINED (S#, C#, CREDIT)

OPINION (S#, C#, RATING)

For the relationship set Examined-by-in

GRADE (S#, P#, C#, RATING)

I.e. that defines the relationship attributes

Credits-obtained.CREDIT

Opinion.RATING (which can later be abbreviated to Opinion)

Grade.RATING (which can be abbreviated to Grade).

The analyst has noted the following.

- Credits-Obtained indicates the credits a student obtains by successfully completing a particular course.
- Opinion indicates how useful a student thought a course was.
- Grade indicates the grade provided by a professor for a student examined in a particular course. For simplicity the dependence on time has been omitted: e.g. it is assumed students could get a grade at a particular date but cannot get another grade at a resit later.

4.2 DETERMINATION OF IRREDUCIBLE UNITS

This section deals with how to transform conceptual objects describing the mini world into irreducible units {4.20}, {4.27}, {4.6} called elementary relations. We first explain irreducibility.

Irreducibility criterion

A relation is irreducible if it cannot be broken down by means of project operations into several relations of smaller degree such that these relations can be joined to reconstitute the original relation {4.20}, {4.27}. A relation that is not reducible is called an elementary relation.

Example 4.2.1

Consider the relation (from Fig. 2.2.29, page 66)
OPINION (S#, C#, Rating)

S#	C#	Rating
S1	C1	Good
S1	C2	Poor
S1	C3	Good
S2	C2	Satisfactory
S2	C3	Satisfactory
S2	C4	Good
S3	C3	Satisfactory

Figure 4.2.1

Suppose we were to split the above relation by means of the project operations

OPINION [S#, C#]
OPINION [C#, Rating]

to give the following two relations
R1 (S#, C#)   and   R2 (C#, Rating)

S#	C#
S1	C1
S1	C2
S1	C3
S2	C2
S2	C3
S2	C4
S3	C3

C#	Rating
C1	Good
C2	Poor
C2	Satisfactory
C3	Good
C3	Satisfactory
C4	Good

Figure 4.2.2

On joining R1 and R2 by

R1 * R2

we obtain

OPINION-J (S#, C#, Rating)

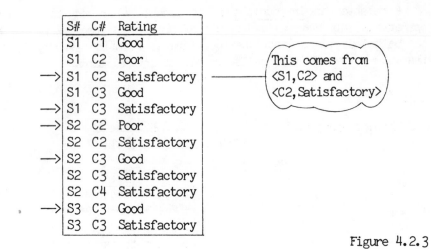

Figure 4.2.3

The result contains tuples (marked with ⟶) that were not in the original. Any other way of splitting the original relation gives the same problem. Thus the relation Opinion is irreducible. It is an elementary relation.

Example 4.2.2

An example of a reducible relation is the relation
        S-HOME-ADDRESS (S#, Street, Number, City)

S#	Street	Number	City
S1	Champel	20	Waterloo
S2	Piccadilly	12	London
S3	Elysee	87	Paris
S4	Louise	5	Brussels

Figure 4.2.4

Breaking down the relation by the project operations
        R1 ⟵ S-HOME-ADDRESS [S#, Street]
        R2 ⟵ S-HOME-ADDRESS [S#, Number]
        R3 ⟵ S-HOME-ADDRESS [S#, City]
into the relations

R1(S#, Street)   R2(S#, Number)   R3(S#, City)

S#	Street
S1	Champel
S2	Piccadilly
S3	Elysee
S4	Louise

S#	Number
S1	20
S2	12
S3	87
S4	5

S#	City
S1	Waterloo
S2	London
S3	Paris
S4	Brussels

Figure 4.2.5

still allows us to reconstitute the original version by means of the natural join operations

$$R1 * R2 * R3.$$

Hence the relation S-Home-address is reducible. Note that R1, R2 and R3 are elementary relations.

The question arises whether or not it is possible to establish precise rules how to break a given collection of relations into irreducible units. This can be done. It needs the following concepts.
- Functional Dependence {4.11}
- Full Functional Dependence {4.11}
- Multivalued Dependence {4.17}, {4.32}
- Transitive Dependence {4.11}
together with
- Candidate Key and Primary Key definitions {4.11}.

Functional Dependence

An attribute B of a relation is <u>functionally dependent</u> on the attribute A of it if at every instant of time each A-value is associated with no more than one B-value {4.11}. For example payment due is functionally dependent on account number.

Equivalently, there exists at every instant of time a simple or conditional association from A to B. It means B is a function of A representable as a relation with two columns. Where the association is conditional there may be some A values that are not associated with a B value. This means tuples with undefined B values, i.e. <u>null</u> or <u>void</u> values, are possible. With time the B value for a particular A value may change. For example Telephone number is functionally dependent on whatever identifies each person (assuming no one has more than one telephone number).

The notation used to indicate that B is functionally dependent on A in the relation R is

$$R.A \longrightarrow R.B$$

whereas

$$R.A \not\longrightarrow R.B$$

denotes that B is not functionally dependent on A in R.

The definition given above can be generalized by saying that a collection of attributes in R, say B_1, ... B_n, is _functionally dependent_ on another collection of attributes in R, say A_1 ... A_m, if, at every instant of time, each list of values

$$\langle r[A_1], r[A_2], \dots r[A_m] \rangle$$

is associated with no more than one list of values

$$\langle r[B_1], r[B_2], \dots r[B_n] \rangle$$

where $r[A_1]$ means a value of attribute A_1 belonging to a particular row of the relation.

The notation $\longrightarrow$, $\not\longrightarrow$ introduced for individual attributes is also used for collections of attributes. Thus

$$R.[A_1, \dots A_m] \longrightarrow R.[B_1, \dots B_n]$$

indicates that the collection of B attributes in R is functionally dependent on the collection of A attributes in R.

The collection of B attributes being functionally dependent on the collection of A attributes implies each individual attribute of the B collection is functionally dependent on the whole of the A collection. Thus

$$R.[A_1, A_2, \dots A_m] \longrightarrow R.B_1$$
$$R.[A_1, A_2, \dots A_m] \longrightarrow R.B_2$$
$$\dots$$
$$R.[A_1, A_2, \dots A_m] \longrightarrow R.B_n$$

Trivial Dependence

A functional dependence of the form

$$R.D \longrightarrow R.E$$

where E is a subset of D is called a _trivial dependence_ {4.11}. We write it for example

$$S\#, \ C\# \ \text{---} \longrightarrow S\#.$$

Candidate Keys, Primary Key and Foreign Keys

We are now in a position to introduce the definitions for candidate and primary key.

We define an attribute (or attribute collection) K as a _candidate key_ {4.11} of a relation R if it has the following properties.

1 In each tuple of R the value of K uniquely identifies that tuple (_Unique Identification_). Corollary: each attribute in R is functionally dependent on K.

2 In the case where K is an attribute collection no attribute in K can be discarded without destroying property 1 (Non-redundancy).   Corollary: every proper subset of the attribute collection K is functionally independent of any other proper subset of the attribute collection K.   In other words there exists a (M:M)-mapping between any two different proper subsets of the attribute collection K.

The existence of a candidate key of any relation R is guaranteed by the fact that the relation is a set.   This means particularly that each tuple in R is unique.   Hence at least the collection of all the attributes in R has the unique identification property.   In practice it is usually not necessary to involve all the attributes since unique identification is normally achievable by choosing an appropriate subset of the attributes in question.

A relation may possess several candidate keys.   One candidate key is always arbitrarily designated as the primary key.   The usual operational distinction between the primary key and other candidate keys (if any) is that no tuple is allowed to have an undefined value for any of the attributes constituting the primary key, whereas any other attribute may have an undefined value {4.11}.

From here on we shall always underline the attribute(s) constituting the primary key of a relation and we shall call these attributes key attributes. Attributes that do not participate in any candidate key will be called non-key attributes.

We now introduce the concept of a foreign key.   An attribute of a relation R1 is a foreign key if it is not the primary key of R1 but its values are values of the primary key of some relation R2.   R1 and R2 are not necessarily distinct {4.13}.

Foreign keys provide - together with primary keys - a means of representing associations between relations.   In the case R1(K, C) and R2(K', D) with
K = the attribute collection constituting the primary key of R1
K' = the attribute collection constituting the primary key of R2
C = the attributes in the complement of K
D = the attributes in the complement of K'
the trivial dependence
$$R1.K \longrightarrow R2.K'$$
holds provided that
$$K' \subseteq K.$$
The collection of attributes in K which are in K' represent a foreign key.

Example 4.2.3

Consider the relation

S-HOME-ADDRESS (S#, Street,   Number, City)

S#	Street	Number	City
S1	Champel	20	Waterloo
S2	Piccadilly	12	London
S3	Elysee	87	Paris
S4	Louise	5	Brussels
S5	Louise	20	Brussels

Figure 4.2.6

The only attribute whose values uniquely identify each tuple in S-Home-address is S#.   Hence S-Home-address possesses a single candidate key which is automatically taken as primary key.

S-Home-address has the following functional dependencies

$$S\# \longrightarrow Street$$
$$S\# \longrightarrow Number$$
$$S\# \longrightarrow City.$$

I.e. each S#-value has no more than one Street, Number and City value associated with it.

We draw functional dependencies as below.

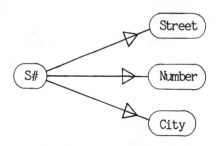

Figure 4.2.7

Each attribute is represented by a box and arrows stand for functional dependencies.   This diagrammatical representation has been found useful to depict complex dependencies within relations.   Usually boxes with soft or rounded ends are drawn in handwriting and the drawings are called <u>bubble charts</u> {4.18}.

Example 4.2.4

This example illustrates compound keys, foreign keys and a diagram style for compound keys.

Consider the relation

OPINION (S#, C#, Rating)

S#	C#	Rating
S1	C2	Poor
S1	C3	Good
S2	C2	Satisfactory
S2	C3	Satisfactory
S2	C4	Good
S3	C3	Satisfactory

Figure 4.2.8

Unique identification is achievable in this case only by means of the attribute collection S#, C#. Hence Opinion possesses a single candidate key which is automatically considered as primary key. Opinion has the following functional dependence

$$S\#, C\# \longrightarrow Rating.$$

I.e. given a particular S#-C# combination there exists precisely one corresponding Rating. This statement reflects the real world fact that a particular student provides a single opinion for a particular course.

The analyst must realize that

$$S\# \not\longrightarrow Rating$$
$$C\# \not\longrightarrow Rating$$

i.e. Rating is not functionally dependent on either S# or C#. Once again these statements reflect precise real world facts. A particular student does not have the same opinion about every course he is enrolled in (S# $\not\longrightarrow$ Rating), and a particular course gets different evaluations from its various students (C# $\not\longrightarrow$ Rating).

This is shown below. The fact that Rating is functionally dependent on the attribute combination S#, C# has been recorded by drawing an arrow from a box which includes boxes for S# and C# to a box representing Rating.

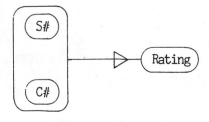

Figure 4.2.9

The attribute S# in Opinion represents a foreign key, since it is not the primary key of Opinion and its values are values of the primary key of the S-Home-address relation (Example 4.2.3). Hence the trivial dependence

$$Opinion.(S\#, C\#) - \to S\text{-Home-address}.S\#$$

holds.

Splitting of Relations

A relation R containing several attributes that are functionally dependent
on other attributes in R can be broken down into several relations of smaller
degree such that these relations can be joined to reconstitute the original
relation.

Example 4.2.5

In the relation
              S-HOME-ADDRESS (S#, Street, Number, City)
there are three dependencies
 S# $\longrightarrow$ Street
 S# $\longrightarrow$ Number
 S# $\longrightarrow$ City.
So the relation can be split by the project operations
                    R1 $\longleftarrow$ S-HOME-ADDRESS [S#, Street]
                    R2 $\longleftarrow$ S-HOME-ADDRESS [S#, Number]
                    R3 $\longleftarrow$ S-HOME-ADDRESS [S#, City].
This gives the following relations.
        R1(S#, Street)   R2(S#, Number)   R3(S#, City)

S#	Street		S#	Number		S#	City
S1	Champel		S1	20		S1	Waterloo
S2	Piccadilly		S2	12		S2	London
S3	Elysee		S3	87		S3	Paris
S4	Louise		S4	5		S4	Brussels
S5	Louise		S5	20		S5	Brussels

Figure 4.2.10

R1, R2 and R3 are not further reducible. Joining R1, R2 and R3 by
                    R1 * R2 * R3
yields the original relation S-Home-address. Hence S-Home-address is reducible,
whereas R1, R2 and R3 are elementary relations.

The general situation is as follows.
Let R(K, A) be a relation where K represents the collection of attributes
constituting a candidate key of R and A the collection of all the other attributes in R. Thus
              $K = K_1, K_2, \ldots K_m$
              $A = A_1, A_2, \ldots A_n.$
Since K represents a candidate key the functional dependences

$$K \longrightarrow A_1$$
$$K \longrightarrow A_2$$
...
$$K \longrightarrow A_n$$

are also valid in R.   One can show {4.11} that in this case R(K,A) is the natural join of its projections $R[K, A_1]$, $R[K, A_2]$, ... $R[K, A_n]$. Thus
$$R(K,A) = R[K,A_1] * R[K,A_2] ... * R[K,A_n].$$
Hence R is reducible.

The reduction criterion is as follows. A relation R with several attributes A that are each functionally dependent on a particular attribute (or attributes) K can always be broken down into several relations of smaller degree. These relations each contain K together with a subset of attributes from A.

A relation which consists of a single attribute that is functionally dependent on a single candidate key may - under certain conditions - further be broken down. The next example illustrates this statement and shows how the reduction criterion established so far requires an important supplement.

<u>Example 4.2.6</u>

Consider the relation
SUPPLIER (S#, Supplier-name, P#, P-name, Qty)

S#	Supplier-name	P#	P-name	Qty
S1	Biggs	P1	Nut	10
S1	Biggs	P2	Screw	15
S1	Biggs	P3	Cam	10
S2	Small Co	P2	Screw	12
S2	Small Co	P3	Cam	18
S2	Small Co	P4	Screw	25
S3	Biggs	P2	Screw	19

Figure 4.2.11

The interpretation of say
<S1, Biggs, P1, Nut, 10>
as a tuple is that the the supplier with the number S1 named Biggs supplies the part with the number P1 named Nut in a quantity of 10.

If different suppliers may have identical names (e.g. S1 and S3) and different parts may have identical part names as well (e.g. P2 and P4) then unique identification is achievable only by means of the attributes S#, P#. Hence the relation Supplier possesses a single candidate key which must become the primary key.

Since
S#, P# $\longrightarrow$ Supplier-name
S#, P# $\longrightarrow$ P-name
S#, P# $\longrightarrow$ Qty

the analyst might (according to the reduction criterion) split the relation Sup-
plier by means of the project operations
  R1 ⟵ SUPPLIER [S#, P#, Supplier-name]
  R2 ⟵ SUPPLIER [S#, P#, P-name]
  R3 ⟵ SUPPLIER [S#, P#, Qty]
to give the following three relations

          R1(S#, P#, Supplier-name)   R2(S#, P#, P-name)   R3(S#, P#, Qty)

S#	P#	Supplier-name
S1	P1	Biggs
S1	P2	Biggs
S1	P3	Biggs
S2	P2	Small Co
S2	P3	Small Co
S2	P4	Small Co
S3	P2	Biggs

S#	P#	P-name
S1	P1	Nut
S1	P2	Screw
S1	P3	Cam
S2	P2	Screw
S2	P3	Cam
S2	P4	Screw
S3	P2	Screw

S#	P#	Qty
S1	P1	10
S1	P2	15
S1	P3	10
S2	P2	12
S2	P3	18
S2	P4	25
S3	P2	19

Figure 4.2.12

  Joining R1, R2 and R3 by
                        R1 * R2 * R3
yields the original relation Supplier. Hence Supplier is reducible.
     The relations R1, R2 and R3 each contain a single non-key attribute (i.e.
Supplier-name, P-name, Qty) that is functionally dependent on a single candidate
key (i.e. S#, P#).
     We next show that R1 and R2 may be further broken down whereas R3 is ir-
reducible. The analyst would have the following dependencies
              in R1:   S# ⟶ Supplier-name
                        P# ⟶̸ Supplier-name
              in R2:   S# ⟶̸ P-name
                        P# ⟶ P-name
              in R3:   S# ⟶̸ Qty
                        P# ⟶̸ Qty.
In R1 the non-key attribute (i.e. Supplier-name) is functionally dependent on a
subset of the candidate key (i.e. S#). R2 is similar, whereas R3 contains no
similar dependence.
     Splitting R1 and R2 (i.e. the relations in which the non-key attribute is
functionally dependent on a subset of the candidate key) by means of the project
operations
                   R1 [S#, Supplier-name]
                     R2 [P#, P-name]
yields the following two relations

R4(S#, Supplier-name)   R5(P#, P-name)

S#	Supplier-name
S1	Biggs
S2	Small Co
S3	Biggs

P#	P-name
P1	Nut
P2	Screw
P3	Cam
P4	Screw

Figure 4.2.13

These can be used to reconstitute the original Supplier relation by means of the natural join R3 * R4 * R5.

R3, R4 and R5 are not further reducible so they are elementary relations. The analyst should include them in the conceptual data model instead of the original Supplier relation.

Full Functional Dependence

The question arises whether or not there is a criterion allowing one to decide if a relation consisting of a single attribute that is functionally dependent on a single candidate key (e.g. the relations R1, R2 and R3 as discussed in Example 4.2.6 or the relation Opinion in Example 4.2.4) is reducible. As it happens full functional dependence is a suitable concept to achieve this.

The attribute (or attribute collection) B in a relation R is fully functionally dependent on the attribute collection A in R if B is functionally dependent on A but not functionally dependent on any proper subset of A {4.11}.

This is equivalent to having either a simple or a conditional association. I.e. the attribute (or attribute collection) B in R is fully functionally dependent on the attribute collection A in R if there exists a simple or conditional association from A to B and every association from any proper subset of A to B is complex.

The notation used to indicate that B is fully functionally dependent on A in R is

$$R.A \implies R.B$$

We write

$$R.A \nRightarrow R.B$$

to mean that B is not fully functionally dependent on A in R.

Example 4.2.7

Consider the relation

S-LANGUAGE (S#, Language, Level)

S#	Language	Level
S1	French	High
S1	German	High
S1	English	Satisfactory
S2	Italian	Low
S2	French	Satisfactory
S2	English	High
S3	English	Satisfactory

Figure 4.2.14

Unique identification is achievable only by the attribute collection S#, Language. So these must be chosen as the primary key.

The dependency is

$$S\#, \text{Language} \longrightarrow \text{Level}$$

i.e. Level is functionally dependent on the attribute collection S#, Language. However

$$S\# \quad\quad \not\longrightarrow \text{Level}$$
$$\text{Language} \not\longrightarrow \text{Level}$$

i.e. Level is not functionally dependent on any proper subset of the attribute collection S#, Language. From that the analyst concludes

$$S\#, \text{Language} \Longrightarrow \text{Level}$$

i.e. Level is fully functionally dependent on the attribute collection S#, Language. This reflects the real world fact that each student has a distinct skill level for each language he or she is familiar with and that each language may be spoken by several students each with a distinct skill level for it.

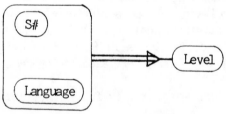

Figure 4.2.15

The fact that Level is fully functionally dependent on the attribute combination S#, Language has been shown by drawing the arrow $\Longrightarrow$ from a box which includes a box for S# and Language to a box representing Level. Double line arrows mean full functional dependency.

Example 4.2.8

Suppose an analyst found a college administrator with the following table, to which he or she gave the name Opinion2.

OPINION2 (S#, Name, C#, Description, Rating)

S#	Name	C#	Description	Rating
S1	Brown	C1	Math	Good
S1	Brown	C2	Chem	Poor
S1	Brown	C3	Physics	Good
S2	Smith	C2	Chem	Satisfactory
S2	Smith	C3	Physics	Satisfactory
S2	Smith	C4	English	Good
S3	Brown	C2	Chem	Satisfactory

Figure 4.2.16

The interpretation of the tuple
<S1, Brown, C1, Math, Good>
is that the student numbered S1 named Brown has a good opinion of course C1 on Math.

The analyst may find from discussion that each course has a distinct description but that student names are not unique. Thus there are two candidate keys for the relation, namely {S#, C#} and {S#, Description}. Assuming that C# is an entity key domain (but Description is not) then the primary key of the relation is S#, C#.

The analyst determines the dependencies on S#, C#.

S#, C# ⟶ Name   (Name is functionally dependent on S#, C#)

S#   ⟶ Name   (Name functionally dependent on
                  S# representing a subset of S#, C#)

C#   ⟶̸ Name   (Name not functionally dependent on
                  C# representing a subset of S#, C#)

Thus the analyst should deduce

S#, C# ⇏ Name   (Name not fully functionally dependent on S#, C#)

Similarly

S#, C# ⟶ Description
S#   ⟶̸ Description
C#   ⟶ Description

imply

S#, C# ⇏ Description.

Similarly

S#, C# ⟶ Rating
S#   ⟶̸ Rating
C#   ⟶̸ Rating

imply

S#, C# ⟹ Rating.

Here are these dependencies drawn.

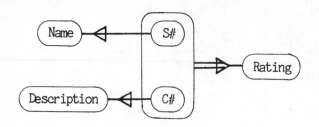

Figure 4.2.17

Name is functionally dependent on S# but not fully functionally dependent on the combination S#, C#. This has been recorded by drawing an arrow from the box representing S# to the box representing Name. Description is similar.

Since there is no difference between functional dependence and full functional dependence in the case of dependence on a single attribute, both can be shown by a single line arrow.

Example 4.2.9

In the relation
$$\text{SUPPLIER (S\#, Supplier-name, P\#, P-name, Qty)}$$
of Example 4.2.6 the following dependencies hold

1.1   S#, P# $\longrightarrow$ Supplier-name
1.2   S# $\longrightarrow$ Supplier-name
1.3   P# $\longrightarrow\!\!\!\!/$ Supplier-name.

Hence because 1.2 holds
$$\text{S\#, P\#} \not\Longrightarrow \text{Supplier-name.}$$

Similarly
2.1   S#, P# $\longrightarrow$ P-name
2.2   S# $\longrightarrow\!\!\!\!/$ P-name
2.3   P# $\longrightarrow$ P-name.

Hence because 2.3 holds
$$\text{S\#, P\#} \not\Longrightarrow \text{P-name.}$$

Similarly
3.1   S#, P# $\longrightarrow$ Qty
3.2   S# $\longrightarrow\!\!\!\!/$ Qty
3.3   P# $\longrightarrow\!\!\!\!/$ Qty.

Hence
$$\text{S\#, P\#} \Longrightarrow \text{Qty.}$$

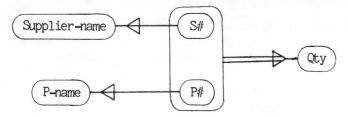

Figure 4.2.18

Splitting into Joinable Relations

Next, can a relation R containing attributes that are fully functionally dependent on an attribute collection K in R be broken down into several relations of smaller degree such that these relations can be joined to reconstitute the original relation?

Example 4.2.10

In the relation of Example 4.2.7
$$\text{S-LANGUAGE (S\#, \underline{Language}, Level)}$$
the only non-key attribute, Level, is fully functionally dependent on the only candidate key S#, Language, so the relation is not reducible, i.e. it is an elementary relation.

The relation
$$\text{OPINION (\underline{S\#}, \underline{C\#}, Rating)}$$
of Example 4.2.4 is a similar case. Opinion contains a single attribute (i.e. Rating) that is fully functionally dependent on the only candidate key S#, C#. Therefore
$$\text{S\#, C\#} \Longrightarrow \text{Rating.}$$
The full functional dependence holds because
$$\text{S\#, C\#} \longrightarrow \text{Rating}$$
$$\text{S\#} \quad \longrightarrow\!\!\!\!/ \;\; \text{Rating}$$
$$\text{C\#} \quad \longrightarrow\!\!\!\!/ \;\; \text{Rating.}$$

The general situation is as follows.
Let R(K, A, B) be a relation where K represents the collection of attributes constituting a candidate key of R, A the collection of attributes that are fully functionally dependent on K and B the remaining attributes in R. Thus
$$K = K_1, K_2, \ldots K_m$$
$$A = A_1, A_2, \ldots A_n$$
$$B = B_1, B_2, \ldots B_o$$
$$K \Longrightarrow A$$
$$K \not\Longrightarrow B.$$

Each of the attributes in B is functionally dependent on K (otherwise K would not represent a candidate key) and on at least one subset of K (otherwise the attributes in B would be fully functionally dependent on K). Thus

$$K \longrightarrow B$$

Suppose there is a subset K' of K such that the attributes in B are all fully functionally dependent on K'. Thus

$$K' \longrightarrow B$$
$$K' \subset K$$
$$K' \Longrightarrow B.$$

The relation R then can be broken down by means of the project operations

$$R[K, A_1], R[K, A_2], \dots R[K, A_n],$$
$$R[K', B_1], R[K', B_2], \dots R[K', B_o].$$

The relation R is reducible as it can be obtained from the join of these projections

$$R[K, A_1] * R[K, A_2] * \dots R[K, A_n] *$$
$$R[K', B_1] * R[K', B_2] * \dots R[K', B_o].$$

The reduction criterion can thus be restated. A relation R containing a collection of attributes A_1, A_2, ... A_n that are functionally dependent on a particular attribute (or a particular attribute collection) K can always be broken down into several relations of smaller degree. These relations each contain K together with a single attribute, say A_i. Irreducible relations are obtained where the dependent A_i is fully functionally dependent on the candidate key K.

Where A_i is not fully functionally dependent on K the analyst should look for a subset K' such that

$$K' \subset K \quad \text{(i.e. a proper subset)}$$

and either

$$K' \Longrightarrow A_i \quad \text{(if K' is an attribute collection)}$$

or

$$K' \longrightarrow A \quad \text{(if K' is a single attribute).}$$

The relation R (K', A_i) is then irreducible. It is always possible to find such a K' (possibly a single attribute) otherwise A_i would be fully functionally dependent on K.

Example 4.2.11

Consider the relation

OPINION2 (S#, Name, C#, Description, Rating)

as discussed in Example 4.2.8. Since

S#, C# $\Longrightarrow$ Rating
S# $\longrightarrow$ Name
C# $\longrightarrow$ Description

the analyst might split the relation by means of the project operations

        R1 ⟵ STUDENT [S#, C#, Rating]
        R2 ⟵ STUDENT [S#, Name]
        R3 ⟵ STUDENT [C#, Description]

to give the relations

R1(S#, C#, Rating)   R2(S#, Name) R3(C#, Description)

S#	C#	Rating
S1	C1	Good
S1	C2	Poor
S1	C3	Good
S2	C2	Satisfactory
S2	C3	Satisfactory
S2	C4	Good
S3	C2	Satisfactory

S#	Name
S1	Brown
S2	Smith
S3	Brown

C#	Description
C1	Math
C2	Chem
C3	Physics
C4	English

Figure 4.2.19

R1, R2 and R3 are not further reducible. Joining R1, R2 and R3 by R1 ∗ R2 ∗ R3 gives the original relation Opinion2. There is no loss of information. Hence Opinion2 is reducible. R1, R2 and R3 cannot be further split. So the analyst should include these three in the conceptual data model instead of the relation Opinion2 that the college administrator had.

Multivalued Dependence

Some associations have a more complicated structure. They are rare, but the analyst should be able to recognize them. An example is where parts are made by employees using machines and the operating of a particular machine is always done by one of a corresponding team of several employees, and there are similar teams for other machines.

Example 4.2.12

Consider the relation

MANUFACTURE1 (P#, M#, E#)

P#	M#	E#
P1	M1	E1
P1	M1	E2
P1	M1	E3
P1	M2	E3
P1	M2	E4
P2	M1	E1
P2	M1	E2
P2	M1	E3
P3	M2	E3
P3	M2	E4

Figure 4.2.20

The tuple <P1, M1, E1> means product P1 can be made on machine M1 operated by employee E1. The meaningful associations are as follows.

P# $\longleftrightarrow\!\!\longrightarrow$ M# i.e. making a product requires several machines and a machine may be used for several products

M# $\longleftrightarrow\!\!\longrightarrow$ E# i.e. a machine can be operated by any one of several employees and an employee may operate several machines

P# $\longleftrightarrow\!\!\longrightarrow$ E# i.e. making a product requires several employees and an employee may be involved in the making of several products.

Thus every proper subset of the attribute collection in Manufacture1 is functionally independent of every other proper subset. Therefore the only candidate key and hence the primary key of Manufacture1 is P#, M#, E# (i.e. the relation is <u>all key</u>).

The essential feature of the example is that a machine is always operated by one of the same set of employees. Therefore the set of employees for a machine essentially depends only on the machine and not on the products produced by the machine. Thus the set of E#-values that appears with a given M#-value appears with every combination of this M#-value and appropriate P#-values. E.g. E3 and E4 can operate M2 to make P1, so they both also occur with M2 for any other product made on M2 such as P3. This is called a multivalued dependence of E# on M# and is written

$$M\# \longrightarrow\!\!\longrightarrow E\#$$

We say M# multidetermines E# in Manufacture1. In other words in Manufacture1 there exists a multivalued dependence from M# to E#.

Here is how to draw this dependence.

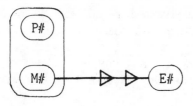

Figure 4.2.21

The general situation is as follows. A relation R may have an attribute (or an attribute collection) B whose values depend on the values of another attribute (or another attribute collection) A in R such that there exists more than one B-value for a given A-value. B then is not functionally dependent on A but it may be multivalued dependent on A in R.

Multivalued dependence can be defined as follows {4.17}, {4.32}. Let R(X) be a relation where X represents the set of all attributes in R. Now let A and B be subsets of X. Thus $A \subset X$ and $B \subset X$. A and B do not have to be disjoint. Let C represent the complement of the union of A and B in X. Thus

$$C = X - (A \cup B).$$

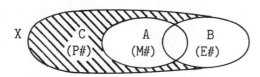

Figure 4.2.22

We say that B is <u>multivalued dependent</u> on A if the set of B-values that appears in R with a given A-value appears with every combination of this A-value and a given C-value. This means that the set of B-values is a function of the A-value only and does not depend on the C-values that appear.

The general notation to indicate that B is multivalued dependent on A in R (or that A multidetermines B in R) is

$$R.A \longrightarrow\!\!\!\rightarrow R.B$$

The R. mean in the relation R. The opposite is

$$R.A \longrightarrow\!\!\!\!/\!\!\!\rightarrow R.B$$

for B is not multivalued dependent on A in R.

The validity of a multivalued dependence depends not only on the A- and B-values but on the values of all the attributes in X. As stated in {4.4} it would be more appropriate, perhaps, to use the notation

$$R.A \longrightarrow\!\!\!\rightarrow R.B(X)$$

to stress the fact that the multivalued dependence involves all the attributes in X. It is common practice to omit the reference to X and write simply

$$R.A \longrightarrow\!\!\!\rightarrow R.B$$

assuming that X is a known set of attributes.

Next, can a relation with a multivalued dependence be broken down into several relations of smaller degree such that these relations can be joined to reconstitute the original relation?

Let R(X) be a relation as before, X being the set of all the attributes. Let A and B be subsets of X and let C be the complement of the union of A and B in X. Assume that

$$A \longrightarrow\!\!\!\!\rightarrow B.$$

One can prove {4.17} {4.32} that R(X) is the natural join of its projections R[A,B] and R[A,C]. Thus R is reducible.

$$R(X) = R(A, B, C) = R[A, B] * R[A, C]$$

Example 4.2.13

MANUFACTURE1 (P#, M#, E#) with M# $\longrightarrow\!\!\!\!\rightarrow$ E# might be split by means of the project operations

$$R11 \longleftarrow MANUFACTURE1\ [P\#,\ M\#]$$
$$R12 \longleftarrow MANUFACTURE1\ [M\#,\ E\#]$$

to give the following two relations

R11 (P#, M#)   R12 (M#, E#)

P#	M#
P1	M1
P1	M2
P2	M2
P3	M2

M#	E#
M1	E1
M1	E2
M1	E3
M2	E3
M2	E4

Figure 4.2.23

All information in the original Manufacture1 can be obtained by joining these. Hence Manufacture1 is reducible. Note however that R1 and R2 are elementary relations. Also note that these elementary relations represent relations that are all key and do not have any multivalued dependence.

This situation needs clarifying by discussing additional cases.

Example 4.2.14

Suppose the analyst finds
MANUFACTURE2 (P#, M#, E#)

P#	M#	E#
P1	M1	E1
P1	M1	E2
P1	M1	E3
P1	M2	E3
P1	M2	E4
P2	M1	E3
P2	M1	E4

Figure 4.2.24

In this relation
P# $\longleftrightarrow\!\!\!\!\gg$ M#
P# $\longleftrightarrow\!\!\!\!\gg$ E#
M# $\longleftrightarrow\!\!\!\!\gg$ E#
but
M# $\longrightarrow\!\!\!\!\!\!/\longrightarrow$ E#.

There is no way to split the above relation into relations of smaller degree such that the original can be reconstituted by means of join operations. Hence the relation is not reducible, i.e. it represents an ER.

Example 4.2.15

Suppose the analyst finds
MANUFACTURE3 (P#, M#, E#)

P#	M#	E#
P1	M1	E1
P2	M2	E2
P3	M1	E2
P4	M1	E1
P5	M3	E3
P6	M4	E1

Figure 4.2.25

Here
P# $\longleftrightarrow$ M# i.e. a particular product can only be made on a single machine but a machine may be used for the production of several products
P# $\longleftrightarrow$ E# i.e. a product is produced by a single employee but an employee may produce several products
M# $\longleftrightarrow\!\!\!\!\gg$ E# i.e. a machine may be operated by several employees and an employee may operate several machines.

This example does not involve a multivalued dependency.

Obviously the only candidate key and hence the primary key is P#. Manufacture3 represents a relation in which two attributes M# and E# are functionally dependent on the same candidate key. Hence Manufacture3 may be split by the project operations

$$R31 \longleftarrow MANUFACTURE3\ [P\#,\ M\#]$$
$$R32 \longleftarrow MANUFACTURE3\ [P\#,\ E\#]$$

to give the following two elementary relations

$$R31\ (\underline{P\#},\ M\#)\ \text{and}\ R32\ (\underline{P\#},\ E\#)$$

P#	M#
P1	M1
P2	M2
P3	M1
P4	M1
P5	M3
P6	M4

P#	E#
P1	E1
P2	E2
P3	E2
P4	E3
P5	E3
P6	E1

Figure 4.2.26

Joining R31 and R32 by

$$R31 * R32$$

yields the original relation Manufacture3. Hence Manufacture3 is reducible. R31 and R32 are elementary relations.

Example 4.2.16

Another situation arises with the relation

MANUFACTURE4 $(\underline{P\#},\ M\#,\ E\#)$

P#	M#	E#
P1	M1	E1
P2	M2	E2
P3	M1	E1
P4	M1	E1
P5	M3	E2
P6	M4	E1

Figure 4.2.27

Here we suppose that the analyst finds

$$P\# \longleftarrow\!\longrightarrow M\#$$
$$P\# \longleftarrow\!\longrightarrow E\#$$
$$M\# \longleftarrow\!\longrightarrow E\#$$

i.e. a machine is always operated by a single employee and an employee may operate several machines.

Fig. 4.2.28 shows this.

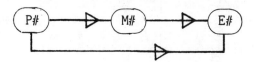

Figure 4.2.28

The analyst should realize the functional dependence
$$P\# \longrightarrow E\#$$
is the product function of
$$P\# \longrightarrow M\#$$
and
$$M\# \longrightarrow E\#.$$

Hence $P\# \longrightarrow E\#$ can be deduced from $P\# \longrightarrow M\#$ and $M\# \longrightarrow E\#$. Splitting Manufacture4 by the project operations
$$R41 \longleftarrow MANUFACTURE4\ [P\#, M\#]$$
$$R42 \longleftarrow MANUFACTURE4\ [M\#, E\#]$$
gives the following relations.

R41 (P#, M#)   R42 (M#, E#)

P#	M#
P1	M1
P2	M2
P3	M1
P4	M1
P5	M3
P6	M4

M#	E#
M1	E1
M2	E2
M3	E2
M4	E1

Figure 4.2.29

The original relation Manufacture4 (and with that the functional dependence $P\# \longrightarrow E\#$) can be obtained by means of the natural join operation
$$R41 * R42.$$
So Manufacture4 is reducible. The relations R41 and R42 are elementary relations.

The analyst must avoid the following pitfall or its equivalent in more complicated cases. Manufacture4 can also be broken down by the project operations
$$MANUFACTURE4\ [P\#, M\#]$$
$$MANUFACTURE4\ [M\#, E\#]$$
$$MANUFACTURE4\ [P\#, E\#]$$
to give the following relations

R41 (P#, M#)   R42 (M#, E#)   R43 (P#, E#)

P#	M#
P1	M1
P2	M2
P3	M1
P4	M1
P5	M3
P6	M4

M#	E#
M1	E1
M2	E2
M3	E2
M4	E1

P#	E#
P1	E1
P2	E2
P3	E1
P4	E1
P5	E2
P6	E1

Figure 4.2.30

Joining R41, R42 and R43 by

R41 * R42 * R43

yields the original relation Manufacture4. The pitfall is R43. The relation R43 is not essential since it can be deduced from the relations R41 and R42.

Transitive Dependence

We say that the attribute E# is transitively dependent on the attribute P# in Manufacture4. The transitivity is through M#. Since the determination of transitive dependence within relations is essential for deriving irreducible units we discuss the concept next.

Transitive dependence can formally be defined as follows {4.11}.

Suppose that A, B, C are three distinct attributes or attribute collections of a relation R (hence R is at least of degree 3). Suppose that the following dependencies always hold.

$$R.A \longrightarrow R.B$$
$$R.B \longrightarrow\!\!\!\!/\ R.A$$
$$R.B \longrightarrow R.C.$$

The analyst should deduce

$$R.A \longrightarrow R.C$$
$$R.C \longrightarrow\!\!\!\!/\ R.A.$$

The next figure shows this.

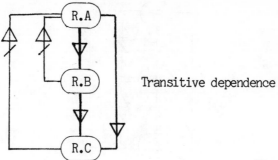

Transitive dependence

Figure 4.2.31

Where
$$R.C \not\longrightarrow R.B$$
(see left figure below) we say that C is <u>strictly transitively dependent</u> on A
under R.   In the case where
$$R.C \longrightarrow R.B$$
(see right figure below) both B and C are transitively dependent on A under R.

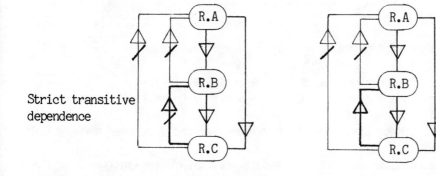

Strict transitive
dependence

Figure 4.2.32

<u>Example 4.2.17</u>

For Manufacture4 (P#, M#, E#) as in Example 4.2.16, Fig. 4.2.33 depicts the
dependencies
$$P\# \longleftrightarrow M\#$$
$$P\# \longleftrightarrow E\#$$
$$M\# \longleftrightarrow E\#.$$
E# is strictly transitively dependent on P# (through M#).

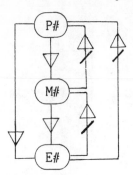

Figure 4.2.33

Example 4.2.18

Suppose an analyst found a user with a relation W concerning employees and their departments

$$W \ (E\#, \ D\#, \ M\#, \ CT)$$

where

E# = employee serial number
D# = department number of employee
M# = serial number of department manager
CT = contract type (government or non-government)

Suppose that the structure is as follows (based on {4.11})

E# ⟵⟶ D# i.e. at any time an employee is assigned to only one department but a department has many employees

D# ⟵⟶ M# i.e. a department has only one manager and a manager manages only one department

D# ⟵⟶ CT i.e. a department is involved in work on either government or non-government contracts, not both, and several departments are involved in work on a particular contract.

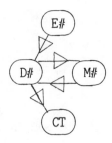

Figure 4.2.34

The analyst deduces the following.

E# ⟵⟶ M# with the interpretation that an employee has only one manager and a manager has several subordinates

M# ⟵⟶ CT i.e. a manager is involved in work on either government or non-government contracts, not both, and several managers are involved in work on a particular contract

E# $\longleftrightarrow$ CT i.e. an employee is involved in work on either government or non-government contracts.

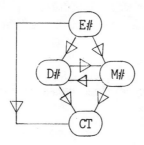

Figure 4.2.35

This figure is complete in that all functional dependencies are shown. Any attribute that is not connected by an arrow from another is not dependent on that other. Arrows corresponding to associations in the direction 'to many' have been omitted.

CT is strictly transitively dependent on E# via either D# (as (a) below) or M# ((b) below) whereas D# and M# are just transitively dependent on E# via respectively M# and D# ((c) and (d)).

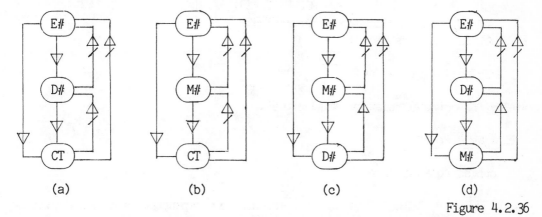

(a)   (b)   (c)   (d)

Figure 4.2.36

The next question is whether or not a relation with transitive dependence can be broken down into relations of smaller degree such that these relations can be joined to reconstitute the original.

A relation with a strict transitive dependence can be split. In the relation R(A, B, C) where A, B and C are three distinct collections of attributes satisfying the conditions as in Fig. 4.2.32 left side, C is strictly transitively dependent on A. In such a case R can be split by the project operations

$$R\ [A,\ B]$$
$$R\ [B,\ C]$$

to give the relations

$$R1 \ (\underline{A}, \ B) \text{ and } R2 \ (\underline{B}, \ C).$$

On joining R1 and R2 by

$$R1 * R2$$

one obtains the original relation R. Hence R is reducible.

In the case shown in Fig. 4.2.32 right side B and C are transitively dependent on A. In this case R can be split in two ways to give
either R1 ($\underline{A}$, B) and R2 ($\underline{B}$, C)
or R3 ($\underline{A}$, C) and R4 ($\underline{C}$, B).

From either pair all information in the original relation can be deduced.

Example 4.2.19

Manufacture4 ($\underline{P\#}$, M#, E#) from Examples 4.2.16 and 4.2.17 had
P# $\longrightarrow$ M#
M# $\longrightarrow\!\!\!/\,$ P#
M# $\longrightarrow$ E#
E# $\longrightarrow\!\!\!/\,$ M#

The analyst realizes that through M#, E# is strictly transitively dependent
on P#. Thus the relation Manufacture4 can be split by means of the project
operations

$$R41 \longleftarrow \text{MANUFACTURE4 } [P\#, \ M\#]$$
$$R42 \longleftarrow \text{MANUFACTURE4 } [M\#, \ E\#]$$

to give the relations

$$R41 \ (\underline{P\#}, \ M\#) \text{ and } R42 \ (\underline{M\#}, \ E\#).$$

Joining R41 and R42 by

$$R41 * R42$$

yields the original relation Manufacture4.

Example 4.2.20

Consider the relation

$$W \ (\underline{E\#}, \ D\#, \ M\#, \ CT)$$

as in Example 4.2.18. CT is strictly transitively dependent on E# via either D#
or M#. So W can be split by the project operations

$$W \ [E\#, \ D\#, \ M\#]$$

and
either W [D#, CT]
or W [M#, CT]
to give the relations

$$R1(\underline{E\#}, \ D\#, \ M\#)$$

and either R2($\underline{D\#}$, CT) or R3($\underline{M\#}$, CT).

By analyzing relation R1 the analyst observes that D# and M# are transitively dependent on E# via respectively M# and D#.

The analyst might split R1 by the project operations
$$\text{R1 } [E\#, \ D\#]$$
$$\text{R1 } [D\#, \ M\#]$$
to give the relations
$$\text{R4 } (\underline{E\#}, \ D\#) \text{ and } \text{R5 } (\underline{D\#}, \ M\#)$$
Alternatively the analyst might split R1 by the project operations
$$\text{R1 } [E\#, \ M\#]$$
$$\text{R1 } [M\#, \ D\#]$$
to give the relations
$$\text{R6 } (\underline{E\#}, \ M\#) \text{ and } \text{R7 } (\underline{M\#}, \ D\#)$$

Thus the analyst may reach any one of four different solutions each allowing the reconstitution of the original relation W by means of appropriate natural join operations. The solutions are as follows.

Solution 1: R4 ($\underline{E\#}$, D#), R5 ($\underline{D\#}$, M#), R2 ($\underline{D\#}$, CT)

Solution 2: R4 ($\underline{E\#}$, D#), R5 ($\underline{D\#}$, M#), R3 ($\underline{M\#}$, CT)

Solution 3: R6 ($\underline{E\#}$, M#), R7 ($\underline{M\#}$, D#), R2 ($\underline{D\#}$, CT)

Solution 4: R6 ($\underline{E\#}$, M#), R7 ($\underline{M\#}$, D#), R3 ($\underline{M\#}$, CT)

The relations R5 and R7 are identical in content. The attributes D# and M# are candidate keys in both relations. The meaning is that the functional dependencies
$$D\# \longrightarrow M\#$$
$$M\# \longrightarrow D\#$$
hold in both relations.

Reduction Procedure

In order to obtain elementary relations (i.e. irreducible units) the analyst should do the following procedure. It starts from a set of relations as produced by the procedure of Section 4.1.

Step 1: Replace the original relations by other new relations to eliminate any nonfull functional dependencies on candidate keys.

Step 2: Replace the relations obtained in Step 1 by other relations to eliminate any transitive dependencies on candidate keys.

Step 3: Replace the relations obtained in Step 2 by other relations to eliminate any multivalued dependencies.

The three steps must be done in that order. In each step the new relations are suitably chosen projections of old relations.

Each new relation is one or other of two kinds.

1 It is all key.

2 It has one or more candidate keys. Also all attributes in the complement of a candidate key are fully functionally dependent and non-transitively dependent on that candidate key. In addition it includes no multi-valued dependencies. The candidate key may be a single attribute or composite. Where the candidate key is a single attribute the above is equivalent to saying that its complement is functionally dependent on it.

The reduction procedure produces a collection of relations. Where a relation is all key or where a relation consists of a single attribute that is fully functionally dependent on a single candidate key the analyst has obtained an elementary relation. Otherwise the analyst needs a Step 4.

Step 4: Determine the primary key for each relation which qualifies for Step 4. The primary key may be a single attribute or may be composite. Take projections of these relations such that each projection contains the primary key and one attribute from the complement of the primary key. Thus create new relations that replace the old.

If the non-key attribute is conditionally dependent then maybe no value for it exists. If its value does not exist when the entity is created then a tuple can be created corresponding to the existence of the entity but it will have a void or null value for the non-key dependent attribute. The existence of the tuple indicates the existence of the entity.

Occasionally - but rarely - the reduction procedure may produce several alternative solutions. The analyst may then choose any one of these alternatives and proceed as in Sections 4.3 and 4.4. Briefly, to the chosen solution the analyst applies a rule that gives a transitive closure {4.14} and then removes redundant elementary relations to give a collection of elementary relations called a minimal cover. The details are in later sections and in Chapter 7.

From the preceding discussion it follows that an elementary relation can be one of

1 a relation that is all key

2 a relation in which a single attribute is functionally dependent on a second single attribute (so this must be a binary relation)

3 a relation in which a single attribute is fully functionally dependent on a collection of attributes (i.e. a n-ary relation where $n \geq 3$).

An irreducible relation never has a key that is less than all but one of its components {4.20}.

Example 4.2.21

   Assume that a mini world consists of entity sets and entity attributes as in
Fig. 4.1.1 and of relationship sets and relationship attributes as in Fig.
4.1.2. Assume further that all entity attributes, relationship sets and rela-
tionship attributes have been defined by means of relations as discussed in Ex-
ample 4.1.1.
   The analyst works through the reduction procedure, using the following ab-
breviations
 CK: Candidate Key
 ER: Elementary Relation
 FD: Functional Dependence
 FFD: Full Functional Dependence
 PK: Primary Key.
   The reader may like to try the analysis for himself or herself. The solu-
tion follows in full on the next two pages.

Analyzing the relations yields the following.

1 S-HOME-ADDRESS (S#, Street, Number, City)
   CK and PK: S#
   FDs: S# $\longrightarrow$ Street, S# $\longrightarrow$ Number, S# $\longrightarrow$ City
   Elementary relations: ER1 (S#, Street), ER2 (S#, Number), ER3 (S#, City)

2 S-LANGUAGE (S#, Language, Level)
   CK and PK: S#, Language (assuming that S# $\longleftarrow\!\!\!\longrightarrow$ Language)
   FFD: S#, Language $\Longrightarrow$ Level
   ER: ER4 (S#, Language, Level)

3 S-LODGING-ADDRESS (S#, Street, Number, City)
   CK and PK: S#
   FDs: S# $\longrightarrow$ Street, S# $\longrightarrow$ Number, S# $\longrightarrow$ City
   Elementary relations: ER5 (S#, Street), ER6 (S#, Number), ER7 (S#, City)

4 STUDENT-NAME (S#, Name)
   CK and PK: S#
   FD: S# $\longrightarrow$ Name
   ER: ER8 (S#, Name)

5 P-HOME-ADDRESS (P#, Street, Number, City)
   CK and PK: P#
   FDs: P# $\longrightarrow$ Street, P# $\longrightarrow$ Number, P# $\longrightarrow$ City
   Elementary relations: ER9 (P#, Street), ER10 (P#, Number), ER11 (P#, City)

6 P-NAME (P#, Name)
   CK and PK: P#
   FD: P# $\longrightarrow$ Name
   ER: ER12 (P#, Name)

7 C-CREDITS-REQUIRED (C#, Credits)
   CK and PK: C#
   FD: C# $\longrightarrow$ Credits
   ER: ER13 (C#, Credits)

8 C-DESCRIPTION (C#, Description)
   CK: C# and Description
   PK: C#
   FD: C# $\longrightarrow$ Description
   ER: ER14 (C#, Description)

9 R-SIZE (R#, Size)
   CK and PK: R#
   FD: R# $\longrightarrow$ Size
   ER: ER15 (R#, Size)

10 ADVISED-BY (S#, P#)
   CK and PK: S#
   FD: S# $\longrightarrow$ P#
   ER: ER16 (S#, P#)

11 ENROLLED-IN (S#, C#)
   CK and PK: S#, C# (assuming that S# $\longleftarrow\!\!\!\longrightarrow$ C#)

FD: -
ER: ER17 (S#, C#) (relation being all key)
12 EXAMINED-BY-IN (S#, P#, C#)
   CK and PK: S#, P#, C# (assuming that S# $\longleftrightarrow\!\!\!\rightarrow$ P#, S# $\longleftrightarrow\!\!\!\rightarrow$ C# and P# $\longleftrightarrow\!\!\!\rightarrow$
C#)
   FD: -
   ER: ER18 (S#, P#, C#) (relation being all key)
13 SEQUENCE (Before.C#, After.C#)
   CK and PK: Before.C#, After.C# (assuming that Before.C#$\longleftrightarrow\!\!\!\rightarrow$After.C#)
   FD: -
   ER: ER19(Before.C#, After.C#) (relation being all key)
14 TAUGHT-BY (S#, P#)
   CK and PK: S#, P# (assuming that S# $\longleftrightarrow\!\!\!\rightarrow$ P#)
   FD: -
   ER: ER20 (S#, P#) (relation being all key)
15 TAUGHT-BY-WHERE (C#, P#, R#)
   CK and PK: C#, P# (assuming that C# $\longleftrightarrow\!\!\!\rightarrow$ P# and C# $\longleftrightarrow$ R#)
   FD: C# $\longrightarrow$ R#
   Elementary relations: ER21 (C#, P#) (relation being all key),
   ER22 (C#, R#)
16 CREDITS-OBTAINED (S#, C#, Credits)
   CK and PK: S#, C# (assuming that S# $\longleftrightarrow\!\!\!\rightarrow$ C#)
   FFD: S#, C# $\Longrightarrow$ Credits
   ER: ER23 (S#, C#, Credits)
17 OPINION (S#, C#, Rating)
   CK and PK: S#, C#
   FFD: S#, C# $\Longrightarrow$ Rating
   ER: ER24 (S#, C#, Rating)
18 GRADE (S#, P#, C#, Rating)
   CK and PK: S#, P#, C# (assuming that S# $\longleftrightarrow\!\!\!\rightarrow$ P#, S# $\longleftrightarrow\!\!\!\rightarrow$ C# and C# $\longleftrightarrow\!\!\!\rightarrow$
P#)
   FFD: S#, P#, C# $\Longrightarrow$ Rating
   ER: ER25 (S#, P#, C#, Rating).

Summary

   The analyst needs to be able to recognize and deal with
   - Functional Dependence
   - Full Functional Dependence
   - Multivalued Dependence
   - Transitive Dependence.
   The derivation of elementary relations from a set of relations representing
conceptual objects (i.e. entity sets, relationship sets, entity attributes and

relationship attributes) follows from analysis of the dependencies. Correctly chosen elementary relations represent in a simple way without loss of information what types of information exist and what dependencies they satisfy. This provides the analyst and database administrator with a precise way of describing the mini world to be modelled. Irreducibility is an inherent property of the meaning of the appropriate relations. As such it is impossible for any computer procedure to automatically check the irreducibility of a collection of relations. The analyst must continually check with future users and managers that the model developed so far is correct. Such people should confirm the choices of primary keys and the meanings of the dependencies and elementary relations.

4.3 THE DETERMINATION OF TRANSITIVE CLOSURES

The rest of this chapter describes the selection of a minimum collection of elementary relations. Initially the analyst has a collection of relations such as Manufacture4. There may be several tens of such. They may overlap in various ways. Some attributes may appear in several relations.

The problem is how to handle the collection systematically. The dependencies and their consequencies can become almost unmanageable where there are lots. The procedure aims to finish up with a minimum collection of elementary relations such that if users' information is represented using them then

1 there can never be any inconsistency − no matter what values occur

2 all possible mini world information can be held − there is no loss of information possibilities from the choice of model

3 all possible meaningful information can be deduced by allowable and feasible operations on the stored data, so the data can later be used for new applications and in new ways that were not necessarily envisaged initially.

The way of determining the minimum collection of elementary relations is roughly two steps.

1 Determine all the possible elementary relations − e.g. including all those in any of the four solutions for the job example (Example 4.2.20). This gives lots of elementary relations, including all those that are transitive dependencies.

2 Reduce these down to a minimal set by a straightforward procedure.

These two steps correspond to Sections 4.3 and 4.4.

However, in most simple examples and in many similar real situations it is fairly easy for the appropriately experienced analyst to see what relations should be selected − i.e. what relations would be in the minimal cover without going through the procedure in full. But when dealing with many users, many overlapping relations, many dependencies, many different local partial models to be combined into a single whole and other complications, there may be situations where the correct choice is not obvious. Experience suggests that in the opinion of their colleagues most people do not manage to model complicated situations correctly at their first attempt.

The procedures below are straightforward algorithms that have been programmed and always yield a resulting set of elementary relations from data representing attributes and their dependencies.

But the amount of computing in a real case may be too large to be cost-effective. In practice the attributes and relations can usually be grouped with little or no overlap (e.g. sales, engineering). Operating separately on such groups avoids useless computing on data that is mostly zeroes that denote the absence of dependencies. Both when working by hand on paper and when doing it by computer it helps to group attributes - e.g. put together in a relation those that depend on the same collection of other attributes which becomes the primary key. This is described in Section 4.5.

The results will be rubbish if the initial list of relations and dependencies does not absolutely correctly correspond to the meanings intended. The analyst must ensure users' agreement that the meanings and associations are correct. No automatic procedure can do that!

Briefly, the first part of the procedure involves using product functions and the theory of directed graphs to derive a complete set of elementary relations - complete in the sense that all elementary relations equivalent to transitive dependencies through others are included. Hence descriptions of product functions and directed graphs comes next, so the reader should be aware of them for where they are needed in the procedure description.

Deriving Additional Elementary Relations

You remember that two functions
$$f: A \longrightarrow B$$
$$g: B \longrightarrow C$$
determine a third function, their product, say h from A to C, written
$$(g \circ f): h: A \longrightarrow C.$$
The products of functional dependencies are transitive dependencies. So from suitable pairs of elementary relations representing functional dependencies further elementary relations can be derived. Deriving all such from some initial collection of elementary relations yields a transitively closed collection of elementary relations, called a transitive closure {4.14}. It is the maximal set of elementary relations derivable from the initial collection. It includes both derived and original elementary relations.

We say that an elementary relation is redundant if it is derivable from other elementary relations. Thus a transitive closure usually contains many redundant elementary relations. However for a given list of elementary relations there exists one and only one transitive closure. The uniqueness of the transitive closure makes it a useful concept.

Before considering the details we discuss two catches when interpreting products of functional dependencies.

1 Whilst, mathematically speaking, one may conclude that

$$A \longrightarrow B$$
$$B \longrightarrow C$$

imply

$$A \longrightarrow C$$

such a conclusion may not be meaningful in the way users want or expect.

Example 4.3.1

Assume the functional dependencies

$$E\# \longrightarrow M\#$$
$$M\# \longrightarrow R\#$$

where
E# = employee serial number
M# = manager serial number
R# = manager's room number.

The composition of the above functional dependencies is the functional dependence

$$E\# \longrightarrow R\#$$

which denotes the room of the manager of an employee. A table of values could wrongly be interpreted as a functional dependence giving an employee's room. Such must be avoided. But more complicated examples may be harder to spot, especially when they are not expected.

2 The analyst must be aware of a similar catch where there are two or more attributes in the middle.

Example 4.3.2

A child has a father and a mother. A man and a woman together make a marriage.

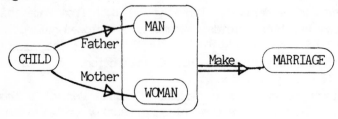

Figure 4.3.1

This does not give the usual expected relationship that a child corresponds to a marriage. For example some people remarry and some children are illegitimate.

In general if A, B and C are attribute collections such as

$$A = A_1, A_2, \ldots A_m$$
$$B = B_1, B_2, \ldots B_n$$
$$C = C_1, C_2, \ldots C_o$$

where B has at least two attributes, the analyst should not conclude that f: A $\Longrightarrow$ B and g: B $\Longrightarrow$ C necessarily imply h: A $\Longrightarrow$ C. Fig. 4.3.2 illustrates this.

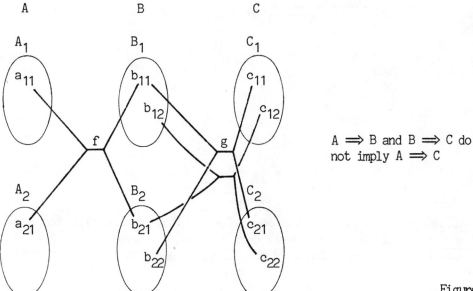

A $\Longrightarrow$ B and B $\Longrightarrow$ C do
not imply A $\Longrightarrow$ C

Figure 4.3.2

In Fig. 4.3.2 the image of say $\langle a_{11}, a_{21}\rangle$ is $\langle b_{11}, b_{21}\rangle$. In other words $f(\langle a_{11}, a_{21}\rangle) = \langle b_{11}, b_{21}\rangle$. For $\langle b_{11}, b_{21}\rangle$ and consequently for $\langle a_{11}, a_{21}\rangle$ there is however no image in C. Hence A $\Longrightarrow$ B and B $\Longrightarrow$ C do not necessarily imply A $\Longrightarrow$ C. Note however that A $\Longrightarrow$ B and B $\longrightarrow$ C imply (mathematically speaking) A $\Longrightarrow$ C if B consists of a single attribute.

From the preceding discussion one should conclude that any transitive closure obtained by a programmed procedure requires further investigation in order to eliminate semantically meaningless dependencies.

Directed Graphs

We describe below only the required features of directed graphs. Fuller treatment is in {4.5}, {4.21}.

A directed graph or a digraph is a figure with nodes and arcs. Each arc is a line with a direction. It starts at a node and finishes at a node. An arc can start and finish at the same node.

The nodes and arcs may be labeled, e.g. N_1, N_2, ... A_1, A_2, ... The nodes may represent attributes and the arcs represent dependencies.

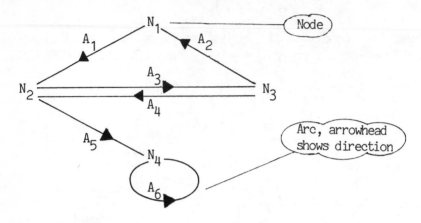

Figure 4.3.3

Outdegree and Indegree of Nodes

The outdegree of a node is the number of arcs directed away from the node. The indegree of a node is the number of arcs directed to the node. For example node N_3 above has outdegree 2 and indegree 1.

Path and Directed Path

A path is an unbroken route alternating through nodes and arcs. It begins and ends at nodes but may not repeat any arc. For example

$$N_1\text{-}A_1\text{-}N_2\text{-}A_3\text{-}N_3$$

in Fig. 4.3.3 is a path.

A directed path is a path that follows arcs in their correct directions.

Length of a Path

The length of a path is the number of arcs in it. For example the length of the directed path

$$N_1\text{-}A_1\text{-}N_2\text{-}A_3\text{-}N_3\text{-}A_4\text{-}N_2\text{-}A_5\text{-}N_4$$

(No arc repeated)

is 4.

Reachability

A node N_j is <u>reachable</u> from a node N_i if there is a directed path from N_i to N_j.

For example node N_4 is reachable from node N_1 along either of the directed paths

$$N_1 - A_1 - N_2 - A_5 - N_4$$
$$N_1 - A_1 - N_2 - A_3 - N_3 - A_4 - N_2 - A_5 - N_4.$$

Distance

The <u>distance</u> between two nodes is the <u>longest</u> possible path between them.

For example the distance between node N_1 and N_4 in Fig. 4.3.3 is 4 since the longest possible path between the nodes is

$$N_1 - A_1 - N_2 - A_3 - N_3 - A_4 - N_2 - A_5 - N_4.$$

Cycle

A <u>cycle</u> is a directed path from a node to itself. It can go through other nodes. The term <u>loop</u> is sometimes used where the path is a single arc that does not go through any other node.

For example

$$N_1 - A_1 - N_2 - A_3 - N_3 - A_2 - N_1 \qquad \text{and} \qquad N_4 - A_6 - N_4$$

are cycles in Fig. 4.3.3.

Tree

A <u>tree</u> is a special type of directed graph where
- there is one <u>root</u> node with no paths into it, i.e. it has indegree 0
- every other node has indegree 1
- there are no cycles, i.e. there is only one path from the root to any other node.

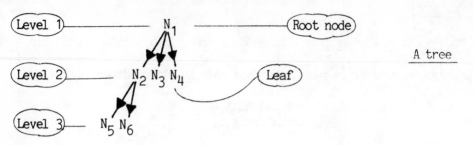

Figure 4.3.4

A node with an outdegree of zero is called a _leaf_. The root is said to be at the first _level_, and a node reached by a path of length n-1 is at level n.

Converse Digraphs and Transitively Closed Digraphs

Reversing the direction of every arc of a directed graph produces the _converse_ directed graph.

The transitively closed directed graph is obtained by adding arcs that satisy the transitive law, i.e. if N_i is joined to N_j and that to N_k then an arc from N_i to N_k is added if not already there.

Example 4.3.3

Fig. 4.3.5 illustrates a converse digraph and a transitively closed digraph each derived from the same digraph. In Fig. 4.3.5

$$A_1 \text{ and } A_3 \text{ imply } A_9$$
$$A_1 \text{ and } A_5 \text{ imply } A_7$$
$$A_3 \text{ and } A_2 \text{ imply } A_{10}$$
$$A_4 \text{ and } A_5 \text{ imply } A_8.$$

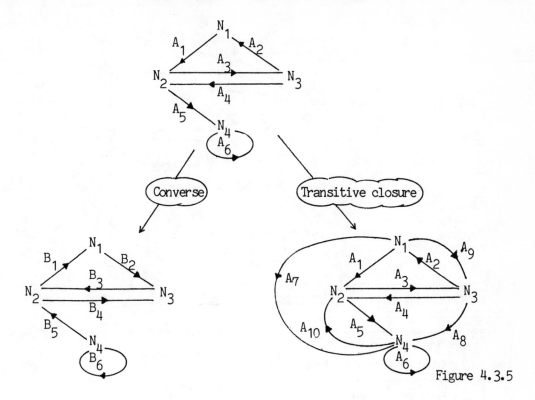

Figure 4.3.5

Representation of Lists of Elementary Relations by Digraphs

Digraphs consist of two kinds of objects, nodes and arcs.

Suppose nodes correspond to attributes and arcs to dependencies - either functional, trivial or full functional dependencies.

A node N_i representing an attribute or a collection of attributes that constitute an entity key is distinguished from other nodes by the fact that N_i participates in a cycle of type

$$N_i - A_j - N_i.$$

Such a cycle corresponds to the trivial dependence

$$N_i \to N_i.$$

Similarly, an elementary relation that is all key is represented by a cycle of the same type.

Example 4.3.4

The list of elementary relations in Example 4.2.21 gives the directed graph shown on the next page.

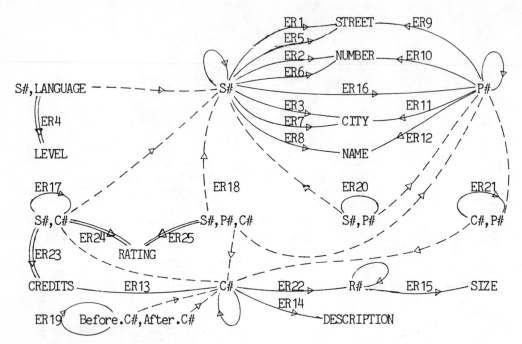

⟹ fully functionally dependent
⟶ functionally dependent
— — ⟶ trivially dependent

Figure 4.3.6

The analyst should be aware of the following.

1 Each node represents either a single attribute or a collection of attributes. Thus, each node denotes essentially a n-ary relation where n $\geq$ 1.

2 Nodes denoting a key attribute or a collection of key attributes are underlined.

3 Nodes denoting an entity key (such as S#, P#, C#, R#) or nodes denoting an ER that are all key (such as ER17, ER18, ER19, ER20 and ER21) participate in a cycle of length 1.

4 Each arc represents a dependence. Functional dependencies (denoted by ⟶) and full functional dependencies (denoted by ⟹) are derived from ERs. The name of such an arc corresponds to the name of the ER whose dependence is represented by the arc.

5 Trivial dependencies (denoted by — — ⟶) are derived where foreign keys and primary keys establish associations between relations.

6 All trivial dependencies between two nodes, say N_i and N_j, are of the type

$$N_i.K \longrightarrow N_j.K'$$

where K = attribute collection constituting the node N_i, K' = attribute collection constituting the node N_j and K' $\subseteq$ K. If the attribute (or attribute collection) K' represented by the node N_j is a subset of the attribute collection K represented by the node N_i then K' is trivially dependent on K.

In such a case a broken arrow ($-\,-\,\longrightarrow$) links N_i to N_j.

Example 4.3.5

The next figure shows the digraphs for the four solutions of Example 4.2.20. The elementary relations R5 and R7 correspond to the two functional dependencies
$$D\# \longrightarrow M\#$$
$$M\# \longrightarrow D\#.$$
Thus two opposite arcs relate the nodes D# and M#.

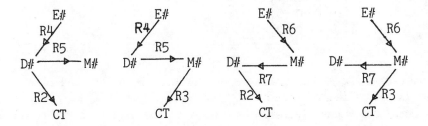

(a) Solution 1   (b) Solution 2   (c) Solution 3   (d) Solution 4

Figure 4.3.7

The graphical representation of elementary relations is useful to visualize the mini world to be modelled.

Connectivity Matrices

For computing purposes matrices are useful at the next stage. A matrix is an array of numbers arranged in rows and columns. The matrix
$$\begin{bmatrix} 1 & 0 & 6 \\ 5 & 8 & 7 \end{bmatrix}$$
is a matrix with two rows and three columns, i.e. size 2 x 3.

A square matrix of size n (i.e. size n x n) has n rows and n columns. E.g. here is a square 3 x 3 matrix
$$\begin{bmatrix} 1 & 0 & 2 \\ 0 & 4 & 2 \\ 1 & 0 & 5 \end{bmatrix}$$

Square matrices can be used to represent directed graphs. If the directed graph has n nodes then a square n x n matrix is used. The first row is associated with the first node, the second row with the second node, and so on. Also the first column is associated with the first node, the second column with the second node, and so on. Using the value 1 to mean the presence of a connection and the value 0 to mean the absence of a connection, a square matrix can represent the connections between the nodes of a directed graph. For example if node 2 is connected to node 4 then the element in row 2 and column 4 will be 1, otherwise it will be 0.

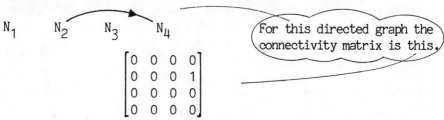

$N_1 \qquad N_2 \qquad N_3 \qquad N_4$

$$\begin{bmatrix} 0 & 0 & 0 & 0 \\ 0 & 0 & 0 & 1 \\ 0 & 0 & 0 & 0 \\ 0 & 0 & 0 & 0 \end{bmatrix}$$

For this directed graph the connectivity matrix is this.

Figure 4.3.8

If there are n nodes in the directed graph the matrix will be square and size n x n. Such a matrix is called a connectivity matrix. The matrix is given a name, usually a single upper case letter. Each node of the digraph corresponds to a row and to a column of the connectivity matrix M. Each row and each column of M is named the same as the corresponding node (i.e. with the name(s) of the attribute(s) constituting the node).

The matrix element in the ith row and the jth column is written $m_{i,j}$ or m_{ij}. In the connectivity matrix the elements have values as follows

m_{ij} = 1 if N_j is dependent (either functionally, fully functionally or trivially) on N_i

m_{ij} = 0 otherwise.

Where a node N_i denotes an entity key or an elementary relation that is all key the fact is recorded by the diagonal element of the matrix

$$m_{ii} = 1.$$

This corresponds to the trivial dependence

$$N_i \longrightarrow N_i$$

which is used to indicate that N_i denotes an entity key or an ER that is all key.

Where a node N_j is repeatedly dependent on an adjacent node N_i, the former has to be represented within the connectivity matrix M by as many rows and columns as are required to record these multiple dependencies. Appropriate role-names are then used to distinguish multiple rows and columns denoting essentially a single node.

Example 4.3.6

The next figure shows the connectivity matrix M to represent the digraph of Fig. 4.3.6. The following abbreviations have been used for role-names

HA = Home Address

LA = Lodging Address

B = Before

A = After.

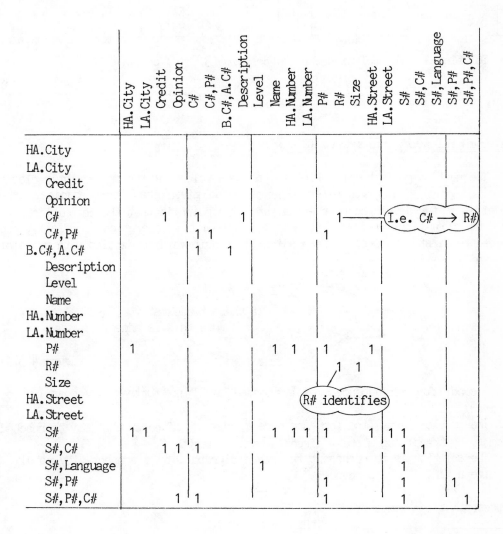

Figure 4.3.9

Example 4.3.7

The next figure shows the four connectivity matrices to represent the four digraphs of Fig. 4.3.7.

M1	CT	D#	E#	M#
CT				
D#	1			1
E#	1			
M#	1			

M2	CT	D#	E#	M#
CT				
D#				1
E#		1		
M#	1	1		

M3	CT	D#	E#	M#
CT				
D#	1			1
E#				1
M#		1		

M4	CT	D#	E#	M#
CT				
D#			1	
E#			1	— R6
M#	1	1		

(a) Solution 1   (b) Solution 2   (c) Solution 3   (d) Solution 4

Figure 4.3.10

Determination of Transitive Closures

The next stage is how to calculate the equivalent of the transitively closed directed graph of a given directed graph. The given graph corresponds to the model as so far developed by the analyst. The point is that the calculation can be done automatically, for example by suitable matrix operations. Briefly, the procedure first adds arcs corresponding to transitive dependencies with paths of length 2.

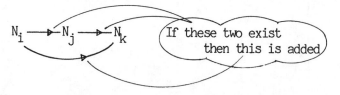

Figure 4.3.11

Second, further dependencies are added until no further new ones can be derived.

The problem is to find for each node N_i the set of nodes that may be reached from N_i by travelling along a directed path of length 2.

The solution is to represent the given digraph D by a connectivity matrix M of size n x n. The dependence

$$N_i \longrightarrow N_k$$

representing the composition

$$N_i \longrightarrow N_j \longrightarrow N_k$$

holds if the conditions

$$C1: M_{i,j} = 1 \text{ and } C2: M_{j,k} = 1$$

hold in M.

The conditions C1 and C2 denote that
$$N_i \longrightarrow N_j \text{ and } N_j \longrightarrow N_k$$
hold in D and hence that
$$N_i \longrightarrow N_k$$
which represents the composition
$$N_i \longrightarrow N_j \longrightarrow N_k.$$
This derived transitive dependence is recorded in M by assinging 1 to $M_{i,k}$.

For preciseness we shall occasionally give an explicit formulation in A Programming Language (APL) {4.19}, {4.22}, {4.26}. Since we do not assume that the reader is familiar with APL we shall briefly explain whenever necessary. In APL the above assignment is done by the statement
$$M_{i,k} \longleftarrow 1$$
Here is a simple example of a connectivity matrix M representing the dependencies
$$N_1 \longrightarrow N_2 \longrightarrow N_3.$$

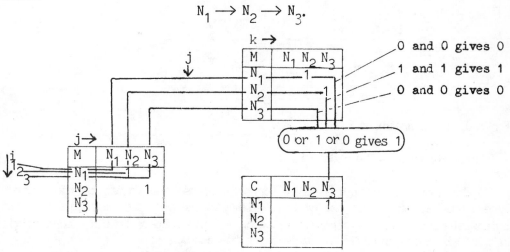

Figure 4.3.12

The lines 1, 2 and 3 symbolize the verification of the conditions C1 and C2 for $N_1 \longrightarrow N_j \longrightarrow N_3$ where $1 \leq j \leq 3$. Obviously the conditions C1 and C2 are satisfied for $j = 2$. Thus
$$N_1 \longrightarrow N_3$$
represents the composition of
$$N_1 \longrightarrow N_2 \longrightarrow N_3.$$
For the sake of clarity, this fact has been recorded in the figure within an additional matrix C (C stands for <u>Composition</u>) by assigning the value 1 to the appropriate element of C
$$C[N_1, N_3] \longleftarrow 1$$

The matrix C has the same dimension as the matrix M.

The generalized procedure for the determination of compositions has to verify the conditions C1 and C2 for all possible i, j and k combinations $1 \leq i,$ j, k $\leq$ n, where n is the number of elementary relations. The procedure is as follows (except as discussed below).

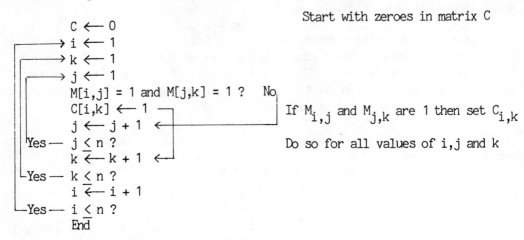

$$C \leftarrow 0$$

Start with zeroes in matrix C

$$i \leftarrow 1$$
$$k \leftarrow 1$$
$$j \leftarrow 1$$
$$M[i,j] = 1 \text{ and } M[j,k] = 1 ? \quad No$$
$$C[i,k] \leftarrow 1$$
$$j \leftarrow j + 1$$

If $M_{i,j}$ and $M_{j,k}$ are 1 then set $C_{i,k}$

Yes — $j \leq n$?
$$k \leftarrow k + 1$$

Do so for all values of i, j and k

Yes — $k \leq n$?
$$i \leftarrow i + 1$$
Yes — $i \leq n$?
End

Figure 4.3.13

For coding see Appendix 1.1 page 282.

Three remarks can be made here.

1 The above is not quite fully correct because the values on the diagonal have a special use. From the diagonal elements the procedure may generate wrong compositions that are not transitive. For example suppose that the connectivity matrix M includes specifications denoting the conditions
$$N_i \longrightarrow N_i \longrightarrow N_i \text{ and } N_i \longrightarrow N_i \longrightarrow N_j.$$
The first case requires that the connectivity matrix includes the element
$$M_{i,i} = 1$$
and the second case requires in addition that
$$M_{i,j} = 1.$$
The procedure shown in Fig. 4.3.13 supposes for the first case the 'composition'
$$N_i \longrightarrow N_i$$
and for the second case
$$N_i \longrightarrow N_j.$$
Yet it is obvious that neither case represents a composition satisfying the transitive law.

This problem can easily be overcome by working with a modified connectivity matrix MM for which all diagonal elements are zero, i.e.
$$MM_{i,i} = 0 \text{ for all } 1 \leq i \leq n.$$

MM then represents a matrix which no longer includes the information as to whether a node denotes an entity key or an elementary relation that is all key.
    For coding see Appendix 1.2.

    2 A similar problem occurs if the connectivity matrix M includes elements denoting the condition

$$N_i \longrightarrow N_j \longrightarrow N_i$$

recorded in M by

$$M_{i,j} = 1 \text{ and } M_{j,i} = 1.$$

    The procedure shown in Fig. 4.3.13 supposes in this case the 'composition'

$$N_i \longrightarrow N_i$$

which again does not satisfy the transitive law.
    We can overcome this second problem, that the procedure shown in Fig. 4.3.13 records the erroneous 'composition' within the matrix C by

$$C_{i,i} \longleftarrow 1$$

by assigning the value 0 to this matrix element.
    For coding see Appendix 1.3.

    3 The procedure in Fig. 4.3.13 has to be repeated until no further compositions are created. The reason is as follows.
    From the functions

$$f: A \longrightarrow B$$
$$g: B \longrightarrow C$$
$$h: C \longrightarrow D$$

one can form the product function

$$g \circ f: A \longrightarrow C$$

and then the function

$$h \circ (g \circ f): A \longrightarrow D.$$

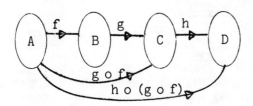

Figure 4.3.14

    One can also form the product function the other way round

$$h \circ g: B \longrightarrow D$$

and then the function

$$(h \circ g) \circ f: A \longrightarrow D.$$

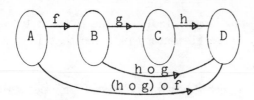

Figure 4.3.15

Both h o (g o f) and (h o g) o f are functions of A into D. A basic theorem on functions states that these functions are equal.

The same applies to a list of elementary relations. Since each elementary relation may denote a functional dependence (i.e. a function) it is usually possible to derive from a list of elementary relations additional elementary relations representing not only the composition of other elementary relations but also of other compositions. This means that the procedure shown in Fig. 4.3.13 has to be repeated until no additional compositions can be created.

Here is a picture of the logic of a procedure for determining a transitive closure given a connectivity matrix M.

1   Create a matrix J such that
       the leading diagonal elements $J_{i,i} = 0$ for $1 \leq i \leq n$
       and the off diagonal elements $J_{i,j} = 1$ for $i \neq j$
2   Derive the modified connectivity matrix MM
       from the given connectivity matrix M
3   Comp: Determine the compositions for MM as in Fig. 4.3.13
4   Remove the erroneous compositions that were derived
       from the situation $N_i \longrightarrow N_j \longrightarrow N_i$
5   Were any new compositions obtained?   No
6   Create a new modified connectivity matrix MM that
       includes the new compositions derived at Step 3
7   Go to Comp to repeat Step 3
8   End

Figure 4.3.16

For coding see Appendix 1.4.

The procedure accepts a connectivity matrix and presents the result in table form as illustrated by the figure in the next example.

Example 4.3.8

The connectivity matrix M in the next figure comes from applying the transitive closure procedure (Fig. 4.3.16) to any one of the connectivity matrices shown in Fig. 4.3.10.

M	CT	D#	E#	M#
CT				
D#	1			1
E#	1	1		1
M#	1	1		

Figure 4.3.17

This connectivity matrix allows the analyst to derive the following elementary relations

ER1 (D#, CT)
ER2 (D#, M#)
ER3 (E#, CT)
ER4 (E#, D#)
ER5 (E#, M#)
ER6 (M#, CT)
ER7 (M#, D#)

These elementary relations correspond to the transitively closed digraph in Fig. 4.2.35. All dependencies derived by the transitive closure procedure are semantically meaningful in this example.

In practice the analyst might check the meanings of new dependencies with users where their usefulness is doubtful. For example the compositions of

E# $\longrightarrow$ M#, i.e. each employee has a manager

M# $\longrightarrow$ R#, i.e. each manager has a room number

mathematically gives E# $\longrightarrow$ R#. This is not useful since users may interpret it as the employee's room number, and anyway will rarely want to find the manager's room number.

Summary

In this section we have presented a procedure allowing automized determination of transitive closures. The procedure may well produce dependencies which are - semantically speaking - meaningless (see the remarks concerning some characteristics of product functions at the beginning of this section). Any transitive closure obtained by an automatic procedure requires further investigations in order to eliminate semantically meaningless dependencies. Since semantic correctness cannot be automatically checked it goes without saying that a considerable human effort - presumably to be performed by the analyst or database administrator - may be required for these additional investigations.

4.4 THE DETERMINATION OF MINIMAL COVERS

The next problem is how to remove from a list of elementary relations (and particularly from a transitive closure) all redundant elementary relations (i.e. elementary relations representing the composition of others). The result of this removing process is one or more minimal covers {4.14}. A _minimal cover_ is a minimal set of elementary relations from which the transitive closure can be derived {4.1}. From a typical set of elementary relations several alternative minimal covers may be derived. The minimal cover is _not_ unique. Each minimal cover is a list of non-redundant elementary relations. Each fully models all the information types in the original elementary relations of the global conceptual data model.

Example 4.4.1

Here is the transitive closure for the elementary relations of Examples 4.2.18 and 4.2.20.

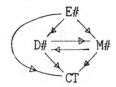

Figure 4.4.1

The family of minimal covers is given in the next figure.

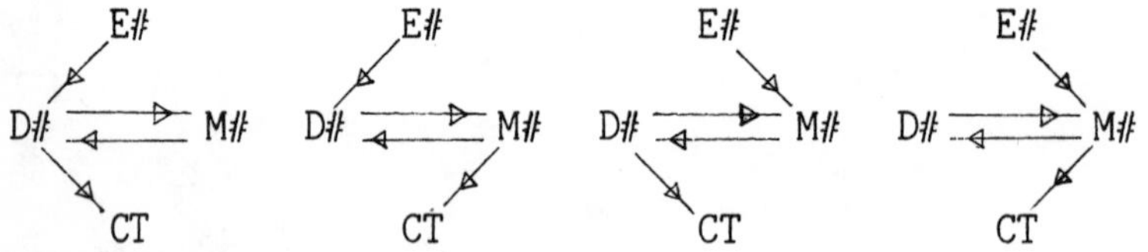

Figure 4.4.2

The transitive closure can be derived from any of these minimal covers.

It may seem amazing to you that we first add to a list of elementary relations redundant (i.e. derivable) elementary relations in order to obtain a transitive closure and that in a subsequent step we remove redundant elementary relations in order to obtain a set of minimal covers. However the approach is justified for the following reason.

Deriving from a transitive closure all the alternative minimal covers guarantees that every possible minimal cover is found. From these the designer should be well placed to select the minimal cover that best fits the organiza-

tion's needs. We shall return to how to do that in Chapter 7. In this section
we concentrate on the procedure for determining minimal covers.

Conditions for the removal of elementary relations

An elementary relation can be removed from a list of elementary relations
provided that the following conditions are met.

1 The elementary relation to be removed, say ER_r, must represent a composition of two other ERs, say ER_i and ER_j where $i \neq j$. We write
$$ER_r = C (ER_i, ER_j)$$
to denote that ER_r represents the <u>composition</u> of ER_i and ER_j.

2 The second condition is best explained by an example.
Suppose the following functional dependencies and their corresponding
elementary relations exist.

$$ER1-A-B : A \longrightarrow B$$
$$ER2-B-C : B \longrightarrow C$$
$$ER3-C-D : C \longrightarrow D$$
$$ER4-A-C : A \longrightarrow C$$
$$ER5-B-D : B \longrightarrow D$$
$$ER6-A-D : A \longrightarrow D$$

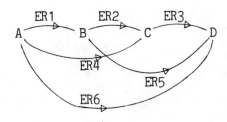

Figure 4.4.3

Then
$$ER4-A-C = C (ER1-A-B, ER2-B-C)$$
$$ER5-B-D = C (ER2-B-C, ER3-C-D)$$
$$ER6-A-D = C (ER4-A-C, ER3-C-D) = C (ER1-A-B, ER5-B-D)$$

Here ER4-A-C and ER5-B-D (both representing compositions of other ERs) appear in the two different compositions of ER6-A-D. Thus ER6-A-D represents a
composition of another composition whichever way one looks at it.

Now suppose that the analyst first removes ER4-A-C and ER5-B-D. In this
case the analyst would still have to be able to recognize that ER6-A-D is redundant; i.e that it can be derived via ER1-A-B, ER2-B-C and ER3-C-D. So the aim
is to remove ER6-A-D first.

To do so one removes in the sequence that ensures that an elementary relation may only be removed if it no longer appears in the composition of another
ER.

Thereby one would remove ER6-A-D before ER4-A-C and ER5-B-D since the latter
occur in compositions of the former.

In {4.31} an algorithm has been proposed which uses the distances between
nodes to determine the removing sequence. We illustrate it with the ERs of Fig.
4.4.3.

Each elementary relation has an associated distance
ER1-A-B, ER2-B-C, ER3-C-D : distances d_1, d_2, d_3 = 1
ER4-A-C and ER5-B-D : distances d_4, d_5 = 2
ER6-A-D : distance d_6 = 3.

It is obvious that the ER with the highest distance will never occur in the
composition of another ER. Thus removing ERs in descending distance sequence
guarantees that we never remove ERs occurring in the composition of other ERs.

3 Where at least two ERs have equal longest distance and also occur in each
other's compositions gives a tie. The next figure illustrates a tie in which
ER1 and ER2 each have the distance 2 and

$$ER1 = C \ (ER2, ER4)$$
$$ER2 = C \ (ER1, ER3).$$

ER1 occurs in the composition of ER2 and vice versa.

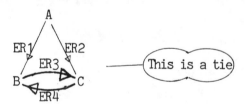

Figure 4.4.4

The minimal cover is either {ER1, ER3, ER4} or {ER2, ER3, ER4}. Hence in
general there exist several minimal covers for a digraph containing a tie.

Algorithm for the Determination of Minimal Covers

The following algorithm was presented originally in {4.29} and was
rediscussed (with slight modifications) in {4.14} and {4.31}.

Let

$$S^z = \{ER1, ER2, \ldots ER_z\}$$

represent the original list of ERs and let

$$MC \ \{S_n^m\}$$

represent the set of minimal covers. Note that z and m represent the cardinality of S and MC respectively, whereas n stands for a running number. Also MC is empty at the beginning of the procedure.

Step 1
Associate a distance to each ER in S^z.

Step 2
Remove ER_r from S^z if it is a longest distance composition of say ER_i and ER_j, i.e. provided that all of
(a) ER_i, ER_j, ER_r belong to S^z
(b) $ER_r = C^J(ER_i, ER_j)$
(c) ER_r possesses maximum distance.
   Call the remaining set
$$S_{nz}^{z-1}.$$
If no element can be removed from S^z, place S^z in the set MC and terminate. In general, one can find a family of collections
$$S_1^{z-1}, S_2^{z-1}, \ldots S_n^{z-1}$$
each containing $z-1$ elements. Note that
$$ER_r \cup S_n^{z-1} = S^z.$$

Step 3
Repeat Step 2 for each
$$S_n^{z-1}$$
to obtain a family of
$$S^{z-2}$$
collections. If no element can be removed from
$$S_n^{z-1}$$
then add to MC those of S not already in MC. I.e. form the union with MC and assign the result to MC by performing
$$MC \leftarrow MC \cup S_n^{z-1}$$
The union operation guarantees that
$$S_n^{z-1}$$
is only added to MC if the former is not already an element of MC.

Step 4
Repeat Step 3 until no element can be removed from any collection. Then terminate. Then
$$MC \{S_n^m\}$$
represents the desired result.

Example 4.4.2

Assume that the transitive closure shown in Fig. 4.4.1 is determined by the following ERs

ER1 ($\underline{E\#}$, CT)
ER2 ($\underline{E\#}$, $D\#$)
ER3 ($\underline{E\#}$, $M\#$)
ER4 ($\underline{D\#}$, CT)
ER5 ($\underline{M\#}$, CT)
ER6 ($\underline{D\#}$, $M\#$)
ER7 ($\underline{M\#}$, $D\#$)

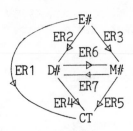

Figure 4.4.5

Thus

$$s^7 = \{ER1, ER2, ER3, ER4, ER5, ER6, ER7\}.$$

Obviously then

$$ER1 = C\ (ER2,\ ER4)\ \text{and distance}\ d_1 = 4$$

(because $E\#\rightarrow D\#\rightarrow M\#\rightarrow D\#\rightarrow CT$), and $ER1 = C\ (ER3,\ ER5)$

$$ER2 = C\ (ER3,\ ER7)\ \text{and}\ d_2 = 2$$
$$ER3 = C\ (ER2,\ ER6)\ \text{and}\ d_3 = 2$$
$$ER4 = C\ (ER6,\ ER5)\ \text{and}\ d_4 = 2$$
$$ER5 = C\ (ER7,\ ER4)\ \text{and}\ d_5 = 2$$
$$ER6\ \text{has}\ d_6 = 1$$
$$ER7\ \text{has}\ d_7 = 1$$

ER2 and ER3 are a tie. So also are ER4 and ER5.
The derivation of minimal covers from s^7 is tabulated below.

Iteration	s_n^z	ER	$C(ER_i,\ ER_j)$	d_r	ER_r removed	s_n^{z-1}	Digraph (before remove)	MC
0	s^7	ER1	$C(ER2,\ ER4)$ $C(ER3,\ ER5)$	4	<-	s_1^6		
		ER2	$C(ER3,\ ER7)$	2				
		ER3	$C(ER2,\ ER6)$	2				no
		ER4	$C(ER6,\ ER5)$	2				
		ER5	$C(ER7,\ ER4)$	2				
		ER6	–	1				
		ER7	–	1				
1	s_1^6	ER2	$C(ER3,\ ER7)$	2	<-	s_1^5		
		ER3	$C(ER2,\ ER6)$	2	<-	s_2^5		
		ER4	$C(ER6,\ ER5)$	2	<-	s_3^5		no
		ER5	$C(ER7,\ ER4)$	2	<-	s_4^5		
		ER6	–	1				
		ER7	–	1				

Iteration	S_n^z	ER	$C(ER_i, ER_j)$	d_r	ER_r removed	S_n^{z-1}	Digraph (before remove)	MC
2	S_1^5	ER3	–	2			E#	
		ER4	$C(ER_6, ER5)$	2	←	S_1^4		
		ER5	$C(ER7, ER4)$	2	←	S_2^4	D# ⇌ M#	no
		ER6	–	1				
		ER7	–	1			CT	
2	S_2^5	ER2	–	2			E#	
		ER4	$C(ER6, ER5)$	2	←	S_3^4		
		ER5	$C(ER7, ER4)$	2	←	S_4^4	D# ⇌ M#	no
		ER6	–	1				
		ER7	–	1			CT	
2	S_3^5	ER2	$C(ER3, ER7)$	2	←	$S_5^4 = S_1^4$	E#	
		ER3	$C(ER2, ER6)$	2	←	$S_6^4 = S_3^4$		
		ER5	–	2			D# ⇌ M#	no
		ER6	–	1				
		ER7	–	1			CT	
2	S_4^5	ER2	$C(ER3, ER7)$	2	←	$S_7^4 = S_2^4$	E#	
		ER3	$C(ER2, ER6)$	2	←	$S_8^4 = S_4^4$		
		ER4	–	2			D# ⇌ M#	no
		ER6	–	1				
		ER7	–	1			CT	
3	S_1^4	ER3	–	2			E#	
		ER5	–	2				
		ER6	–	1			D# ⇌ M#	yes
		ER7	–	1				
							CT	
3	S_2^4	ER3	–	2			E#	
		ER4	–	2				
		ER6	–	1			D# ⇌ M#	yes
		ER7	–	1				
							CT	

Iteration	S_n^z	ER	$C(ER_i, ER_j)$	d_r	ER_r removed	S_n^{z-1}	Digraph (before remove)	MC
3	S_3^4	ER2	–	2			E# → D# ⇄ M# (D# → M#), M# → CT, E# → D#	
		ER5	–	2				
		ER6	–	1				yes
		ER7	–	1				
3	S_4^4	ER2	–	2			E# → D# ⇄ M#, D# → CT	
		ER4	–	2				
		ER6	–	1				yes
		ER7	–	1				

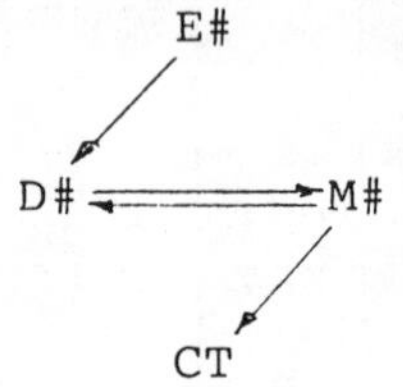

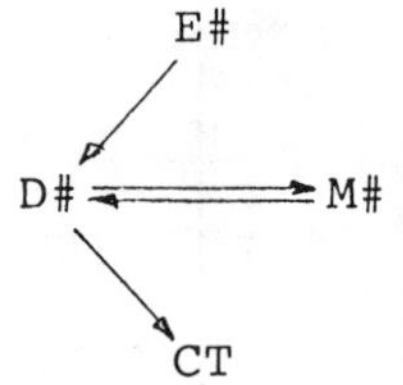

Figure 4.4.6

After the third iteration MC (i.e. the set of minimal covers) consists of
$$MC \{S_1^4, S_2^4, S_3^4, S_4^4\}$$
with

$$S_1^4 = \{ER3, ER5, ER6, ER7\}$$
$$S_2^4 = \{ER3, ER4, ER6, ER7\}$$
$$S_3^4 = \{ER2, ER5, ER6, ER7\}$$
$$S_4^4 = \{ER2, ER4, ER6, ER7\}$$

These are four alternative minimal covers.

Summary

This section discussed an algorithm for the determination of a set of minimal covers starting with a redundant list of elementary relations (e.g. a transitive closure. Each minimal cover is a list of non-redundant ERs reflecting appropriately the portion of the real world modelled. An important problem still has to be solved; namely how the analyst should select the minimal cover which fits the organization's needs in an optimum way. Consideration of this problem will be in Chapter 7.

4.5 REDUCING THE NUMBER OF ELEMENTARY RELATIONS

In a practical case the analyst may have thousands of ERs to describe appropriately the real world portion. In view of the various processing steps already presented and still to be discussed in succeeding sections it is desirable to reduce the number of ERs as much as possible.

The following way to do this is adapted from {4.14}.

Step 1
Select all ERs having a non-key attribute occurring solely in the selected ER.

Step 2
Create subsets of the ERs from Step 1 such that all ERs within a subset have identical keys.

The non-key attributes of all ERs within a set, say A_1, A_2, ... A_n, all depend on the same key attribute, say K. We may write

$$K \longrightarrow \{A_1, A_2, ... A_n\}$$

i.e. simply

$$K \longrightarrow T_1$$

where

$$T_1 = \{A_1, A_2, ... A_n\}.$$

Where K is a collection of attributes then all the attributes in T_1 are fully functionally dependent on K. Thus

$$K \Longrightarrow \{A_1, A_2, ... A_n\}$$

i.e. simply

$$K \Longrightarrow T_1.$$

Step 3
Each subset obtained in Step 2 is replaced and represented by a single ER of the form

$$ER\ (\underline{K}, T_1).$$

In practice this process considerably reduces the number of ERs to be handled.

For coding see Appendix 1.5.

The procedure accepts a connectivity matrix and produces a table as below. Each row indicates elementary relations that constitute a subset.

Example 4.5.1

Assume the following domains
E# = employee serial number
EN = employee name
SX = sex

BD = birth date
AD = address
D# = department number of employee
DI = division number of employee
DN = department name
DL = department location.
    Assume that the mini-world is described by the following ERs
ER1 (E#, EN)
ER2 (E#, SX)
ER3 (E#, BD)
ER4 (E#, AD)
ER5 (E#, D#)
ER6 (E#, DI)
ER7 (D#, DI)
ER8 (D#, DN)
ER9 (D#, DL).
    The analyst proceeds through the Steps 1 to 3.

Step 1
The ERs having a non-key attribute occurring solely in a single ER are
$$\text{ER1, ER2, ER3, ER4, ER8, ER9}$$

Step 2
The analyst obtains a first subset with ERs whose key is E# (i.e. ER1, ER2, ER3, ER4) and a second subset with ERs whose key is D# (i.e. ER8, ER9). Note that
$$E\# \longrightarrow \{EN,\ SX,\ BD,\ AD\} \text{ and } D\# \longrightarrow \{DN,\ DL\}$$

Step 3
The analyst replaces the subsets from Step 2 by the following ERs
$$\text{ER10 } (\underline{E\#},\ T_1) \text{ and ER11 } (\underline{D\#},\ T_2)$$
where
$$T_1 = \{EN,\ SX,\ BD,\ AD\} \quad \text{and} \quad T_2 = \{DN,\ DL\}.$$
The mini world may now be defined by means of the following ERs, which is fewer ERs, thus reducing the amount of processing in later design steps
$$\begin{array}{l}
\text{ER5 } (\underline{E\#},\ D\#) \\
\text{ER6 } (\underline{E\#},\ DI) \\
\text{ER7 } (\underline{D\#},\ DI) \\
\text{ER10 } (\underline{E\#},\ T_1) \\
\text{ER11 } (\underline{D\#},\ T_2)
\end{array}$$

Example 4.5.2

The ERs discussed in Example 4.5.1 are represented by the connectivity matrix below.

M	E#	EN	SX	BD	AD	D#	DI	DN	DL
E#	1	1	1	1	1	1	1		
EN									
SX									
BD									
AD									
D#						1	1	1	1
DI									
DN									
DL									

Figure 4.5.1

The reduction procedure yields the following matrix. (In APL this is done by REDUCE M.)

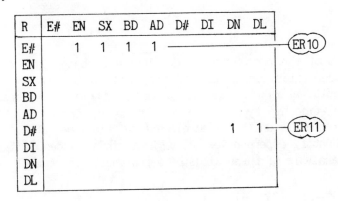

R	E#	EN	SX	BD	AD	D#	DI	DN	DL	
E#		1	1	1	1					ER 10
EN										
SX										
BD										
AD										
D#							1	1		ER 11
DI										
DN										
DL										

Figure 4.5.2

The matrix shown in Fig. 4.5.2 immediately tells the analyst the elementary relations

$$\text{ER10 } (\text{E\#, } \overline{T_1}) \text{ and}$$
$$\text{ER11 } \overline{(\text{D\#, } T_2)}$$

where again

$$T_1 = \{\text{EN, SX, BD, AD}\} \text{ and } T_2 = \{\text{DN, DL}\}.$$

The reduction procedure can be coded as follows. The assignment statement

$$D \leftarrow M > \text{REDUCE M}$$

will yield the matrix D below, showing

$$ER5 \ (E\#, \ D\#)$$
$$ER6 \ (\overline{E\#}, \ DI)$$
$$ER7 \ (\underline{D\#}, \ DI)$$

still have to be included. The assignment statement means compare corresponding elements of the matrices M and REDUCE M; if M_{ij} is greater then assign 1 to D_{ij}, otherwise assign 0. The result is the following matrix D.

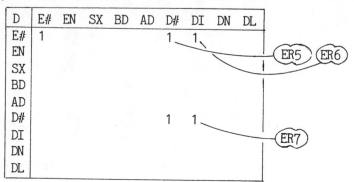

Figure 4.5.3

Summary

Chapter 4 described part of the procedure for developing a conceptual data model. The analyst first identifies conceptual objects; that is to say entity sets, relationship sets, entity attributes and relationship attributes. These lead to entity types and relationship types. The collection of conceptual objects are represented by irreducible units called elementary relations (ERs).

The analyst needs to identify dependencies of various kinds to deduce the elementary relations. The analysis of these kinds of dependencies is crucial
- Functional Dependence
- Full Functional Dependence
- Multivalued Dependence
- Transitive Dependence.

Correct analysis - expressing the meaning in terms of such dependencies - leads to a collection of elementary relations. This collection - because of the way it is produced - may be incomplete or not satisfactory in some way.

To improve the collection a transitively closed equivalent is formed. From this redundant relations are removed thus giving a minimal set, or in general several alternative minimal sets called minimal covers.

Substantial simplification comes from handling as a group all the elementary relations whose non-key attributes have the same dependencies on the same key.

In detail the transitive law was used to determine a transitive closure of a collection of elementary relations. A transitive closure represents the maximal set of all ERs and contains (usually) many redundant (i.e. derivable) ERs. We then showed how a transitive closure can be transformed into a set of minimal covers. Each minimal cover is a non-redundant list of ERs and is an appropriate model of the real world portion whose information is to be held as data in the database. We pointed out that an important problem - the selection of the minimal cover which fits the organization's needs in the best way - still has to be solved and that an appropriate procedure will be discussed in Chapter 7.

EXERCISES

1 What are the four kinds of conceptual objects? Summarize the steps used by analysts to identify real world occurrences of these from interviews and study of documents. Which of the four types of conceptual object does the analyst assign names to the types of real world occurrences of?

2 Identify the entity types, relationship types, entity attributes and relationship attributes in the following. Suggest entity keys.

There are several airlines, Pan-Am, British Airways, and so on. Each makes scheduled flights between certain airports such as Denver, Chicago, Heathrow. The airports are identified by three character codes such as HRW for Heathrow. The flights are numbered, e.g. the daily flight BA103 is at a particular departure time and has a particular arrival time. A passenger can book a trip consisting of several flights on different dates and using more than one airline.

3 Why are elementary relations important? What kind of association or relationship does an elementary relation correspond to?

4 Which of the following are elementary relations, making any reasonable assumptions?
EMPLOYEE (Employee#, Employee-name, Employee-room#)
TOWN (Name, Population)
GREY-TROUSERS-IN-STOCK (Waist, Leg)
ORDER (Order#, Supplier#, Order-date)
PART (Part#).
Explain any assumptions made.

5 Does a project operation correspond to any of the following?
A Selecting a single row from a relation
B Selecting none, one or more rows from a relation
C Selecting the primary key columns from a relation
D Selecting one column from a relation
E Selecting one or more columns from a relation
F Making a new relation from two existing relations.

6 Does a join operation correspond to any of the following?
A to F as in the question above.
G Specifying certain columns of two relations that have values from the same
domains and forming a tuple of the resulting relation .for each pair of tuples
from the original relations that have equal values in the columns
H Specifying certain columns of two relations that have attributes that have
the same names and forming a tuple of the resulting relation for each pair of
tuples of the original relations that have equal values for the common attibute.

7 What is the difference between functional dependence and full functional
dependence?

8 If two elementary relations are derived from a relation correctly can the
original relation always be reconstructed by a join operation?
What are the elementary relations corresponding to
        PASSPORT (Passport#, Surname, Given-names, Address-City, Date)
Can the Passport relation be calculated from a join?

9 What is the concept of multivalued dependence about?

10 What is the term for the following situation?

Machine-operation# $\longrightarrow$ Method# $\longrightarrow$ Part#

I.e. Operation 1478 is one of the operations in making by method 174 part 1690.

11 In representing elementary relations by directed graphs, what do the
nodes correspond to and what do the arcs correspond to? Can a node correspond
to more than one attribute? What kind of nodes have a loop?

12 For what purpose are matrices introduced?

13 What is a minimal cover? Is the minimal cover for a particular conceptual model unique? If not, what kind of situation can lead to more than one?
What is the minimal cover for the following list of dependencies between attributes named a, b, ...?
a $\longrightarrow$ b
a $\longrightarrow$ d
a $\longrightarrow$ c
b $\longrightarrow$ e
d $\longrightarrow$ b
c $\longrightarrow$ f
d $\longrightarrow$ f
b $\longrightarrow$ c

Assume these are the only dependencies identified by the analyst.

14 Derive a collection of elementary relations for the dependencies of the previous question with **e ——) c also.**

15 Suppose a conceptual data model includes the following relations.
STUDENT (S#, S-name, S-year)
COURSE (C#, C-title, C-level)
ENROLMENT (S#, C#, Grade)
What operations such as project and join operations would be required to produce a relation answering each of the following queries, assuming the stored data had exactly the same structure as the conceptual data model?
Assume there is also available a Select operation which will select those tuples of a relation that have a particular value for a particular attribute (or satisfy a combination of such conditions using 'and', 'or', 'not'). For example
STUDENT2 ←— Select STUDENT tuples satisfying S-year = 1980
will form a new relation STUDENT2 which has the same named attribute columns as STUDENT but only has those tuples that have 1980 as the value of S-year. The left facing arrow means the result of the expression to its right is assigned the name to its left.
(i) What is the title and level of course C12?
(ii) List the S#, C# and grade for each student of course C12.
(iii) List the S# only of those students of course C12.
(iv) List the S-name of those same students.
(v) List the C# values and grades for student S45.
(vi) Did any student get grade C for the Physics course?

16 (i) Specify the elementary relations corresponding to the three relations Student, Course and Enrolment of the previous question.
(ii) Draw these elementary relations so as to show the dependencies to which they correspond.
(iii) Draw them as a directed graph.
(iv) Write down the corresponding connectivity matrix.

17 Determine the transitive closure and minimal cover(s) for the following.
In the relation
            EMPLOYEE5 (E#, E-name, D#, D-name, M#, P-name, P#)
which represents employees in departments making parts on machines, the attributes and dependencies are as follows.
E# = Employee serial number
E-name = Employee name
D# = Department identification
D-name = Department name
M# = Machine number

P# = Part number
P-name = Part name
E# $\longrightarrow$ E-name and E# $\longrightarrow$ D#
D# $\longleftrightarrow$ D-name
P# $\longrightarrow$ M# and P# $\longrightarrow$ P-name
M# $\longrightarrow\!\!\!\!\!\rightarrow$ P#
E# $\longrightarrow$ M#

The above is intended as an exercise and is not necessarily realistic.

   18 Do as the previous question for the following.
T = Teacher
D = Date and time
R = Room number
Y = Year level
C = Course
T $\longrightarrow$ C
T,D $\longrightarrow$ Y
T,D $\longrightarrow$ R
D,R $\longrightarrow$ T
D,R $\longrightarrow$ Y
D,Y $\longrightarrow$ T; D,Y $\longrightarrow$ C
Y,D $\longrightarrow$ R

REFERENCES AND BIBLIOGRAPHY

   4.1 Aho, A.V.; Garey, M.R.; Ullman, J.D.: 'The Transitive Reduction of a Directed Graph', SIAM J. Comp., Vol. 1, No. 2, 1972, Pages 131-137

   4.2 ANSI/X3/SPARC: Interim Report: Study Group on Data Base Management Systems. FDT ... Bulletin of ACM - SIGMOD the Special Interest Group on Management of Data, Volume 7, Number 2, 1975

   4.3 ANSI/X3/SPARC DBMS Framework, 'Report of the Study Group on Database Management Systems', Tsichritzis, D.; Klug, A.: Eds., AFIPS PRESS, 210 Summit Avenue, Montvale, New Jersey 07645, 1978

   4.4 Beeri, C; Fagin, R.; Howard, J.H.: 'A Complete Axiomatization for Functional and Multivalued Dependencies in Database Relations', IBM Research Laboratory, San Jose, California, RJ 1977, April 1977

   4.5 Berge, C.: 'The Theory of Graphs', Methuen and Co. Ltd., London, 1966

   4.6 Bernstein, P.A.; Swenson, J.R.; Tsichritzis, D.C.: 'A Unified Approach to Functional Dependencies and Relation', ACM-SIGMOD International Conference on Management of Data, San Jose, California, May 1975, Pages 237-245

   4.7 Bernstein, P.A.: 'Synthesizing Third Normal Form Relations from Functional Dependencies', ACM Transactions on Database Systems, Vol. 1, No. 4, December 1976, Pages 277-298

4.8 Bracchi, G.; Fedeli, A.; Paolini, P.: 'A Multilevel Relational Model for Data Base Management Systems', Proc. of the IFIP Working Conference on Data Base Management, Cargese, Corsica, France, 1974, Klimbie, J.W.; Koffeman, K.L.: Eds., North-Holland Pub. Co., Amsterdam, Pages 211-223

4.9 Bracchi, G.; Paolini, P.; Pelagatti, G.: 'Binary Logical Associations in Data Modelling', Proc. of the IFIP Working Conference on Modelling in Data Base Management Systems, Freudenstadt, Germany, 1976, Nijssen, G.M.: Ed., North-Holland Pub. Co., Amsterdam, Pages 125-148

4.10 Burnside, W.: 'Theory of Groups of Finite Order', Cambridge University Press, Cambridge, 1911

4.11 Codd, E.F.: 'Further Normalization of the Relational Model', in 'Data Base Systems', Courant Computer Science Symposium 6, 1971, Rustin, R.: Ed., Prentice-Hall Inc., Englewood Cliffs, New Jersey, 1972, Pages 33-64

4.12 Codd, E.F.: 'Relational Completeness of Data Base Sublanguages', in 'Data Base Systems', Courant Computer Science Symposium 6, 1971, Rustin, R.: Ed., Prentice-Hall Inc., Englewood Cliffs, New Jersey, 1972, Pages 65-98

4.13 Date, C.J.: 'An Introduction to Database Systems', Addison-Wesley Publishing Company, 1977

4.14 Delobel, C.: 'A Theory About Data in an Information System', IBM Research Laboratory, San Jose, California, RJ 964, January 28, 1972

4.15 Delobel, C.; Casey, R.G.: 'Decomposition of a Data Base and the Theory of Boolean Switching Functions', IBM Journal of Research and Development, Vol. 17, No. 5, 1973, Pages 374-386

4.16 Fagin, R.: 'Multivalued Dependencies and a New Normal Form for Relational Databases', IBM Research Laboratory, San Jose, California, RJ 1812 (26109), 1976

4.17 Fagin, R.: 'Multivalued Dependencies and a New Normal Form for Relational Databases', ACM Transactions on Database Systems, Vol. 2, No. 3, 1977, Pages 262-278

4.18 Fagin, R.: 'The Decomposition Versus the Synthetic Approach to Relational Database Design', Proc. of the 3rd Int. Conf. on Very Large Data Bases, Tokyo, Japan, 1977, Pages 441-446

4.19 Gilman, L.; Rose, A.J.: 'APL: An Interactive Approach', John Wiley and Sons, Inc., New York, 1976

4.20 Hall, P.; Owlett, J.; Todd, S.: 'Relations and Entities', Proc. of the IFIP Working Conference on Modelling in Data Base Management Systems, Freudenstadt, Germany, 1976, Nijssen, G.M.: Ed., North-Holland Pub. Co., Amsterdam, Pages 201-220

4.21 Harary, F.; Norman, R.Z.; Cartwright: 'Structural Models: An Introduction to the Theory of Directed Graphs', John Wiley, 1965

4.22 Harms, E.; Zabinski, M.P.: 'Introduction to APL and Computer Programming', John Wiley and Sons, Inc., New York, 1977

4.23 Hitchcock, P.; Pace, F.: 'An Approach to Conceptual Data Analysis', IBM UK Scientific Centre, Neville Road, Peterlee, UKSC 0090, 1977

4.24 Martin, J.: 'Computer Data-Base Organization', 2nd Ed., Prentice-Hall Inc., Englewood Cliffs, New Jersey 07632, 1977

4.25 Nijssen, G.M.: Ed.: 'Architecture and Models in Data Base Management Systems', Proc. of the IFIP Working Conference on Modelling in Data Base Management Systems, Nice, France, 1977, North-Holland Pub. Co., Amsterdam

4.26 Polivka, R.P.; Pakin, S.: 'APL: The Language and Its Usage', Prentice-Hall Inc., Englewood Cliffs, New Jersey, 1975

4.27 Rissanen J., Delobel, C.: 'Decomposition of Files, a Basis for Data Storage and Retrieval', IBM Research Report No. RJ 1220, San Jose, California, May 1973

4.28 Schmid, H.A.; Swenson, J.R.: 'On the Semantics of the Relational Data Model', Proc. ACM SIGMOD, San Jose, California, May, 1975, King, W.F.: Ed., Pages 211-223

4.29 Wang, C.P.; Wedekind, H.H.: 'Segment Synthesis in Logical Data Base Design', IBM Journal of Research and Development, Jan. 1975, Pages 71-77

4.30 Webster's Dictionary, G. and C. Merriam Company, Springfield, Massachusetts

4.31 Wedekind, H.H.: 'Datenbansysteme I', B.I. Wissenschaftsverlag, Reihe Informatik 16, 1974

4.32 Zaniolo, C.: 'Analysis and Design of Relational Schemata for Database Systems', Ph.D. Dissertation, University of California, Los Angeles, UCLA-ENG-7669, 1976.

5

The Internal Realm

The preceding chapters gave an approach to data modelling. The approach aims to

1 avoid duplication that could lead to inconsistency in the stored data by ensuring that facts each only occur once

2 have a sound theoretical basis

3 avoid depending on the peculiarities of a particular hardware system or on the facilities of a particular database management system

4 provide stability of application programs to real world changes, i.e. growth independence

5 provide stability of such programs to storage structure changes, i.e. storage structure independence.

So far we have deliberately completely neglected any considerations related to computer efficiency. Now we are primarily concerned with economical use of the computing facility. The database administrator's problem is to find an internal model (i.e. a physical structure) which supports the conceptual model in a machine efficient way. The internal model must be consistent with the conceptual model.

Basically, one could individually store the tuples of the elementary relations constituting the conceptual model. However, such an approach - requiring an awful number of accesses to determine the facts for an entity - would be extremely machine inefficient. Clearly, the principle needed is how to determine which tuples from different elementary relations one can glue together and store as a unit in order to minimize the number of accesses. This chapter addresses aspects of that problem.

We behave first of all as if we were able to define the internal model by means of relations. A central problem for the database administrator is to find relations that are consistent with the conceptual model and that minimize the number of accesses required to obtain all the facts for an entity. For that

Section 5.1 introduces the normalization criteria proposed by E.F. Codd, R.F. Boyce, W. Kent, R. Fagin and C. Zaniolo and discusses their usefulness.

In Section 5.2 we describe how the internal model as described in Section 5.1 would have to be interpreted when working with a CODASYL-based database management system (DBMS) i.e. a DBMS based on the DBTG-proposal {5.2}, {5.3}, {5.4}, {5.5}. DBTG is an acronym for Data Base Task Group (a subgroup of the CODASYL Programming Language Committee). Founded in 1968 the mission of DBTG was 'to develop the specifications of a common language and functions for a unified database system' {5.2}.

5.1 RELATIONS AS INTERNAL DATA MODEL

The logical organization of data to be stored on physical storage devices is described by means of an internal data model. The internal data model essentially specifies which attributes will have their values stored as a unit and how the relationships between these units will be represented. In this section we discuss how to describe the internal data model by relations. We particularly show how normalization criteria can be used to obtain an internal data model which is consistent with the conceptual data model and - for all that - reduces the number of accesses required when a user wants to obtain facts about an entity.

We first review some concepts of relations and introduce a few additional definitions.

Relations

Given a collection of domains (i.e. sets) D_1, D_2, ... D_n (not necessarily distinct), R is a relation on these n sets if it is a set of ordered n-tuples $\langle d_1, d_2, \ldots d_n \rangle$ such that each d_j belongs to D_j for j = 1, 2, ... n {5.6}, {5.7}. Here 'ordered' means the order of the element values d_1, ... d_n must be the same in each tuple. The tuples can be in any order.

Another - equivalent - definition is the following. R is a relation on the domains (i.e. sets) D_1, D_2, ... D_n (not necessarily distinct) if it is a subset of the Cartesian product $D_1 \times D_2 \times \ldots \times D_n$. Thus

$$R \subseteq D_1 \times D_2 \times \ldots \times D_n.$$

The value n represents the degree of the relation R. The relation is usually written in the style

$$R (D_1, D_2, \ldots D_n).$$

In the above expression D_1, D_2, ... D_n are called the <u>attributes</u> of the relation R. The values for the attributes are taken from the corresponding domains D_1, D_2, ... D_n. Note that attribute and domain are different concepts although analysts usually give pairs of them the same name. A <u>domain</u> is a set of values whereas an <u>attribute</u> is a list of values. A particular value may occur just once in a set (domain) but several times in a list (values of an attribute). An attribute (or possibly several attributes) in a relation R is (are) drawn from a domain and represents (represent) the use of that domain within the relation R. Role names are needed where two or more attributes have values from the same domain.

Since - according to the definition - a relation represents a set of ordered n-tuples there is - strictly speaking - no ordering defined among the tuples of a relation (remember that the order of the elements within a set is immaterial). For most applications it may be useful, however, to be able to provide and guarantee a particular sequence. So analysts and database administrators usually consider relations to have a certain ordering. The database administrator may choose for each relation the order most commonly required and provide that. But - and this is the crucial point - for reasons of data independence the user should always be able to define a desired ordering in terms of values appearing in some attribute(s) of the relation and should never depend on any system-related sequence.

Similar remarks apply to the order of the attributes within a relation. Since a relation is a set of ordered n-tuples (i.e. the jth value in each n-tuple is taken from the jth domain), the attribute ordering is - mathematically speaking - relevant. Presenting a relation in table form allows one, however, to refer to columns by names rather than by relative positions. This means that the ordering of columns (representing attributes) can be treated as irrelevant just like the ordering of rows (representing tuples), provided that the names of the columns of the relation are unique. Attribute names should preferably be distinct even where they are in different relations.

<u>Example 5.1.1</u>

Fig. 5.1.1 shows a relation defined on the five domains S# (student number), Name, Street, Number, City. The name of the relation is Student and its degree is 8. A tuple, such as

        <S1, Brown, Champel, 20, Brussels, Elysee, 87, Paris>

indicates that the student with student number S1 named Brown has Champel 20, Brussels as home address and Elysee 87, Paris as lodging address.

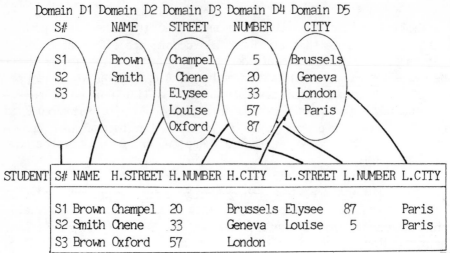

Figure 5.1.1

Note that the degree of the relation Student does not equal the number of domains. Several attributes may take their values from a single domain. Home and Lodging streets are an example. The prefixes H. (for Home-address) and L. (for Lodging-address) are role names and indicate the functions played by a domain underlying several attributes.

Candidate Key

K is a Candidate Key (CK) of a relation R if it is an attribute or an attribute collection of R with the following properties
1 In each tuple of R the value of K uniquely identifies that tuple (Unique Identification). Corollary: each attribute in R is functionally dependent on K.
2 In the case where K is an attribute collection no attribute in K can be discarded without destroying property 1 (Non-redundancy). Corollary: every proper subset of the attribute collection K is functionally independent of any other proper subset of the attribute collection K. In other words there exists a (M:M)-mapping between any two different proper subsets of the attribute collection K. For a group of students who are employees going abroad the candidate keys include
Social security number
Passport number
Employer name and Employee number
Surname and first names (if unique)
Student number.

Primary Key

A relation R may possess several candidate keys. One candidate key is always arbitrarily chosen as the Primary Key (PK) of R. Primary key attribute names or domain names are underlined. The usual operational distinction between the primary key and other candidate keys (if any) is that no tuple is allowed to have an undefined value for any of the attributes constituting the primary key, whereas any other attribute may have an undefined value (so called null value).

Determinant

An attribute (possibly a collection of attributes) of a relation R on which some other attribute of R is functionally (fully functionally) dependent is called a determinant (D).

Prime Attribute

A prime attribute (PA) of a relation R is an attribute participating in at least one candidate key of R.

Non-Prime Attribute

An attribute of a relation R which does not participate in any candidate key of R is called a non-prime attribute (NPA).

Example 5.1.2

Consider the relation

EMPLOYEE (E#, Name, Sex, Location)

E#	Name	Sex	Location
E1	Brown	Male	London
E2	Jones	Female	Brussels
E3	Brown	Male	Paris
E4	Smith	Male	London

Figure 5.1.2

The tuple <E1, Brown, Male, London> means the employee number E1 is called Brown, male and in London.

An analysis of the relation Employee yields

Candidate Key (CK): E#

Primary Key (PK): E# (Since the relation Employee has only one candidate key, this candidate key is automatically taken as the primary key of the relation.)

Determinant (D): E#

Prime Attribute (PA): E#

Non-Prime Attributes (NPA): Name, Sex, Location.

Example 5.1.3

Consider the relation

EMPLOYEE-B (E#, Soc-Sec#, Name)

E#	Soc-Sec#	Name
E1	SS1	Brown
E2	SS2	Jones
E3	SS3	Brown
E4	SS4	Smith

Figure 5.1.3

The tuple <E1, SS1, Brown> means the name of the employee with the employee number E1 and social security number SS1 is Brown.

The analyst should realize the following.

Candidate Keys (CK): E#, Soc-Sec#

Primary Key (PK): E#. Remember that one candidate key is always arbitrarily designated as the primary key. E# is chosen because of the operational distinction that no tuple is allowed to have an undefined value for any of the attributes constituting the primary key. A new employee's social security number might not be known when first creating data about him or her.

Determinants (D): E#, Soc-Sec#

Prime Attributes (PA): E#, Soc-Sec#

Non-Prime Attribute (NPA): Name.

Example 5.1.4

Consider the relation

STUDENT (S#, S-name, C#, C-Name, Opinion)

S#	S-name	C#	C-name	Opinion
S1	Brown	C1	Math	Good
S1	Brown	C2	Chem	Poor
S1	Brown	C3	Phys	Good
S2	Smith	C2	Chem	Satisfactory
S2	Smith	C3	Phys	Satisfactory
S2	Smith	C4	Math	Poor
S3	Brown	C2	Chem	Good
S3	Brown	C3	Phys	Good

Figure 5.1.4

The tuple <S1, Brown, C1, Math, Good> means student S1, Brown, attends course C1 on mathematics and thinks it good.

The analyst notes the following.

Candidate Key (CK): (S#, C#). The unique identification of tuples requires the compound key (S#, C#). Every proper subset of the compound key is functionally independent of any other proper subset e.g. S# is independent of C#. From S# to C# is a many to many mapping.

Primary Key (PK): (S#, C#)

Determinant (D): (S#, C#), S#, C#

Prime Attributes (PA): S#, C#

Non-Prime Attributes (NPA): S-name, C-Name, Opinion.

Normalization

You should now be in a position to appreciate the normalization of relations. We introduce this subject next because analysts and database administrators can thus determine relations that are consistent with a conceptual model specified according to the suggestions made in Chapter 4 but which do not have undesirable dependencies that would give trouble when updating, i.e. when creating, modifying or deleting data item values. These troubles are sometimes called anomalies in storage operations.

Originally Codd defined three levels of normalization, called first normal form (1NF), second normal form (2NF) and third normal form (3NF) {5.7}.

Roughly speaking, each normalized relation is in 1NF (we shall introduce the concept of unnormalized relations later). Some 1NF relations are also in 2NF and some 2NF relations are finally also in 3NF. The point is that 3NF relations are best because they do not allow various inconsistencies in the stored data.

The normalization process as first suggested by Codd {5.7} enables the analyst or database administrator to convert any relation into a set of semantically equivalent 3NF relations. The intention is to implement a database that avoids undesired properties such as anomalies in storage operations.

Schmid and Swenson {5.15} later recognized that even if the internal model is a collection of relations each relation of which is in Codd's 3NF there can still be certain rarer undesirable anomalies in storage operations. Later, Fagin {5.11}, {5.12} defined a fourth normal form (4NF) which overcomes the anomalies recognized by Schmid and Swenson. Briefly, 4NF relations are a subset of 3NF relations and prevent these rarer undesirable inconsistencies.

So we next describe normalization, including how to convert a non-4NF relation into a set of semantically equivalent 4NF relations.

Unnormalized relations and 1NF relations

The examples of relations in Chapter 4 and earlier in this chapter are characterized by the fact that each attribute value in each tuple is atomic (i.e. not decomposable). Such a table or relation presented in table form contains at each row-column-intersection precisely one value, never a set of values. Undefined values (i.e. null values) are allowed for attributes that do not constitute the primary key. Relations satisfying the description above are said to be in first normal form. The word normalized is sometimes used to mean in 1NF, but such usage can be confusing if the same word is used for meaning fully normalized as described later in this chapter.

By contrast a relation that has multiple values at some row-column intersections is not in 1NF. In such an unnormalized structure not all the underlying domains are simple (a non-simple domain is one which contains elements that themselves are relations).

Example 5.1.5

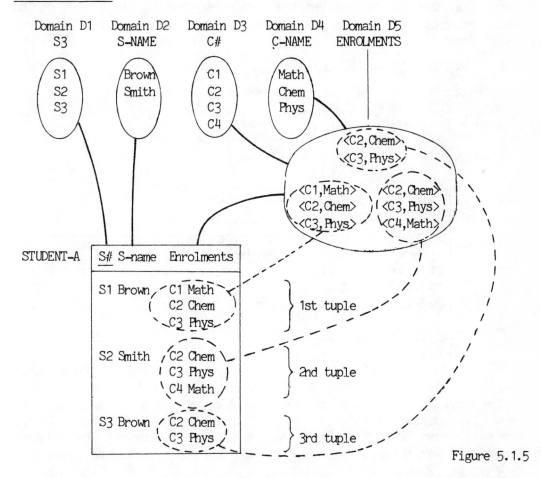

Figure 5.1.5

The above relation is <u>not</u> in 1NF. It is defined on three domains S#, S-name and Enrolments. The name of the relation is Student-a and its degree is, mathematically speaking, three. Here is a tuple of it.

$$\left\langle \begin{array}{lll} \text{S\#} & \text{S-name} & \text{Enrolments} \\[1em] \text{S1,} & \text{Brown,} & \begin{array}{l}\langle \text{C1, Math}\rangle \\ \langle \text{C2, Chem}\rangle \\ \langle \text{C3, Phys}\rangle\end{array} \end{array} \right\rangle$$

Figure 5.1.6

This means Student S1, Brown, is enrolled in those three courses.

The trouble is that the domain Enrolments contains elements which are not atomic, i.e. they can be resolved into two other domains. An element of the domain Enrolments represents a set of binary tuples whose values are taken from the two domains C# and C-name.

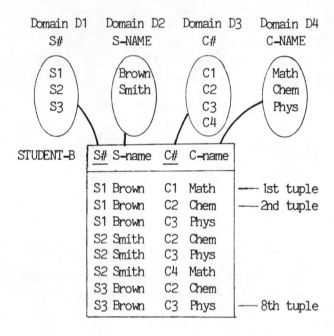

Figure 5.1.7

The above figure shows a relation Student-b that is in 1NF and means the same. The relation Student-b is defined on four domains S#, S-name, C# and C-name, i.e. on domains in which all elements are atomic. The relation Student-b is a relation of degree four. The primary key is compound, consisting of S# and C#.

The analyst should similarly replace any tentative relation that is unnormalized - i.e. with multiple values in elements - by a 1NF relation. That is the first step of the normalization procedure.

Any unnormalized relation can be represented by a semantically equivalent relation in first normal form. The real advantage of 1NF relations as opposed to unnormalized relations is that the operations required for applications are less complicated. Users can understand them. The facilities required in programming languages are also less complex.

Before discussing the undesirable properties of 1NF relations such as Student-b we need to give its analysis.

Suppose the analyst decided students and courses were considered as entities and replaced the entity types by their primary keys. Each student and each

course has one name, not two or more alternatives. A student may attend several courses and a course may have several enrolled students. So there exists a (M:M)-mapping between S# and C#.
    The conceptual data model is as follows.

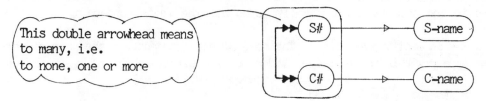

Figure 5.1.8

ER1 (S#, S-name)
ER2 (C#, C-name)
ER3 (S#, C#).
    ER1 and ER2 reflect the functional dependencies
S# $\longrightarrow$ S-name
C# $\longrightarrow$ C-name.
    ER3 corresponds to the (M:M)-mapping between S# and C#.
    Suppose the analyst decided for the internal model to represent these dependencies by a single relation; in other words the analyst combines the attributes S#, C#, S-name and C-name obtaining the Student-b relation in Fig. 5.1.7. The associations in this relation Student-b are as follows.

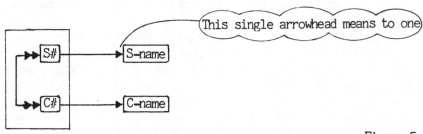

Figure 5.1.9

    All attribute values mentioned in Fig. 5.1.7 obey the dependencies reflected by ER1, ER2 and ER3. Hence the relation Student-b is (with the values above, which correspond to a particular time) consistent with the conceptual data model. However (and we now start to discuss the undesirable properties of the 1NF relation Student-b), we recognize the following anomalies in storage operations.
Anomalies in insert operations: Users cannot enter facts concerning a student without knowing at least one course in which this student is enrolled. The reason is that in such a case part of the primary key (S#, C#) is not known. Similarly, users cannot enter facts concerning a course without knowing at least

one student attending this course (in such a case again they do not know part of the primary key).

Anomalies in delete operations: If users delete all the students attending a particular course the database automatically loses all the facts concerning this course. Similarly if users delete all the courses a particular student is enrolled in the database automatically loses all the facts concerning this student.

Anomalies in modify operations: The name of each student and the name of each course appear within the relation Student-b many times, in general. At the internal level this redundancy has two disadvantages.

- Extra storage space is needed.

- It increases the effort required to modify the relation Student-b. For example if the name of a particular student changes the DBMS would be faced with the problem of changing every tuple containing the name in question. Otherwise the functional dependence

$$S\# \longrightarrow S\text{-name}$$

as reflected by the elementary relation ER1 is not valid any more; i.e. the relation Student-b would no longer be consistent with the conceptual model.

The worst feature is that Student-b allows users to break the rules of the real world conceptual model (e.g. to violate rules such as that each student has only one name). For example suppose that a user tries to insert into Student-b the extra tuple

$$\langle S3, \text{ Jones, } C4, \text{ Chem}\rangle.$$

We can recognize that this tuple contains two 'facts' that do not satisfy the conceptual model

- the student S3 would have two names, i.e. Brown and Jones

- course C4 would be both math and chemistry.

But the database management system would find the attempted insertion acceptable, since the new tuple has a primary key value of $\langle S3, C4\rangle$ that does not already exist, and it cannot check for the inconsistency.

To allow users to work with Student-b would require complicated verification programs to ensure the integrity of the stored data. If such verification were provided in application programs it would be extremely difficult to ensure their completeness and consistency. A more feasible method is needed.

To sum up, the relation Student-b does not enable users to consider students and courses as entities. The conclusion is that the designer is not allowed to replace the conceptual model elementary relations ER1, ER2 and ER3 by an internal model having the single 1NF relation Student-b.

2NF relations

We now go on to discuss the definition of 2NF relations. Thus we get a first hint of whether or not it is feasible to represent several elementary relations (as defined within the conceptual data model) by means of a wider 2NF relation.

We first introduce Codd's original definition {5.7}. A relation R is in second normal form (2NF) if it is in first normal form (1NF) and every non-prime attribute of R is fully functionally dependent on each candidate key of R.

Example 5.1.6

Consider the relation

STUDENT-B (S#, S-name, C#, C-name)

as in Example 5.1.5. The analyst distinguishes the following elements
Candidate Key (CK): (S#, C#)
Primary Key (PK): (S#, C#)
Prime Attributes (PA): S#, C#
Non-Prime Attributes (NPA): S-name, C-name.

The analyst would check if - according to Codd's original definition - every non-prime attribute (NPA) is fully functionally dependent on each candidate key (CK). For the first non-prime attribute S-name

1.1 S#, C# $\longrightarrow$ S-name
1.2 S# $\longrightarrow$ S-name
1.3 C# $\nrightarrow$ S-name

hence (because 1.2 holds)

$$S\#, C\# \nRightarrow S\text{-name}$$

i.e. S-name is not fully functionally dependent on (S#, C#). The attribute S-name would be fully functionally dependent on the attribute collection (S#,C#) if S-name were functionally dependent on (S#,C#) and not functionally dependent on any proper subset of (S#,C#).

Similarly for the non-prime attribute C-name

2.1 S#, C# $\longrightarrow$ C-name
2.2 S# $\nrightarrow$ C-name
2.3 C# $\longrightarrow$ C-name

hence (because 2.3 holds)

$$S\#, C\# \nRightarrow C\text{-name}$$

i.e. C-name is not fully functionally dependent on (S#, C#).

Since neither S-name nor C-name are fully functionally dependent on the candidate key (S#, C#) the relation Student-b is not in 2NF.

Conversion of the relation Student-b to a set of semantically equivalent 2NF relations consists of replacing Student-b by three of its projections. The figure below shows how the dependencies in the relation Student-b (in Fig. 5.1.8) can be used to determine the projections required to obtain a semantically equivalent set of 2NF relations (respectively called Student, Course and SC here).

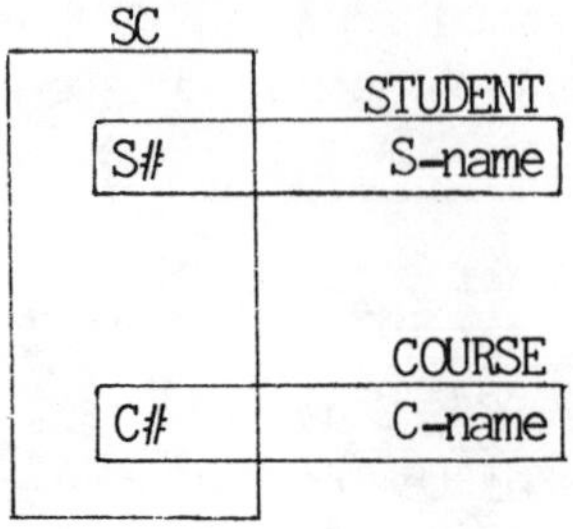

Figure 5.1.10

The analyst may form the project operations

STUDENT ← STUDENT-B [S#, S-name]
COURSE ← STUDENT-B [C#, C-name]
SC   ← STUDENT-B [S#, C#]

and obtains

STUDENT(S#, S-name) COURSE(C#, C-name) SC(S#, C#)

S#	S-name
S1	Brown
S2	Smith
S3	Brown

C#	C-name
C1	Math
C2	Chem
C3	Phys
C4	Math

S#	C#
S1	C1
S1	C2
S1	C3
S2	C2
S2	C3
S2	C4
S3	C2
S3	C3

Figure 5.1.11

The above relations Student, Course and SC are all in 2NF. This follows because a 1NF relation which does not possess any composite candidate key (e.g. the relations Student and Course) or which is just all key (e.g. the relation SC) can never violate Codd's 2NF definition.

The designer should recognize that the relations Student, Course and SC do not lead to anomalies in storage operations and that they enable users to consider students and courses as entities.

He or she should also realize that with this model it is impossible for users to insert 'facts' that violate the conceptual data model. E.g. a user cannot add to the data of Fig. 5.1.11 new tuples such as

<S3, Jones>   or   <C4, Chem>

since these have the same primary key values as existing tuples and duplicates are not allowed.

By splitting the original 1NF relation Student-b into several 2NF relations, no essential information has been lost, since it is always possible to reconstitute the original relation by means of the following natural join operations
$$\text{STUDENT-B} \longleftarrow \text{STUDENT} * \text{SC} * \text{COURSE}.$$

For the above example the set of 2NF relations corresponds to the set of elementary relations required to represent the perception of the real world. The reader should be aware, however, that we have discussed an exceptional case and that in general fewer 2NF relations than elementary relations are required to model a particular perception of the real world.

The following example illustrates that Codd's original definition may lead to problems as soon as a relation possesses overlapping candidate keys.

Example 5.1.7

Let us extend the assumptions concerning students and courses and characterize a student (again represented by a S#-value) not only by his or her name but also by sex and age. Also assume a student may evaluate the courses (represented by C#-values) he or she is enrolled in. This requires three additional attributes - Sex, Age and Opinion. Finally we assume that we have unique course names (i.e. a course name could also be used as an entity key).

This perception of the real world may be represented by the following elementary relations

ER1 ($\overline{\text{S\#}}$, S-name)
ER2 ($\overline{\text{S\#}}$, Sex)
ER3 ($\overline{\text{S\#}}$, Age)
ER4 ($\overline{\text{C\#}}$, C-name)
ER5 ($\overline{\text{S\#}, \text{C\#}}$, Opinion)

These elementary relations reflect the following dependencies

S# $\longrightarrow$ S-name
S# $\longrightarrow$ Sex
S# $\longrightarrow$ Age
C# $\longrightarrow$ C-name
S#, C# $\Longrightarrow$ Opinion.

The elementary relation ER4 possesses two candidate keys because the example assumes unique course names. This means that the dependency
$$\text{C-name} \longrightarrow \text{C\#}$$
also holds in ER4. The five elementary relations are the conceptual model.

Suppose the designer chose to represent this conceptual model by an internal model that has a single relation such as

STUDENT-C(S#, S-name, Sex, Age, C#, C-name, Opinion)

S#	S-name	Sex	Age	C#	C-name	Opinion
S1	Brown	Female	25	C1	Math	Good
S1	Brown	Female	25	C2	Chem	Poor
S1	Brown	Female	25	C3	Phys	Good
S2	Smith	Male	22	C2	Chem	Satisfactory
S2	Smith	Male	22	C3	Phys	Satisfactory
S2	Smith	Male	22	C4	Stat	Poor
S3	Brown	Male	27	C2	Chem	Good
S3	Brown	Male	27	C3	Phys	Good

Figure 5.1.12

All attribute values in the relation Student-c obey the dependencies reflected by the elementary relations ER1, ER2, ER3, ER4 and ER5. Hence the relation Student-c is (with the values above, which correspond to a particular time) consistent with the conceptual model. However the analyst should recognize again insert, delete and update dependencies which are similar to the anomalies discussed for the relation Student-b (see Example 5.1.5).

An analysis of the relation Student-c yields

Candidate Keys (CK): (S#, C#), (S#, C-name) (Note the overlap of the two candidate keys caused by the attribute S#)

Primary Key (PK): (S#, C#)

Prime Attributes (PA): S#, C#, C-name

Non-Prime Attributes (NPA): S-name, Sex, Age, Opinion.

To determine whether or not the relation Student-c is in 2NF (according to Codd's original definition) the analyst has to check if each non-prime attribute of Student-c is fully functionally dependent on each candidate key of Student-c.

For the candidate key (S#, C#) the analyst determines

$S\#, C\# \nRightarrow$ S-name (since: $S\# \longrightarrow$ S-name)

$S\#, C\# \nRightarrow$ Sex (since: $S\# \longrightarrow$ Sex)

$S\#, C\# \nRightarrow$ Age (since: $S\# \longrightarrow$ Age)

$S\#, C\# \Longrightarrow$ Opinion

and for the candidate key (S#, C-name)

$S\#, C\text{-name} \nRightarrow$ S-name (since: $S\# \longrightarrow$ S-name)

$S\#, C\text{-name} \nRightarrow$ Sex (since: $S\# \longrightarrow$ Sex)

$S\#, C\text{-name} \nRightarrow$ Age (since: $S\# \longrightarrow$ Age)

$S\#, C\text{-name} \Longrightarrow$ Opinion.

The next figure shows all dependencies involving non-prime attributes.

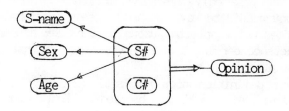

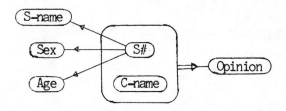

Figure 5.1.13

The relation Student-c is not in 2NF because it contains non-prime attributes that are not fully functionally dependent on candidate keys (i.e. S-name, Sex and Age).

Following Codd's original 2NF definition the analyst has to eliminate from the relation Student-c all non-prime attributes that are not fully functionally dependent on any candidate key. The analyst therefore eliminates S-name, Sex and Age (which are all functionally dependent on S# and therefore can be considered in a separate relation with S# as primary key) and obtains

R1(<u>S#</u>,S-name,Sex,Age)   R2(<u>S#</u>,<u>C#</u>,C-name,Opinion)

S#	S-name	Sex	Age
S1	Brown	Female	25
S2	Smith	Male	22
S3	Brown	Male	27

S#	C#	C-name	Opinion
S1	C1	Math	Good
S1	C2	Chem	Poor
S1	C3	Phys	Good
S2	C2	Chem	Satisfactory
S2	C3	Phys	Satisfactory
S2	C4	Stat	Poor
S3	C2	Chem	Good
S3	C3	Phys	Good

Anomaly: if a user changed this Phys to Engl then the name of C3 would become inconsistent

Figure 5.1.14

Although relation R2 is in 2NF (the only non-prime attribute Opinion is fully functionally dependent on any candidate key), it still leads to anomalies in storage operations and still does not enable the users to consider a course as an entity (because to store facts concerning a course would require that the user knows of at least one student attending the course).

The fact that Codd's original definition does not satisfactorily handle relations with overlapping candidate keys was first observed by Kent. Subsequently Kent proposed the following revised 2NF definition {5.13}.

A relation is in second normal form (2NF) if it is in first normal form (1NF) and every attribute in the complement of a candidate key is fully functionally dependent on that candidate key.

We immediately apply Kent's definition to the relation Student-c.

Example 5.1.8

Consider the relation
           STUDENT-C(S#, S-name, Sex, Age, C#, C-name, Opinion)
as in Example 5.1.7.

The analyst distinguishes the following elements

Candidate Key (CK)	Attributes in CK's complement
(S#, C#)	S-name, Sex, Age, C-name, Opinion
(S#, C-name)	S-name, Sex, Age, C#, Opinion

Figure 5.1.15

To determine whether or not the relation Student-c is in 2NF (according to Kent's definition) the analyst has to check if every attribute in the complement of a candidate key is fully functionally dependent on that candidate key.

For the candidate key (S#, C#) the analyst determines

S#, C#	$\not\Rightarrow$ S-name	(since: S# $\longrightarrow$ S-name)
S#, C#	$\not\Rightarrow$ Sex	(since: S# $\longrightarrow$ Sex)
S#, C#	$\not\Rightarrow$ Age	(since: S# $\longrightarrow$ Age)
S#, C#	$\not\Rightarrow$ C-name	(since: C# $\longrightarrow$ C-name)
S#, C#	$\Longrightarrow$ Opinion	

and for the candidate key (S#, C-name)

S#, C-name	$\not\Rightarrow$ S-name	(since: S# $\longrightarrow$ S-name)
S#, C-name	$\not\Rightarrow$ Sex	(since: S# $\longrightarrow$ Sex)
S#, C-name	$\not\Rightarrow$ Age	(since: S# $\longrightarrow$ Age)
S#, C-name	$\not\Rightarrow$ C#	(since: C-name $\longrightarrow$ C#)
S#, C-name	$\Longrightarrow$ Opinion	

The next figure shows the above dependencies and illustrates how to perform the split of the relation Student-c in order to obtain 2NF relations satisfying Kent's definition.

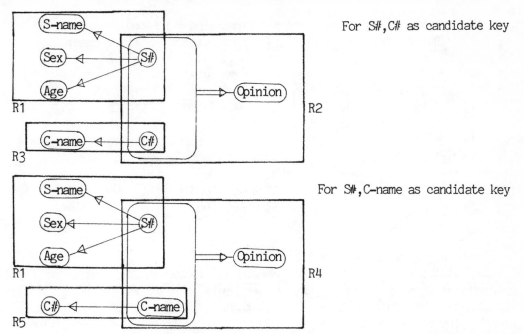

For S#,C# as candidate key

R1   R2   R3

For S#,C-name as candidate key

R1   R4   R5

Figure 5.1.16

By performing the project operations (see Fig. 5.1.16 upper)
R1 ⟵ STUDENT-C [S#, S-name, Sex, Age]
R2 ⟵ STUDENT-C [S#, C#, Opinion]
R3 ⟵ STUDENT-C [C#, C-name]
the analyst obtains for the above example (1st solution)
R1(S#,S-name,Sex,Age)   R2(S#,C#,Opinion)   R3(C#,C-name)

S#	S-name	Sex	Age
S1	Brown	Female	25
S2	Smith	Male	22
S3	Brown	Male	27

S#	C#	Opinion
S1	C1	Good
S1	C2	Poor
S1	C3	Good
S2	C2	Satisfactory
S2	C3	Satisfactory
S2	C4	Poor
S3	C2	Good
S3	C3	Good

C#	C-name
C1	Math
C2	Chem
C3	Phys
C4	Stat

Figure 5.1.17

A semantically equivalent solution may be obtained by performing the project operations (see Fig. 5.1.16 lower)
R1 ⟵ STUDENT-C [S#, S-name, Sex, Age]
R4 ⟵ STUDENT-C [S#, C-name, Opinion]
R5 ⟵ STUDENT-C [C-name, C#]

The analyst thereby obtains the relations (2nd solution)
       R1(S#,S-name,Sex,Age) R4(S#,C-name,Opinion)   R5(C-name,C#)

S#	S-name	Sex	Age
S1	Brown	Female	25
S2	Smith	Male	22
S3	Brown	Male	27

S#	C-name	Opinion
S1	Math	Good
S1	Chem	Poor
S1	Phys	Good
S2	Chem	Satisfactory
S2	Phys	Satisfactory
S2	Stat	Poor
S3	Chem	Good
S3	Phys	Good

C-name	C#
Math	C1
Chem	C2
Phys	C3
Stat	C4

Figure 5.1.18

The analyst should realize the following

1 The relations of both solutions are in 2NF (according to Kent's and Codd's definitions). Note, however, that we were only able to derive these 2NF relations from the 'ancestor' relation Student-c (which, remember, contains two overlapping candidate keys) by using Kent's more restrictive 2NF definition.

2 The relations of both solutions do not lead to any anomalies in storage operations and retain all the essential information of the 'ancestor' relation Student-c. This means that Student-c can be recovered by joining the relations of a particular solution. Thus

       STUDENT-C ←R1 * R2 * R3 or
       STUDENT-C ←R1 * R4 * R5.

3 The elementary relations ER1, ER2, ER3, ER4 and ER5 are represented in both solutions by three relations. Hence the number of elementary relations required to model the perception of the real world has been reduced from five to three. The conceptual data model was elementary relations but the internal model need not be.

Unless otherwise specified, subsequent references to 2NF relations refer to Kent's more restrictive definition.

Optimal 2NF relations

A collection of relations C is in optimal second normal form (with respect to a relation T) if

1 all the relations in C are in 2NF

2 the relations in C retain all the essential information in the relation T (i.e. T can be recovered by joining the relations in C)

3 there is no smaller collection with these properties {5.13}.

This combines Kent's 2NF with the grouping of attributes that are fully functionally dependent on the same key.

Example 5.1.9

Consider the 1NF relation
$$\text{STUDENT-C}(S\#, S\text{-name}, Sex, Age, C\#, C\text{-name}, Opinion)$$
as in Example 5.1.7. As illustrated by Example 5.1.8 Student-c can be trans-
formed into the following collections of 2NF relations
C_1 = {R1 (S#, S-name, Sex, Age),
            R2 (S#, C#, Opinion),
            R3 (C#, C-name)}   and
C_2 = {R1 (S#, S-name, Sex, Age),
            R4 (S#, C-name, Opinion),
            R5 (C-name, C#)}.
The relation R1 can be replaced by the 2NF relations
            R6 (S#, S-name)
            R7 (S#, Sex)
            R8 (S#, Age)
since R1 can be obtained by
            R1 ⟵ R6 * R7 * R8.
This means that Student-c can also be transformed into the following collec-
tions of 2NF relations
C_3 = {R6 (S#, S-name),
            R7 (S#, Sex),
            R8 (S#, Age),
            R2 (S#, C#, Opinion),
            R3 (C#, C-name)}   and
C_4 = {R6 (S#, S-name),
            R7 (S#, Sex),
            R8 (S#, Age),
            R4 (S#, C-name, Opinion),
            R5 (C-name, C#)}.
The collections C_1 and C_2 are in optimal 2NF whereas the collections C_3 and
C_4 are not in optimal 2NF since there are smaller collections (i.e. C_1 and C_2)
representing the same information.

Relations that are in 2NF may - under some conditions - still lead to
anomalies in storage operations. The next example shows how.

Example 5.1.10

Assume that the perception of the real world is as follows.
1 Products (represented by a product number P#) and machines (represented by a
machine number M#) are entities.

2 A product is always manufactured by a single machine but a machine may manufacture several products. Hence the mapping

$$P\# \Longleftrightarrow M\#$$

always holds.

3 A product is always manufactured by a single employee (represented by the employee number E#) but an employee may manufacture several products. Hence the mapping

$$P\# \Longleftrightarrow E\#$$

always holds.

4 A machine is always operated by a single employee but an employee may operate several machines. Hence the mapping

$$M\# \Longleftrightarrow E\#$$

always holds.

The perception of the real world can be represented by the following elementary relations

ER1 ($\overline{P\#}$, M#)
ER2 ($\overline{P\#}$, E#)
ER3 ($\overline{M\#}$, E#).

These elementary relations correspond to the functional dependencies

$P\# \longrightarrow M\#$
$P\# \longrightarrow E\#$
$M\# \longrightarrow E\#.$

The designer glues the elementary relations ER1, ER2 and ER3 together and obtains the relation

MANUFACTURE ($\underline{P\#}$, M#, E#)

P#	M#	E#
P1	M1	E1
P2	M2	E3
P3	M1	E1
P4	M1	E1
P5	M3	E2
P6	M4	E1

Figure 5.1.19

The tuple <P1, M1, E1> means product P1 is manufactured on machine M1 which is operated by the employee E1.

Analysis of the relation Manufacture yields

Candidate Key (CK): P#
Primary Key (PK): P#
Prime Attribute (PA): P#
Non-Prime Attributes (NPA): M#, E#.

The relation is in 2NF since it is in 1NF and its key consists of a single attribute only.

However this relation is still not satisfactory. It can lead to other problems with storage operations. For example if a user changed the E1 in the first tuple to say E3 then the first tuple would be inconsistent with the other tuples involving M1 which would still have E1. This is not consistent with M# $\longrightarrow$ E#. The problems are as follows.

<u>Anomalies in insert operations</u>: It is not possible for a user to store the fact that a particular machine is operated by a particular employee without knowing at least one product produced by this machine (otherwise the primary key value is not known). This means that a machine cannot be considered on its own: it cannot be handled as a real entity.

<u>Anomalies in delete operations</u>: If all the products manufactured by a particular machine are deleted then the relationship between this machine and the employee operating this machine is also deleted. E.g. if products P1, P3 and P4 are deleted then the fact that machine M1 is operated by employee E1 also disappears.

<u>Anomalies in modify operations</u>: If the employee responsible for a machine changes then several tuples would have to be modified. Otherwise the functional dependence

$$M\# \longrightarrow E\#$$

corresponding to the elementary relation ER3 would no longer be valid, i.e. the internal model would no longer be consistent with the conceptual model.

The worst point is that Manufacture allows users to violate the conceptual data model rule that a machine is operated by only one employee. E.g. suppose a user tries to insert the tuple

<P7, M4, E2>.

This tuple corresponds to including a 'fact' that is not allowed, i.e. that M4 has two operators E1 and E2. But to the DBMS this attempted insertion is acceptable since the tuple has a new key value P7 that does not already exist. So to use Manufacture as part of the internal model would require application programs to apply verification procedures in a way that would not be feasible.

3NF relations

We go on to discuss the concept of third normal form (3NF) which may help to overcome the above mentioned anomalies in storage operations.

We introduce Codd's definition {5.7} first.

A relation R is in third normal form (3NF) if it is in second normal form (2NF) and every non-prime attribute of R is non-transitively dependent on each candidate key of R.

Example 5.1.11

Consider the relation
                    MANUFACTURE (P#, M#, E#)
as in Example 5.1.10. The mappings are

P# $\longleftrightarrow$ M#
M# $\longleftrightarrow$ E#
P# $\longleftrightarrow$ E#.

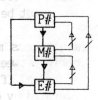

                                                    Figure 5.1.20

The non-prime attribute E# is strictly transitively dependent on the candidate key P#. Hence the relation Manufacture is not in 3NF according to Codd's definition.

You will remember from Section 4.2 that the attribute C of a relation R is strictly transitively dependent on the attribute A of R if R contains a third attribute B such that

A $\longrightarrow$ B
B $\nrightarrow$ A
B $\longrightarrow$ C
C $\nrightarrow$ B.

These dependencies imply (mathematically speaking)

A $\longrightarrow$ C and
C $\nrightarrow$ A.

The above anomalies in storage operations are because E# is transitively dependent on P# via M#. Conversion of the relation Manufacture to a set of semantically equivalent 3NF relations consists of replacing Manufacture by two of its projections. Since the functional dependence

                    P# $\longrightarrow$ E#

represents the product function of

                    P# $\longrightarrow$ M# and M# $\longrightarrow$ E#

and hence can be deduced from P# $\longrightarrow$ M# and M# $\longrightarrow$ E#, the designer may split Manufacture by the project operations

                    R1 $\longleftarrow$ MANUFACTURE [P#, M#]
                    R2 $\longleftarrow$ MANUFACTURE [M#, E#]

to give the relations

R1 (P#, M#)   and   R2 (M#, E#)

P#	M#
P1	M1
P2	M2
P3	M1
P4	M1
P5	M3
P6	M4

M#	E#
M1	E1
M2	E3
M3	E2
M4	E1

Figure 5.1.21

The functional dependence

$$P\# \longrightarrow E\#$$

is still derivable (i.e. all the essential information of Manufacture is retained). The original relation Manufacture (and with that the functional dependence $P\# \longrightarrow E\#$) can be reconstituted by means of the join operation

MANUFACTURE ← R1 * R2.

The above insert, delete and update anomalies have disappeared with the removal of the transitive dependence. This means that both a machine and a product can each be considered as an entity. It is also impossible for a user to insert a tuple such as <M4, E2> which does not conform to the dependencies in the conceptual data model; the DBMS would not allow it to be added to R2.

Again one can show that Codd's original 3NF definition does not satisfactorily handle the case of a relation possessing two overlapping candidate keys. Kent therefore proposes in {5.13} an alternative 3NF definition as follows.

A relation in 2NF is in 3NF if every attribute in the complement of a candidate key is nontransitively dependent on that candidate key.

This definition is more restrictive than Codd's original definition and has similar characteristics to Kent's alternate definition of 2NF presented earlier.

The concepts of 1NF and 2NF are not very important in themselves. They just lead to the more desirable 3NF and (as we shall see later) 4NF. As a matter of fact, it is possible to give a 3NF definition which makes no reference to 2NF, nor to the concepts of full functional dependence and transitive dependence. Such a definition is due to Boyce and Codd {5.8} and is as follows.

A relation R is in 3NF if it is in 1NF and, for every attribute collection C of R, if any attribute not in C is functionally dependent on C, then all attributes in R are functionally dependent on C. (To appreciate that think of C as a candidate key.)

Relations satisfying Boyce/Codd's 3NF definition (which is logically equivalent to Kent's alternative definition) are sometimes said to be in Boyce/Codd normal form (BCNF).

Still another (but logically equivalent definition) has been given in {5.9} by Date. This definition is based on the concept of candidate keys and determinants as follows.

A normalized relation R is in 3NF if every determinant is a candidate key.

Example 5.1.12

Consider the relation
$$STUDENT\text{-}C(S\#, S\text{-}name, Sex, Age, C\#, C\text{-}name, Opinion)$$
as discussed in Example 5.1.7.

The analyst distinguishes the following elements
Candidate Key (CK): (S#, C#)
Determinants (D):
  (S#, C#) because S#, C# $\Longrightarrow$ Opinion
  S# because S# $\longrightarrow$ S-name, S# $\longrightarrow$ Sex and S# $\longrightarrow$ Age
  C# because C# $\longrightarrow$ C-name.

The relation Student-c is not in 3NF according to Date's definition because the determinants S# and C# are not candidate keys.

Consider the relations
$$R1(S\#, S\text{-}name, Sex, Age)$$
$$R2(S\#, C\#, C\text{-}name, Opinion)$$
obtained by splitting the relation Student-c using Codd's original 2NF definition (see Example 5.1.7).

For R1 the analyst distinguishes the elements
Candidate Key (CK): S#
Determinant (D): S# because S# $\longrightarrow$ S-name, S# $\longrightarrow$ Sex and S# $\longrightarrow$ Age.

The relation R1 is in 3NF because the only determinant S# is also a candidate key.

For R2 the analyst distinguishes the elements
Candidate Key (CK): (S#, C#)
Determinants (D):
  (S#, C#) because S#, C# $\Longrightarrow$ Opinion
  C# because C# $\longrightarrow$ C-name.

The relation R2 is not in 3NF because the determinant C# is not also a candidate key.

Now consider the relations
$$R1(S\#, S\text{-}name, Sex, Age)$$
$$R2(S\#, C\#, Opinion)$$
$$R3(C\#, C\text{-}name)$$
obtained by splitting the relation Student-c using Kent's alternative 2NF definition (see Example 5.1.8). R1 is - as already pointed out - in 3NF.

For R2 the analyst has
Candidate Key (CK): (S#, C#)
Determinant (D): (S#, C#) because S#, C# $\implies$ Opinion.
Hence the relation R2 is in 3NF.
    Similarly the analyst obtains for R3
Candidate Key (CK): C#
Determinant (D): C# because C# $\longrightarrow$ C-name.
Hence the relation R3 is also in 3NF.
    Unless otherwise specified, subsequent references to 3NF relations refer not
to Codd's original 3NF definition but to the alternatives given by Kent,
Boyce/Codd and Date which are all logically equivalent.

Optimal 3NF relations

    Like optimal 2NF, there exists also a notion of optimal 3NF. The following
definition is taken from {5.13}.
    Let C2 be a collection of relations in optimal 2NF, and C3 a collection of
relations in 3NF obtained by projections from the relations in C2. Then the
collection C3 is in optimal third normal form (with respect to C2) if
 1 All the relations in C3 are in 3NF
 2 The relations in C3 retain all the essential information in C2 (i.e. the collection C2 can be recovered by joining relations in C3)
 3 No relation in C3 contains any two attributes which are strictly transitively
dependent in any relation in C2
 4 No smaller collection of relations has these properties.

Example 5.1.13

    Assume that the collection C2 consists just of the relation
                    MANUFACTURE (P#, M#, E#)
as discussed in Example 5.1.10. The analyst recognizes that the attribute E#
(in the complement of the candidate key P#) is strictly transitively dependent
on P# via M#. Hence Manufacture is not in 3NF. However Manufacture is in optimal 2NF (a single relation in 2NF is always in optimal 2NF).
    Conversion to 3NF consists in removing the transitive dependence in Manufac-
ture. This can be achieved either by excluding E# (as suggested in Example
5.1.11) or by excluding M#. At first glance one might be tempted to take one of
the following solutions.

Solution 1
Replace Manufacture (as suggested in Example 5.1.11) by
                R1 (P#, M#)   and   R2 (M#, E#)

P#	M#
P1	M1
P2	M2
P3	M1
P4	M1
P5	M3
P6	M4

M#	E#
M1	E1
M2	E3
M3	E2
M4	E1

Figure 5.1.22

and let $C3_1$ represent these relations.

Solution 2
Replace Manufacture by
                R1 (P#, M#)   and   R3 (P#, E#)

P#	M#
P1	M1
P2	M2
P3	M1
P4	M1
P5	M3
P6	M4

P#	E#
P1	E1
P2	E3
P3	E1
P4	E1
P5	E2
P6	E1

Figure 5.1.23

and let $C3_2$ represent the above mentioned relations.

'Solution 3'
Replace Manufacture by
                R3 (P#, E#)   and   R2 (M#, E#)

P#	E#
P1	E1
P2	E3
P3	E1
P4	E1
P5	E2
P6	E1

M#	E#
M1	E1
M2	E3
M3	E2
M4	E1

Figure 5.1.24

and let $C3_3$ represent these relations.

We now go on to discuss whether or not the collections $C3_1$, $C3_2$ and $C3_3$ are in optimal 3NF. The analyst would work through the four conditions for optimal 3NF.

1 All the relations in $C3_1$, $C3_2$ and $C3_3$ are in 3NF (a relation with only two attributes can never produce a transitive dependence).

2 The relations $C3_1$ and $C3_2$ allow recovery of the relation in C2 by means of

MANUFACTURE ← R1 * R2   or   ← R1 * R3.

However, a join of the relations in $C3_3$ yields tuples (marked —>) which were not in the collection C2.

MANUFACTURE-MODIFIED (P#, M#, E#) = R3 * R2

	P#	M#	E#
	P1	M1	E1
—>	P1	M4	E1
	P2	M2	E3
	P3	M1	E1
—>	P3	M4	E1
	P4	M1	E1
—>	P4	M4	E1
	P5	M3	E2
—>	P6	M1	E1
	P6	M4	E1

Figure 5.1.25

Hence the collection $C3_3$ does not satisfy the second criterion for optimal 3NF and has to be excluded from consideration.

3 No relation in $C3_1$ contains two attributes which are strictly transitively dependent in C2. The collection $C3_2$ contains the relation R3 with the attribute E# strictly transitively dependent on P# in C2. Hence the collection $C3_2$ does not satisfy the third criterion for optimal 3NF and has to be excluded from consideration.

The third criterion has the effect of minimizing storage requirements in terms of the total number of tuples. The collection $C3_1$ comprises ten tuples and the collection $C3_2$ twelve tuples.

The third criterion has a psychological attractiveness since it tends to preserve direct relationships rather than allowing them to be buried in indirect relationships {5.13}.

4 $C3_1$ represents the smallest possible collection of 3NF relations retaining the essential information in Manufacture. Hence, $C3_1$ is in optimal 3NF.

Fourth Normal Form

A relation may be in 3NF and may yet still possess undesirable properties.

Example 5.1.14

Assume that the perception of the real world is as follows

1 Products (represented by a product number P#) and machines (represented by a machine number M#) are entities.

2 A product is usually manufactured by several machines and a machine may manufacture several products. Hence the mapping

$$P\# \ll\!\!-\!\!\gg M\#$$

always holds.

3 A machine is usually operated by several employees (represented by an employee number E#) and an employee may operate several machines. Hence the mapping

$$M\# \ll\!\!-\!\!\gg E\#$$

always holds.

4 It is assumed that whenever making a product requires a machine then this machine is always operated by the same set of employees.

The perception of the real world can be represented by the following elementary relations as a conceptual data model

ER1 (P#, M#) and   ER2 (M#, E#).

These elementary relations are all key.

The designer might join the elementary relations ER1 and ER2 together and obtain the relation

MANUFACTURE-B (P#, M#, E#)

P#	M#	E#
P1	M1	E1
P1	M1	E2
P1	M1	E3
P1	M2	E3
P1	M2	E4
P2	M1	E1
P2	M1	E2
P2	M1	E3
P3	M2	E3
P3	M2	E4

Figure 5.1.26

The tuple <P1, M1, E1> means product P1 is manufactured (among others) on machine M1 which is operated (among others) by employee E1.

Analysis of the relation Manufacture-B yields

Candidate Key (CK): (P#, M#, E#) (thus the relation is all key)
Primary Key (PK): (P#, M#, E#)
Prime Attributes (PA): P#, M#, E#
Non-Prime Attribute (NPA): −

The relation Manufacture–B is in 3NF since – being all key – it cannot violate any of the normalization criteria discussed so far. But there are still storage problems.

Anomalies in insert operations: It is not possible to store the relationship between a product and the machine(s) required to manufacture this product without knowing at least one person operating the machine(s) (otherwise part of the primary key is not known).

Likewise, it is not possible to store the relationship between a machine and the set of persons operating this machine without knowing at least one product manufactured by this machine.

Also, if the operation of a machine requires an additional person then it is usually necessary to create several new tuples. E.g. if machine M2 is operated in addition by the employee E5 then the user needs to insert

<P1, M2, E5>
<P3, M2, E5>.

Anomalies in delete operations: If all the products manufactured by a particular machine are deleted then the relationship between this machine and the employee(s) operating this machine is also deleted. Likewise, if all the employees operating a machine are deleted then the relationship between this machine and the product(s) manufactured by this machine will also disappear. Also, if the operation of a machine requires a person less then it is usually required to delete several tuples. E.g. if E1 is no longer responsible for machine M1 the user must delete

<P1, M1, E1>
<P2, M1, E1>.

Anomalies in modify operations: If an employee responsible for a machine changes then several tuples have to be updated.

The worst feature is that Manufacture–b allows users to violate the conceptual data model, e.g. that each machine is always operated by the same set of employees. For if a user attempts to insert

<P3, M2, E5>

you can recognize that that tuple is not consistent with Fig. 5.1.26 since machine M2 would be operated by
– E3 and E4 for P1
– E3, E4 and E5 for P3.
But the insertion is acceptable to a DBMS since the tuple has a new key <P3, M2, E5> that is different from all existing keys. So to work with Manufacture–b would require complicated application software that is not feasible.

We go on to discuss the concept of fourth normal form (4NF) which overcomes these anomalies in storage operations.

4NF relations

In the following no attempt will be made to present the concept of 4NF in a formal way (for a formal treatment the reader is referred to {5.12} and {5.19}). However the basic ideas of 4NF will be explained in the context of the relation

$$\text{MANUFACTURE-B (P\#, M\#, E\#)}$$

as introduced in Example 5.1.14 page 202.

We recognize first of all that the relation Manufacture-b contains a multivalued dependence. Since the set of E#-values that appears with a given M#-value appears with every combination of this M#-value and a given P#-value the multivalued dependence

$$\text{M\#} \longrightarrow\longrightarrow \text{E\#}$$

holds (i.e. M# multidetermines E# in Manufacture-b). This multivalued dependence causes the above anomalies in storage operations. Conversion to 4NF consists of eliminating the multivalued dependence. This can be achieved by replacing Manufacture-b by two of its projections

$$\text{R1} \longleftarrow \text{MANUFACTURE-B [P\#, M\#]}$$
$$\text{R2} \longleftarrow \text{MANUFACTURE-B [M\#, E\#].}$$

The resulting relations R1 and R2 are as follows.

R1 (P#, M#)   and   R2 (M#, E#)

P#	M#
P1	M1
P1	M2
P2	M1
P3	M2

M#	E#
M1	E1
M1	E2
M1	E3
M2	E3
M2	E4

Figure 5.1.27

All undesired anomalies of the relation Manufacture-b have disappeared.

Moreover, it is impossible for the dependencies of the conceptual data model to be violated, e.g. by an attempted insertion of <M2, E5>.

The essential information of Manufacture-b has been retained since it is always possible to recover Manufacture-b by means of the join operation

$$\text{MANUFACTURE-B} \longleftarrow \text{R1} * \text{R2.}$$

Relating the Conceptual Realm to the Internal Realm

So far we have discussed the justification for choosing a design using relations in 4NF. We have illustrated how normalization reduces redundancy, eliminates undesired anomalies in storage operations and guarantees certain kinds of integrity of the stored values in the database, i.e. making them conform to the dependencies.

It should perhaps be emphasized that all 4NF relations derived were consistent with the corresponding conceptual model view of the real world. The procedure to resolve a 1NF relation into a set of semantically equivalent 4NF relations follows the same steps as the reduction procedure for the determination of irreducible units (Section 4.2) {5.9}. At each step unsatisfactory relations are replaced by others.

Step 1: Take projections of 1NF relations to eliminate any nonfull functional dependencies. The result is a collection of 2NF relations.

Step 2: Take projections of the relations obtained in step 1 to eliminate any transitive dependencies. The result is a collection of 3NF relations.

Step 3: Take projections of the relations obtained in step 2 to eliminate multivalued dependencies producing undesired side effects (i.e. anomalies in storage operations). The result is a collection of 4NF relations.

The fact that the reduction procedure for the determination of elementary relations follows the above steps means that any elementary relation is in 4NF. However in general the collection of all the elementary relations is not in optimal 4NF. I.e. it is usually possible to find a smaller collection of 4NF relations retaining all the information.

Using CER as an abbreviation for the collection of all the elementary relations of the conceptual data model, the procedure required to obtain the optimal 4NF relations is as follows.

Step 1

Create subsets, say S_j, of the relations in CER such that each subset S_j contains only elementary relations with identical keys K_j, i.e. ER_i (K_j, A_i). Each subset S_j will, in general, contain several elementary relations ER_i (with i = 1, 2, ...n) satisfying this condition.

Step 2

Combine the elementary relations of a subset S_j such that the resulting relation, say R_j, contains the key K_j and all non-key attributes A_i of the elementary relations ER_i in S_j. Thus, create for each subset S_j a single relation of the form

$$R_j (K_j, A_1, A_2, A_3, \ldots A_i, \ldots A_n).$$

Where several attributes A_i have the same name distinguish these attributes by means of role names.

The resulting relation R_j is free both of any nonfull functional dependencies and of multivalued dependencies.

However, as shown below, it is possible for the combination process to produce transitive dependencies. This is unsatisfactory so a third step is needed.

Example 5.1.15

Assume the elementary relations
ER1 ($\underline{A}$, B)
ER2 ($\underline{A}$, C)
ER3 ($\underline{B}$, C).
ER2 represents the composition of ER1 and ER3 i.e.
$$ER2 = C \ (ER1, \ ER3).$$
The subset creation (Step 1) yields
S_1 = {ER1, ER2}
S_2 = {ER3}.
The combination of the elementary relations in each subset (Step 2) yields
R_1 (A, B, C)
R_2 ($\underline{B}$, C).
R_1 and R_2 correspond to the functional dependencies
$R_1.A \longrightarrow R_1.B$
$R_1.A \longrightarrow R_1.C$
$R_2.B \longrightarrow R_2.C.$
From that one may conclude that C is (mathematically speaking) transitively dependent on A in R_1. Thus the procedure for the determination of optimal 4NF requires an extra step.

Step 3
Take projections of the relations obtained in Step 2 to eliminate any transitive dependencies. This step is only required if the collection of all elementary relations contains elementary relations representing the composition of other elementary relations.

Example 5.1.16

This example shows in full the working of the procedure for the collection of 25 elementary relations of Example 4.2.21, pages 135-7, i.e. the following.
ER1 ($\underline{S\#}$, Street)
ER2 ($\underline{S\#}$, Number)
ER3 ($\underline{S\#}$, City)
ER4 ($\underline{S\#}$, $\underline{Language}$, Level)
ER5 ($\underline{S\#}$, $\underline{Street}$)
ER6 ($\underline{S\#}$, Number)
ER7 ($\underline{S\#}$, City)
ER8 ($\underline{S\#}$, Name)
ER9 ($\underline{P\#}$, Street)
ER10 ($\underline{P\#}$, Number)
ER11 ($\underline{P\#}$, City)
ER12 ($\underline{P\#}$, Name)

ER13 (C#, Credits)
ER14 ($\overline{C\#}$, Description)
ER15 ($\overline{R\#}$, Size)
ER16 ($\overline{S\#}$, P#)
ER17 ($\overline{S\#}$, C#)
ER18 ($\overline{S\#}$, $\overline{P\#}$, C#)
ER19 ($\overline{\text{Before.}C\#}$, $\overline{\text{After.}C\#}$)
ER20 ($\overline{S\#}$, $\overline{P\#}$)
ER21 (C#, $\overline{P\#}$)
ER22 ($\overline{C\#}$, $\overline{R\#}$)
ER23 ($\overline{S\#}$, $\overline{C\#}$, Credits)
ER24 ($\overline{S\#}$, $\overline{C\#}$, Opinion.Rating)
ER25 ($\overline{S\#}$, $\overline{P\#}$, $\overline{C\#}$, Grade.Rating)

As an exercise you may like to try the procedure before reading the following solution.

The designer does Step 1 of the optimization procedure. The subset creation (Step 1) yields
S_1 (with K_1 = S#) = {ER1, ER2, ER3, ER5, ER6, ER7, ER8, ER16}
S_2 (with K_2 = P#) = {ER9, ER10, ER11, ER12}
S_3 (with K_3 = C#) = {ER13, ER14, ER22}
S_4 (with K_4 = R#) = {ER15}
S_5 (with K_5 = S#, Language) = {ER4}
S_6 (with K_6 = S#, C#) = {ER17, ER23, ER24}
S_7 (with K_7 = S#, P#, C#) = {ER18, ER25}
S_8 (with K_8 = Before.C#, After.C#) = {ER19}
S_9 (with K_9 = S#, P#) = {ER20}
S_{10} (with K_{10} = C#, P#) = {ER21}.
Next the designer works through Step 2 of the optimization procedure. The combination of the elementary relations in each subset (Step 2) yields the following, where the role names H and L stand for Home-address and Lodging-address.
R_1 (S#, H.Street, H.Number, H.City, L.Street, L.Number, L.City, Name, P#)
R_2 (P#, Street, Number, City, Name)
R_3 (C#, Credits, Description, R#)
R_4 ($\overline{R\#}$, Size)
R_5 ($\overline{S\#}$, Language, Level)
R_6 ($\overline{S\#}$, $\overline{C\#}$, Credits, Opinion.Rating)
R_7 ($\overline{S\#}$, $\overline{P\#}$, $\overline{C\#}$, Grade.Rating)
R_8 ($\overline{\text{Before.}C\#}$, $\overline{\text{After.}C\#}$)
R_9 ($\overline{S\#}$, $\overline{P\#}$)
R_{10} ($\overline{C\#}$, $\overline{P\#}$)
Step 3 of the optimization procedure determines - mathematically speaking - one transitive dependence in R_1 because

$R_1.S\# \longrightarrow R_1.P\#$

$R_1.S\# \longrightarrow R_1.Name$

$R_2.P\# \longrightarrow R_2.Name.$

i.e. Name is (mathematically speaking) transitively dependent on S# via P#. However, it would - semantically - be wrong to replace R_1 by the projections

RA = R_1 {S#, H.Street, H.Number, H.City, L.Street, L.Number, L.City, P#}

RB = R_1{P#, Name}

since the functional dependence

$R_2.P\# \longrightarrow R_2.Name$

as defined by the relation R_2 denotes the name of the professor advising a student and not the name of the student himself. Hence the above ten relations already represent an optimal 4NF solution. They are consistent with the 25 elementary relations required to model the perception of the ·real world. They are fully normalized. They guarantee consistency with real world dependencies.

Summary

The justification for designing internal realm models based on collections of relations in 4NF is
- reduction of redundancy
- elimination of undesired anomalies in storage operations and
- ensuring database integrity in conforming to dependencies.

The procedure for resolving a 1NF relation into equivalent 4NF relations follows the same steps as the reduction procedure for determining irreducible units, replacing unsatisfactory relations by better ones.

Elementary relations are necessarily in 4NF since their determination is based on the same concepts.

An optimization procedure allows transformation of a collection of elementary relations into a collection of semantically equivalent optimal 4NF relations. This optimization process usually reduces the number of relations required to model the mini world.

Any collection of real world entity types, attributes and relationships can be expressed in terms of dependencies between attributes, giving a conceptual data model expressible as elementary relations. These can then be internally modelled as a collection of relations that are in optimal 4NF. In optimal 4NF the attributes are grouped in the best way to represent the conceptual model. If each relation in the optimal 4NF collection corresponds to a type of stored record and each tuple to a stored record occurrence then there will be as few record types and record occurrences as possible.

5.2 THE CODASYL APPROACH

This section describes how a collection of optimal 4NF relations could be implemented with a CODASYL-based database management system {5.2}, {5.3}, {5.4}, {5.5}.

The plan of this section is as follows. We first introduce the relevant CODASYL features such as the concept of a set type which is the most important feature. That leads on to how to produce a global logical model for a CODASYL-based DBMS that is equivalent to a collection of optimal 4NF relations. That global logical model will be theoretically sound, i.e. such that all currently proposed and all future possible uses of the data as information can be handled. However for a particular organization it may be desirable to implement a slightly different global logical model for detailed technical reasons. Such reasons may depend on the patterns of use and the detailed features of the DBMS in use and are somewhat specialist.

The CODASYL Data Model

We briefly describe only the relevant CODASYL features. For a complete treatment see references {5.2}, {5.3}, {5.4}, {5.5}, {5.14}.

A CODASYL global logical model consists essentially of types of records and types of relationships between these record types. Each record type consists of a collection of data item types.

The data item types roughly correspond to the attributes or columns of the 4NF relations. The relationship types are called set types. Each set type roughly corresponds to a mapping, such as a one-to-many mapping, between two record types. Each record type, data item type and set type is named.

For example the relation R_1 above becomes a record type named say Student with data item types S#, H.Street, H.Number, H.City, L.Street, L.Number, L.City, Name. The relation R_2 similarly becomes a record type named Professor with data item types P#, Street, Number, City, Name.

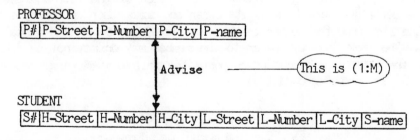

Figure 5.2.1

The P# which was in the optimal 4NF relation R_1 has been omitted from the Student record type. It corresponds to the mapping that each one Professor has a relationship with many Students. This becomes a set type as explained below.

Each Professor record occurrence will have a corresponding set of Student record occurrences. So we say the Professor is the <u>owner record type</u> and the Student record type is the <u>member record type</u>. Each owner occurrence can have none, one or many member occurrences.

Although this brief example does not tell the whole story, you see that whereas P# occurred twice in the optimal 4NF relations it only occurs once in the data item types of the CODASYL record types. Thus the stored records cannot have incosistencies in the values of P# that occur and each Student record occurrence is a member of only one of the sets owned by the various Professor record occurrences.

A unit of stored data item values is usually called a <u>record occurrence</u> (or a <u>record instance</u>). A <u>record type</u> is a description that contains just the names of the data items but not the values. The record type may be considered as a framework into which the data item values can be fitted yielding thereby record instances. For brevity authors occasionally omit the word "type" e.g. some literature uses the term "record" for "record type".

The set of record types and set types conform to the following {5.16}.

1 There is a set of record types $\{R_1, R_2, \ldots R_n\}$.

2 There is a set of named links (called set types) connecting the record types according to a so called <u>data structure diagram</u> {5.1}.

3 Every link is <u>functional</u> (i.e. there exists a simple association) in at least one direction (partial functionality is allowed).

4 A record type may be linked to itself. This means the same record type can be both owner and member of a set type. For example in a management reporting structure a Person (owner) may have none, one or many Persons (member) reporting to him or her. And a (member) person may report to none or one.

The CODASYL Set Concept

A set type is a named type of link between two record types. It is described in the schema which is the coded description of the global logical model to have a certain record type as its owner and some other record type as its member. The link from the member to the owner is <u>always</u> functional (totally or partially). The link from the owner to the member may or may not be functional. Thus, the CODASYL set concept supports the following mappings between owner record (OR) and member record (MR)

OR $\longleftrightarrow$ MR

OR $\longleftarrow$ MR

OR $\longleftrightarrow\!\!\!\!\!\succ$ MR   All combinations of

OR $\longleftarrow\!\!\!\succ$ MR   - insertion manual or automatic

OR $\longleftarrow$ MR   - retention fixed, mandatory or optional

OR $\longleftarrow\!\!\!\!\!\!\succ$ MR

The CODASYL term "set" is completely different from a mathematical set as defined in Section 2.1. To avoid confusion some authors therefore employ different terms such as "DBTG set", "coset" (for CODASYL set), "owner-coupled set", "fan set", etc. We shall continue to use the term "set", except where ambiguity may arise.

A set type may also contain more than one type of member. We ignore this possibility because it is not usually needed in simple cases.

From the above you realize that (M:M)-mappings are not supported directly. This is, however, not a serious restriction since every (M:M)-mapping can be replaced by introducing an intermediate record type and two (M:1)-mappings.

Example 5.2.1

Assume a (M:M)-mapping between students (represented by S#) and courses (represented by C#). The mapping

$$S\# \Longleftrightarrow C\#$$

then denotes that a student may follow several courses and that a course may be attended by several students. The next figure shows that student S1 is enrolled for Math, Chem and Phys, and that Student S2 is enrolled for Chem, Phys and Computer science (Cosc).

Mapping type $S\# \Longleftrightarrow C\#$

Mapping occurrences

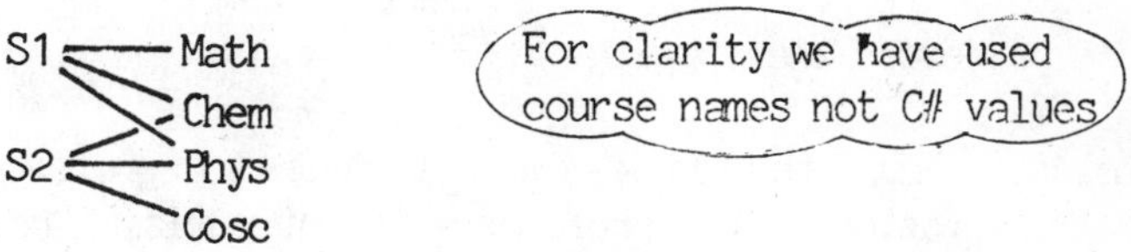

S1 ——— Math
      Chem
S2 ———— Phys
        Cosc

For clarity we have used course names not C# values

Figure 5.2.2

The designer would replace the (M:M)-mapping $S\# \Longleftrightarrow C\#$ by two (M:1)-mappings and an intermediate record type with the compound key S#, C# (i.e. the attributes involved in the (M:M)-mapping) and obtain thereby

$$S\# \longleftrightarrow \{S\#, C\#\} \longleftrightarrow C\#.$$

Figure 5.2.3

S# and C# are subsets of the compound key S#, C#. Both S# and C# are each trivially dependent on (S#, C#).

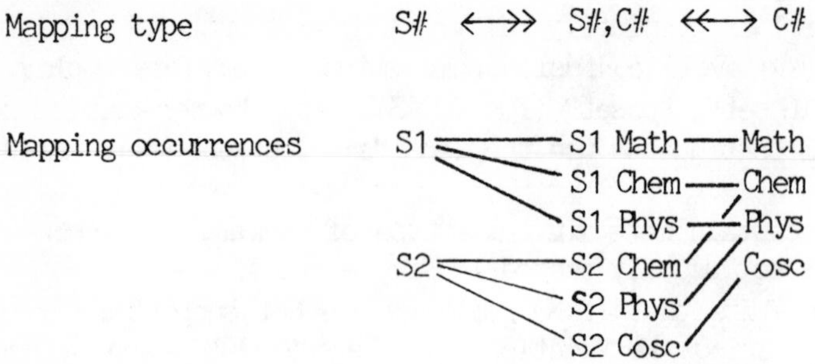

Mapping type $S\# \longleftrightarrow\!\!\!\gg S\#,C\# \ll\!\!\!\longleftrightarrow C\#$

Mapping occurrences

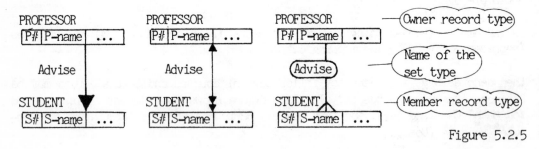

Figure 5.2.4

For clarity course names have been shown instead of $C\#$ values.

Set types are usually represented by means of <u>data structure diagrams</u> as suggested in {5.1}. Here are three ways of drawing such a diagram for the professor-student advising relationship. Combinations of these are also used.

Figure 5.2.5

Since a professor (represented by the professor number $P\#$) can advise several students (represented by a student number $S\#$) and a student is advised by just one professor the mapping

$$P\# \longleftrightarrow\!\!\!\gg S\#$$

holds. Thus the link from student to professor is functional, allowing representation of the professor-student advising relationship by a set type.

The link between the owner (representing the entity type professor) and the member (representing the entity type student) is labeled with a name for the set type. In addition the link is directed such that the to-many arrow points from the owner to the member. This allows a clear distinction between the owner and the member.

For each set type there will be a <u>set occurrence</u> for each owner record occurrence. Each set occurrence has the owner record occurrence and a collection of none, one or many member record occurrences. Each record occurrence of the member type can only belong to at most one set occurrence of each particular set type. Where a set occurrence has no member record occurrences it is said to be <u>empty</u>. It still has the owner record occurrence.

A set type can be considered as a framework into which record occurrences can be fitted yielding thereby set occurrences. The word "set" alone may be used to mean either set type or set occurrence depending on context, like "record". Here are two set occurrences for the set type Advised-by.

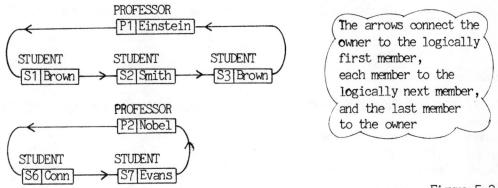

Figure 5.2.6

An owner occurrence (e.g. the owner occurrence representing the professor P1) is logically connected to the corresponding member occurrences (i.e. the member occurrences representing the students S1, S2 and S3). One way (not the only way) to implement these logical connections is by pointers. There can be a pointer chain that starts at the owner occurrence, runs through all the member occurrences, and finally returns to the owner occurrence (as illustrated by the figure above). The owner record has a hidden pointer to the first member record. That has a hidden pointer to the next member, and so on. The last member record has a pointer to the owner. Hidden means the application programmers and users need not be concerned with the details. However, you should think of the diagram showing the set occurrence as a convention. The lines between the records are a way of showing that they all belong together to the same owner, the lines are not indicating that those are the physically available pointers. For example there could be, or need not be physical pointers from each member record to the owner. And there might or might not be physical pointers from each record to the prior (i.e. previous in the chain drawn). It is a logical diagram.

Set types have the following properties.

P1: Any record type may be declared as the owner record type of one or more sets.

P2: Any record type may be declared as a member record type of one or more sets.

P3: Any record type may be specified as both an owner record type in one or more sets and a member record type in one or more different sets.

P4: A record type may participate as both owner record type and member record type in the same set type.

P5: A member record occurrence cannot appear in more than one set occurrence of a particular set type. The relationship from member to owner is either to one or else to none or one.

These properties allow any number of set types to be combined together in the global logical model to give satisfactorily any complex data structure.

Example 5.2.2

Suppose in developing a model for a college that entities are represented as follows
Students: by means of a student number S#
Professors: by means of a professor number P#
Courses: by means of a course number C#
Classrooms: by means of a room number R#.

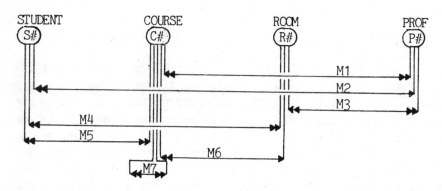

Figure 5.2.7

Suppose the analyst has found the following mappings, which are not necessarily realistic
M1: For the Professors–Courses relationship: $P\# \longleftrightarrow C\#$
M2: For Professors–Students: $P\# \longleftrightarrow S\#$ (This represents counselling and advising.)
M3: For Professors–Classrooms: $P\# \longleftrightarrow R\#$
M4: For Students–Classrooms: $S\# \longleftrightarrow R\#$
M5: For Students–Courses: $S\# \longleftrightarrow C\#$
M6: For Classrooms–Courses: $R\# \longleftrightarrow C\#$
M7: For Courses–Courses: (i.e. for the course sequence and course prerequisites) Before.$C\# \longleftrightarrow$ After.$C\#$
The designer now replaces each (M:M)–mapping by an intermediate record type and two (M:1)–mappings and obtains thereby
M8: For the Professors–Courses relationship: (replaces M1)
$$P\# \longleftrightarrow P\#,\ C\# \longleftrightarrow C\#$$

M9: For the Professors-Classrooms relationship: (replaces M3)

P# ⟷⟫ P#, R# ⟪⟶ R#

M10: For the Students-Classrooms relationship: (replaces M4)

S# ⟷⟫ S#, R# ⟪⟶ R#

M11: For the Students-Courses relationship: (replaces M5)

S# ⟷⟫ S#, C# ⟪⟶ C#

M12: For the Courses-Courses relationship: (replaces M7)

Before.C# ⟷⟫ Before.C#, After.C# ⟪⟶ After.C#

The mappings M2, M6 and M8 to M12 define the data structure shown in Fig. 5.2.8.

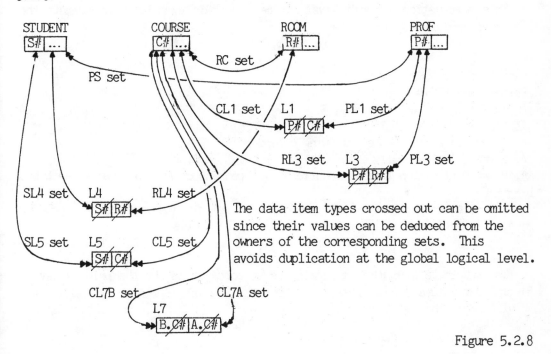

The data item types crossed out can be omitted since their values can be deduced from the owners of the corresponding sets. This avoids duplication at the global logical level.

Figure 5.2.8

This illustrates the following.

1 A single record type can be owner of several sets (property P1). For example the record type Professors acts as owner of the sets PL1, PL3 and PS. These set types could alternatively be replaced by a single set type having more than one member record type for some special reason depending on the special circumstances of the implementation.

2 There are record types acting as members of several sets (property P2). The record type L1 acts as a member of the sets PL1 and CL1.

3 The record type Student acts as an owner of the sets SL4 and SL5 and as a member in the set PS (property P3).

Interpreting n-ary Relations as CODASYL Sets

We are now in a position to discuss how to form the global logical model for a CODASYL-based DBMS from an internal model defined in terms of relations.

You remember that the normalization process usually leads to a collection of optimal 4NF relations associated through primary and foreign keys. You remember that an attribute (or an attribute combination) of a relation R1 is a foreign key if it is not the primary key of R1 but its values are values of the primary key of some relation R2. R1 and R2 do not have to be distinct.

This association through keys can be seen for example by analysing the result of normalizing a relation

$$R (\underline{A}, \underline{B}, C, D)$$

with
 Candidate Key (CK): (A, B)
 Primary Key (PK): A, B
 Prime Attributes (PA): A, B
 Attributes in the complement of CK (or Non-Prime Attributes (NPA)): C, D.
    Assume in addition the following dependencies
A, B $\Longrightarrow$ C (i.e. C fully functionally dependent on A, B)
A, B $\nRightarrow$ D (i.e. D not fully functionally dependent on A, B because A $\longrightarrow$ D but B $\nrightarrow$ D).

The relation R is not in 2NF because D is not fully functionally dependent on A, B. The normalization process (Section 5.1) yields

$$R1 (\underline{A}, \underline{B}, C)$$
$$R2 (\underline{A}, D).$$

The attribute A in R1 is a foreign key because it is not the primary key of R1 but its values are values of the primary key of R2. Also note that the trivial dependence

$$R1.(A, B) - \text{>} R2.A$$

holds because A represents a subset of (A, B).

 Example 5.2.3

This example illustrates relationships and situations that can occur with primary and foreign keys.

Consider again the relation

STUDENT (S#, S-name, C#, C-name, Opinion)

S#	S-name	C#	C-name	Opinion
S1	Brown	C1	Math	Good
S1	Brown	C2	Chem	Poor
S1	Brown	C3	Phys	Good
S2	Smith	C2	Chem	Satisfactory
S2	Smith	C3	Phys	Satisfactory
S2	Smith	C4	Math	Poor
S3	Brown	C2	Chem	Good
S3	Brown	C3	Phys	Good

Figure 5.2.9

The meaning is as before, e.g. student S1 named Brown has a good opinion of the math course C1.

For this example the analyst distinguishes
Candidate Key (CK): (S#, C#)
Primary Key (PK): (S#, C#)
Prime Attributes (PA): S#, C#
Attributes in the complement of CK (or Non-Prime Attributes (NPA)):S-name, C-name, Opinion.

The following are the dependencies
S#, C# $\not\Rightarrow$ S-name (because S# $\longrightarrow$ S-name)
S#, C# $\not\Rightarrow$ C-name (because C# $\longrightarrow$ C-name)
S#, C# $\Longrightarrow$ Opinion (because S# $\not\longrightarrow$ Opinion and C# $\not\longrightarrow$ Opinion).

The relation Student is not in 2NF because S-name and C-name are not fully functionally dependent on S#, C#.

Fig. 5.2.10 shows the result of the normalization process and illustrates that the dependencies
R2.(S#, C#) $\longrightarrow$ R1.S# and
R2.(S#, C#) $\longrightarrow$ R3.C#
hold because S# and C#, respectively, are both subsets of (S#, C#).

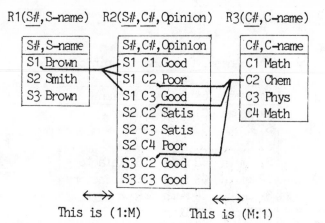

Figure 5.2.10

Assume a relation of the form R ($\underline{A}$, B, C)
with: Candidate Key (CK): A
Primary Key (PK): A
Prime Attribute (PA): A
Attributes in the complement of CK or Non-Prime Attributes (NPA)): B, C
   The dependencies are
A $\longrightarrow$ B
A $\longrightarrow$ C
B $\longrightarrow$ C.
   The relation R is not in 3NF because the attribute C is transitively dependent on A. The normalization process yields
R1 ($\underline{A}$, B)
R2 ($\underline{B}$, C).
   The attribute B in R1 is a foreign key because it is not the primary key of R1 but its values are values of the primary key of R2. In this case the dependence

$$R1.A \longrightarrow R2.B$$

holds because a particular A value in R1 is always associated via a particular B value in R1 with a single B value in R2 (otherwise the normalization process would have destroyed the functional dependence R.A $\longrightarrow$ R.B which holds in the original relation R).

Example 5.2.4

Consider the relation

MANUFACTURE (P#, M#, E#)

P#	M#	E#
P1	M1	E1
P2	M2	E3
P3	M1	E1
P4	M1	E1
P5	M3	E2
P6	M4	E1

Figure 5.2.11

The tuple <P1, M1, E1> means product P1 is manufactured by machine M1 operated by the employee E1.

For this example we distinguish

Candidate Key (CK): P#

Primary Key (PK): P#

Prime Attribute (PA): P#

Attributes in the complement of CK (or Non-Prime Attributes (NPA)): M#, E#

The dependencies are

P# ⟶ M#

P# ⟶ E#

M# ⟶ E#.

The relation Manufacture is not in 3NF because the attribute E# is transitively dependent on P#.

The result of the normalization process illustrates that the dependence

$$R1.P\# \longrightarrow R2.M\#$$

holds.

R1(P#,M#)   R2(M#,E#)

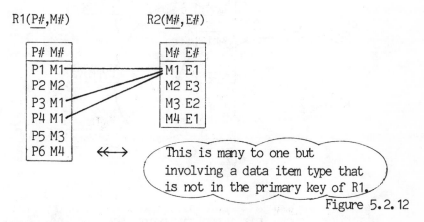

P# M#		M# E#
P1 M1		M1 E1
P2 M2		M2 E3
P3 M1		M3 E2
P4 M1		M4 E1
P5 M3		
P6 M4	⟷	This is many to one but involving a data item type that is not in the primary key of R1.

Figure 5.2.12

The preceding discussion shows how by consistently applying the normalization process one gets a set of mutually linked relations such that every link is functional in at least one direction. This perception permits physical im-

plementation of relations by means of CODASYL sets. It is important to recognize that such an implementation
 - is consistent with a conceptual model
 - does not lead to any anomalies in storage operations
 - preserves integrity concerning dependencies.
In addition it is computer efficient because all the attributes describing an
entity (i.e. those dependent only on its primary key) may be reached by means of
a single logical access operation.

    In practice less than one physical access is required for each logical ac-
cess, because the record occurrences that are the members of a set occurrence
can be physically stored together in the same physical block or page as the
owner record occurrence. So for example one physical access will be needed to
find the owner, but thereafter few or no more physical transfers will be needed
to retrieve data items of the member record occurrences. Such member records
usually give values of relationship attributes and other similar facts.

    The next figure shows a data structure diagram together with some set occur-
rences derived from the relations shown in Fig. 5.2.10.

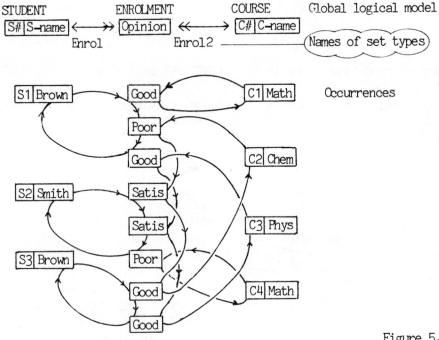

Figure 5.2.13

    This figure shows the important point that S# and C# do not have to be
present in Enrolment. The relation R2 contained these foreign keys to model the
relationships to R1 and R3 in Fig. 5.2.10, but the set types Enrol and Enrol2
model these.

As drawn Fig. 5.2.13 is the global logical model. The physical model could be the same, but need not be. Whatever is chosen for the physical model, the application programs will always be able to manipulate the stored data to derive any fact that can be derived from the global logical model. E.g. an application having, say, currently found the record for S2 could find the first Enrolment, Satisfactory, and find its owner course C2. From that Enrolment it could find the next Enrolment, and thus having made that the current record it could later find the original Enrolment record by finding the prior of the current Enrolment. The physical structure might be any structure that makes all manipulations possible; e.g. it could be a mixture of pointers (i.e. links), indexes and tree structures (e.g. B* trees).

Fig. 5.2.14 illustrates the same concept of a data structure diagram and some occurrences but derived from the relations shown in Fig. 5.2.12.

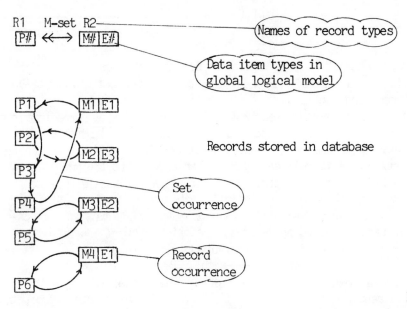

Records stored in database

Figure 5.2.14

Example 5.2.5

This example shows how the normalization procedure finally leads to a correct optimal 4NF collection of relations, and how these can be satisfactorily converted into a satisfactory global logical model for a CODASYL-based DBMS.

Assume that a database designer would like to establish a bill of material database for the products and product structures shown in Fig. 5.2.15.

The perception of the real world can be described as follows.

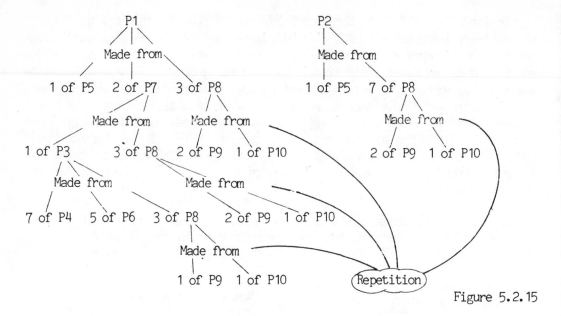

Figure 5.2.15

1 Products (represented by a product number P#) are entities.

2 A product is characterized (in addition to the product number P#) by a product name P-name and a color.

3 The production of a product requires several products as immediate components. The larger product is called the major one and each smaller component product is a minor one. The major- minor relationship is usually called an explosion relationship. This relates a particular product to the many others from which it is made. For example a chair as major product is made from seat, leg, back ... There may be one or more of each minor product such as leg. Similarly, a minor product is used in several major products. The minor-major relationship is usually called an implosion relationship. The explosion and implosion relationships are completely determined by the mapping

$$\text{Major.P\# } \longleftrightarrow \text{ Minor.P\#.}$$

We first give an example of an explosion. The production (1 unit) of the major product P1 requires the following quantities of various minor products: P5 (1 unit), P7 (2 units) and P8 (3 units). At the next level in the bill of materials structure one considers product P7 as a major product. Its production (1 unit) requires the minor products P3 (1 unit) and P8 (3 units).

An example of an implosion is that the minor product P8 is used in the major products P1, P2, P3 and P7. The production (1 unit) of the major products in question requires 3, 7, 3 and 3 units respectively of the minor product P8.

Fig. 5.2.16 shows a relation R defined on the domains P#, P-name, Color and Qty (for quantity). The relation R is of degree 5 and its tuples represent the products and product structures as in Fig. 5.2.15.

The relation R is subject to the following anomalies in storage operations.

P#: P1 P2 P3 P4 P5 P6 P7 P8 P9 P10

P-NAME: PA PB PC PD PE PF PG PH PI PK

COLOR: Green Red Blue Brown Yellow

QTY: 1 2 3 5 7

R (Major.P#, P-name, Color, Minor.P#, Qty)

Major.P#	P-name	Color	Minor.P#	Qty
P1	PA	Green	P5	1
P1	PA	Green	P7	2
P1	PA	Green	P8	3
P2	PB	Red	P5	1
P2	PB	Red	P8	7
P3	PC	Blue	P4	7
P3	PC	Blue	P6	5
P3	PC	Blue	P8	3
P4	PD	Red	-	-
P5	PE	Brown	-	-
P6	PF	Yellow	-	-
P7	PG	Green	P3	1
P7	PG	Green	P8	3
P8	PH	Green	P9	2
P8	PH	Green	P10	1
P9	PI	Red	-	-
P10	PK	Blue	-	-

Figure 5.2.16

Anomalies in insert operations: In principle it is not possible to store tuples representing major products having no minor products as immediate components (otherwise part of the primary key Major.P#, Minor.P# is not known). Hence the tuples representing the major products P4, P5, P6, P9 and P10 should in principle be removed from R.

Anomalies in delete operations: Deleting all the tuples for a given major product also destroys the relationship between this product and its immediate components which we may want to preserve for future use.

Anomalies in modify operations: It is impossible to change the name or the color of a product without search problems or inconsistent results.

It is also possible to update tuples inconsistently, e.g. each product should have a single name and a single color.

The anomalies are because the relation R is not in 2NF. Analysis of R yields

Candidate Key (CK): (Major.P#, Minor.P#)

Primary Key (PK): (Major.P#, Minor.P#)

Prime Attributes (PA): Major.P#, Minor.P#

Attributes in the complement of CK (Non-Prime Attributes (NPA)): P-name, Color, Qty.

The dependencies are

Major.P#, Minor.P# $\not\Rightarrow$ P-name (because: Major.P# $\longrightarrow$ P-name)

Major.P#, Minor.P# $\not\Rightarrow$ Color (because: Major.P# $\longrightarrow$ Color)

Major.P#, Minor.P# $\Longrightarrow$ Qty (because: Major.P# $\not\rightarrow$ Qty and Minor.P# $\not\rightarrow$ Qty).

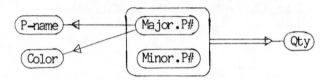

Figure 5.2.17

The relation R is not in 2NF because P-name and Color are not fully functionally dependent on Major.P#, Minor.P#. The conversion to 2NF yields

R1(P#, P-name, Color)   R2(Major.P#, Minor.P#, Qty)

P#	P-name	Color
P1	PA	Green
P2	PB	Red
P3	PC	Blue
P4	PD	Red
P5	PE	Brown
P6	PF	Yellow
P7	PG	Green
P8	PH	Green
P9	PI	Red
P10	PK	Blue

Major-P#	Minor-P#	Qty
P1	P5	1
P1	P7	2
P1	P8	3
P2	P5	1
P2	P8	7
P3	P4	7
P3	P6	5
P3	P8	3
P7	P3	1
P7	P8	3
P8	P9	2
P8	P10	1

Figure 5.2.18

The undesirable anomalies have disappeared and it is no longer possible for users to break the integrity of the modelled real world dependencies. The P# appears only once in the data item types of R1 so does not require a role name, whereas in the two places in R2 role names are needed.

The data items Major.P# and Minor.P# are both foreign keys because each – considered individually – is not the primary key of the relation R2 but its values are values of the primary key of the relation R1. Hence the trivial dependence

R2.(Major.P#, Minor.P#) $\longrightarrow$ R1.P#

holds twice, i.e. for the explosion relationship and for the implosion relationship.

Fig. 5.2.19 shows the global logical model for a CODASYl-based database.

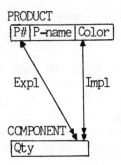

Figure 5.2.19

The record type named Product corresponds exactly to R1 and Component to R2. The Component record only holds how many of a particular minor product is used in a major product. There is one occurrence of a Component record for each product such as leg in a product such as chair. The figure below shows some record occurrences and set occurrences.

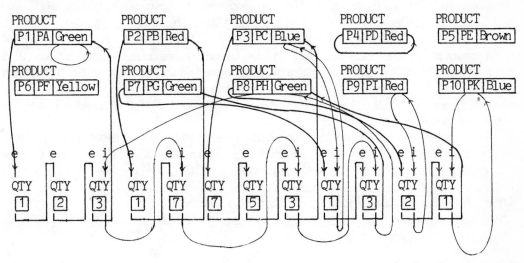

Figure 5.2.20

Physical implementation of CODASYL sets

The pre-1978 CODASYL proposals {5.2, 5.3, 5.4} did not give full physical data independence. The schema coding mixed the logical and physical models, so the physical structures could not be changed without creating a new logical model, since the whole was in one piece of coding that had to be translated at one computer run. Further, subsets of the same mixture had to be available in each subschema, thus application programs could make use of physical model details. Physical independence was not enforcable. Minor physical model changes required undesirable minor reprogramming of applications - though far less than with the file structures of the 1960s.

The 1978 CODASYL proposals {5.20} specify a Data Description language (DDL) for describing the global logical model and separate coding of the physical model in a data storage description language (DSDL). Thus each application program interface is described by a subschema that must be consistent with the schema but the design of the languages and DBMSs ensure that the subschemas cannot be affected by physical model changes. Physical data independence is thus improved, as our design aim (c) of Chapter 1 and Fig. 1.1.6.

The designer has to choose each detail of the physical model. The initial design will include guesses, possibly based on estimates of cardinalities and the frequencies of various types of activities.

Normally the physical record types will correspond closely to the global logical record types. Their physical placement pattern involves compromises. Records such as Student and Part will be used as entry points so it must be possible for the DBMS to calculate the address of each such record and thus retrieve it efficiently, knowing only the key that the user has quoted.

On the other hand records that are members of sets need to be stored near to other members of the same set and to the owner record since applications will tend to access these sets of records together. Thus a compromise has to be made, since it is impossible for all records to be together. Usually some record types are best placed near their owner record where accessed usually after the owner has been found.

Each record can have various pointers stored with it. These pointers will be in the same physical block as the record and not visible to application programs and not mentioned in the global logical model. The simplest such pointer is a <u>physical next pointer</u> which points
   from the owner to the logically first member record
   from each member to the logically next member
   from the last member to the owner record.

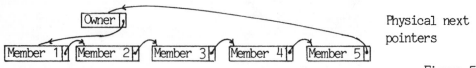

Physical next
pointers

Figure 5.2.21

Theoretically, physical next pointers alone are enough to implement all sets. All manipulations that could possibly be required can be achieved - though not efficiently, by following the chain of pointers until the desired record is found. For example an application program which has found a current record of interest may want
   - the owner to be found starting from a current member
   - the logically last member to be found starting from the owner

- the member immediately prior to the current member
- the logically first member starting from having found the owner
- the member logically next after the currently found member.

Only the last two of the above are efficient if only physically next pointers are available as links - for sets with large numbers of members.

So other types of physical pointers may be used. These include
physical pointers from every member to the owner
physical pointers from every member to the logically prior member (i.e. opposite to physical next pointers)
physical pointers from owner to logically last members.

Such physical pointers can make finding records substantially faster. The choices of which to include for each set type depend closely on the pattern of use in current applications.

However there is extra work to be done by the DBMS to create and maintain these physical pointers, so whether or not to include them involves compromises. And in some situations such pointers cannot provide a structure giving good enough performance. For example with sets each of which has about 900 members it may be an improvement to provide every 30th member record with physical pointers to the 30th record logically forwards and to the 30th backwards. Then any record can be reached from any other by at most less than 30 steps at multiples of 30 records followed by less than 30 steps of physical next or physical prior pointers.

Even that may not be the best possible. Various implementation techniques have been researched {5.21}. The main modes of physical implementation of a set type are

(a) mode is <u>chain</u>, i.e. the owner record and all member records are connected in logical set order by physical next pointers embedded in (or in the same physical blocks as) the records.

(b) mode is chain as above but also each record is also linked to its logically prior record similarly. Further possibilities include for example a pointer in the owner to the logically last member but not prior pointers in the members.

(c) mode is <u>pointer array</u>, which means the creation of an index or table for each set occurrence. The index contains pointers to all member records. The index entries are in logical set member order. They may contain physical pointers to the addresses of the member records or a key from which a required member record can be efficiently found. The physical address of the pointer array itself is physically stored alongside the owner record.

(d) mode is <u>list</u> means member records are stored one after another on a physical page and the pages are connected by physical pointers. This clusters the logically consecutive records. For simplicity think of a page as a physical block; in some implementations it may be possible to have say three physical blocks per page, giving the possibility of the database administrator having physical pages that are multiples of physical blocks and of changing the page size.

Mode is list is possible only if the set membership is automatic insertion and fixed retention. Otherwise alterations of set membership lead to problems of moving the record physically. Retention mandatory can be handled with some extra work when a member is changed from one set to another.

Some recommendations about the choices between these physical set implementations are given in {5.22}.

Part of the point of the discussion here is to help you appreciate that the physical implementation of a database may involve many different kinds of structures for the various set types in the global logical model. In principle the physical design can be changed without affecting the global logical model or the application programs, thus achieving the desired physical efficiency and also the data independence.

To tune the physical model the designer and database administrator must have facilities to monitor performance. Then from evaluation they can refine the physical model in justified steps. Physical model detailed design is a specialist subject. It is not possible to give rules for every situation. For example the optimum structures for on-line updating are different from those for on-line retrieval with overnight updating. There are also many advantages in having several physically separate databases. Then for example both security and recovery can be improved, accidental corruption due to hardware or software or human error is limited, computer runs can perhaps be shorter, and several similar databases can be described by the same schema. E.g. these could be for different users in different locations or organizations or could be for different kinds of electrical and mechanical parts.

The main points are

(a) finish the development of the conceptual model before the global logical model

(b) finish the global logical model before the physical model

(c) group data items into aggregates where these correspond to attributes that are each functionally or fully functionally dependent on the same collection of attributes, thus having fully normalized record types

(d) evaluate fully the alternatives for physical modelling of each set type since the choices may substantially improve or impair performance.

Summary

The concept of set types is central to the CODASYL approach. Any conceptual data model can be implemented as CODASYL record types and set types without anomalies. Each record type corresponds to a collection of data item types that are stored together as a unit. Each attribute in the conceptual data model corresponds to a data item type. This appears in exactly one record type in the global logical model (except in cases where this has been violated for specialist reasons). Thus all the attribute values describing an entity are stored as a unit and may be reached by means of a single access operation.

EXERCISES

1 (i) Which are important and which relatively unimportant of the following?
A 1NF, B 2NF, C Optimal 2NF, D 3NF, E Optimal 3NF, F 4NF.
  (ii) Is being in 3NF a property of
A each individual relation
B a collection of relations as a whole
C a single relation
  (iii) Which of A to C above is optimal 3NF a property of?

2 (i) Is a single relation that is in 2NF also in optimal 2NF?
  (ii) Is a single relation that is in 3NF also in optimal 3NF?
  (iii) Does the concept of optimal 4NF exist?

3 (i) What does the degree of a relation mean?
  (ii) What is the difference between a domain and an attribute?
  (iii) What is the difference between a primary key and a candidate key?
  (iv) What is the difference between a prime attribute and a non-prime attribute?
  (v) What is a determinant (in the context of relations)? Can a collection of attributes be a determinant?
  (vi) What are anomalies in storage operations?
  (vii) Give an example of a relation that includes a domain that contains atomic elements.
  (viii) What are the disadvantages of redundancy in the internal model?
  (ix) Is the layout of the records on disk in physical blocks as one block per record of the internal model?

4 Which of the options A, B and so on apply to the situations (i), (ii) and so on?
 A The relation is in 1NF
 B It is in 2NF
 C It is in optimal 2NF
 D It is in 3NF
 E It is in optimal 3NF
 F It is in 4NF
 G Optimal 4NF
 H None of these.

(i) A relation is in 1NF and for every candidate key C if any attribute not in C is functionally dependent on C then all attributes of the relation are functionally dependent on C.

(ii) Every determinant is a candidate key.

(iii) Every non-prime attribute is transitively dependent on every candidate key.

(iv) Every non-key attribute is dependent on the primary key and the primary key is the only candidate key.

(v) Every domain contains atomic elements.

(vi) Every domain contains atomic elements. Undefined values are allowed for attributes that are not the primary key. Every attribute in the complement of a candidate key is fully functionally dependent on that candidate-key.

(vii) As (vi) and every attribute in the complement of a candidate key is nontransitively dependent on that candidate key.

(viii) As (vii) and there are no multivalued dependencies.

(ix) Every determinant is potentially the primary key.

5 An internal realm model with the following record structure has been suggested by an analyst and designer.

EMPLOYEE (Emp#, Emp-name, Dept#, Dept-name, Machine#, Machine-name)

There are no other record types that involve any of the above data types. The dependencies were originally correctly analysed as follows.

Emp# $\longrightarrow$ Emp-name
Emp# $\longrightarrow$ Dept-name
Emp# $\longrightarrow$ Dept#
Emp# $\longrightarrow$ Machine#
Dept# $\longrightarrow$ Dept-name
Dept-name $\longrightarrow$ Dept#
Dept# $\longrightarrow$ Machine#
Machine# $\longrightarrow$ Dept-#
Machine# $\longrightarrow$ Machine-name.

Could the use of the proposed record type as an internal model ever give rise to difficulties? If so, explain briefly.

6 Transform the record structure proposed in the previous question into the collection of record structures that are in optimal 4NF. You may express your answer either as a collection of relations, in which case some data item types may appear in more than one relation, or as a collection of record and set types to fit a CODASYL-based model, in which case it should not have any data item type appearing more than once.

7 Derive the optimum internal model for the following situation, expressing your model both as relations and as for a CODASYL-based DBMS.

A course is taught by several teachers. Each teacher may be involved in the teaching of several courses. For each course there may be several text books. A text book can be used for more than one course. Each of the teachers for a particular course uses the same text books. (Notice the independence of teachers and text books.)

8 Is the following a satisfactory internal model? Make any reasonable assumptions that fit the given occurrences.

ADULT (Passport#, Child-name, Town-of-marriage, Date-of-marriage)

Passport#	Child-name	Town-of-marriage	Date-of-marriage
P246357	Roy Conn	Hampton	5 Jan 1936
P246357	Sue Conn	Hampton	5 Jan 1936
P246357	Di Conn	Boston	19 Aug 1948
P246357	Joe Conn	Boston	19 Aug 1948
P679432	Fred Ash	York	25 Sept 1951
P679432	Bill Ash	York	25 Sept 1951
P679432	Pat Ash	York	31 March 1957

Figure 5.2.22

The meaning is that each child is a dependent of the adult passport holder and that the appropriate marriage took place at the stated place and date.

REFERENCES AND BIBLIOGRAPHY

5.1 Bachman, C.W.: 'Data Structure Diagrams', Data Base (journal of ACM SIGBDP) 1, No. 2 (summer 1969). Available from ACM.

5.2 CODASYL Data Base Task Group: 'April 1971 Report' (available from IFIP Administrative Data Processing Group, 40 Paulus Potterstraat, Amsterdam)

5.3 CODASYL Data Base Language Task Group: 'Proposal for a data base facility in COBOL', Jan. 1973 (available from Technical Services Branch, Dept. of Supply and Services, Ottawa, Canada

5.4 CODASYL Data Description Language Committee, 'Journal of Development', June 1973 (available from British Computer Society, London, and IFIP Applied Information Processing Group (IAG) HQ, Amsterdam, and ACM HQ, New York)

5.5 CODASYL COBOL Journal of Development, 1976 (available from Technical Services Branch, Dept. of Supply and Services, Ottawa, Canada

5.6 Codd, E.F.: 'A Relational Model of Data for Large Shared Data Banks', CACM 13, 6, June 1970, Pages 377-387

5.7 Codd, E.F.: 'Further Normalization of the Relational Model', in 'Data Base Systems', Courant Computer Science Symposium 6, 1971, Rustin, R.: Ed., Prentice-Hall, Inc., Englewood Cliffs, New Jersey, 1972, Pages 33-64

5.8 Codd, E.F.: 'Recent Investigations in Relational Data Base Systems', Proc. IFIP Congress 74, August 5-10, Stockholm Sweden, Pages 1017-1021

5.9 Date, C.J.: 'An Introduction to Database Systems', Addison-Wesley Publishing Company, 1977 and 2nd ed. 1979

5.10 Engles, R.W.: 'An Analysis of the April 1971 DBTG Report', Proc. of ACM SIGFIDET Workshop on Data Description Access and Control, Nov. 1971, Pages 68-91

5.11 Fagin, R.: 'Multivalued Dependencies and a New Normal Form for Relational Databases', IBM Research Laboratory, San Jose, California, RJ 1812 (26109), 1976

5.12 Fagin, R.: 'Multivalued Dependencies and a New Normal Form for Relational Databases', ACM Transactions on Database Systems, Vol. 2, No. 3, 1977, Pages 262-278

5.13 Kent, W.: 'A Primer of Normal Forms (in a Relational Data Base)', IBM Technical Report TR-02.600, Dec. 17, 1973

5.14 Olle, T.W.: 'The Codasyl Approach to Data Base Management', John Wiley & Sons, 1978

5.15 Schmid, H.A.; Swenson, J.R.: 'On the Semantics of the Relational Data Model', Proc. ACM SIGMOD, San Jose, California, May, 1975, King, W.F.: Ed., Pages 211-223

5.16 Tsichritzis, D.C.; Lochovsky, F.H.: 'Data Base Management Systems', Academic Press, Inc., 1977

5.17 Vetter, M.: 'Problem Solving Capabilities of the Relational Algebra', Proc. of the International Technical Conference on Relational Data Base Systems, IBM Scientific Center, Bari (Italy), June 23rd to 25th, 1976, IBM Form No. G513-3566, Pages 193-229

5.18 Wedekind, H.H.: 'Datenbanksysteme I', B.I. Wissenschaftsverlag, Reihe Informatik/16, 1974

5.19 Zaniolo, C.: 'Analysis and Design for Relational Schemata for Database Systems', Doctoral dissertation, Computer Science Department, University of California, Los Angeles, UCLA-ENG-7669, 1976

5.20 Report of the CODASYL Data Description Language Committee. Information Systems, Vol 3 No 4 (1978) Pages 247-320

5.21 Deen, S. M. and Hammersley, P. Eds: Proceedings International Conference on Data Bases, University of Aberdeen, July 1980, Heyden, 1980

5.22 Effelsberg, W.; Haerder, T.; Reuter, A.: Measurement and evaluation of techniques for implementing Cosets - a case study, in {5.21} Pages 135-159

6

The External Realm

<u>Aim</u>

In the preceding chapter we were primarily concerned with the problem of computer efficiency. Now we are faced with the problem of human efficiency. This requires that data can be presented to a user in a form suited to both his or her skills and the application requirements. Unfortunately it is not possible to isolate the problem of human efficiency from other problems occurring in the database design process. Once an internal model that is consistent with a conceptual model has been determined, the design of external data models has to follow precise constraints.

Users retrieve and update stored data through application programs and query language programs. Each user has a local conceptual model, consisting of the relevant subset of the global conceptual data model and the relevant subset of the application functions. The users must see these as consistent. Both data models for different users and corresponding functional models overlap.

So the many external data models are each mapped by users to the conceptual model which on its part is mapped in the design process to the internal model. This multi-level mapping is called <u>superimposition</u> of data models.

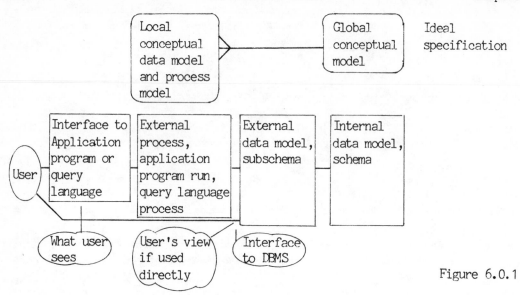

Figure 6.0.1

Any retrieval requested by a user has to be implemented as a retrieval of physically stored data followed by a suitable transformation to rearrange the data into a form accepted by the application program, possibly followed by further processing within the application program to present the data suitably to the user. The same applies if a query language is used.

Any update requested has to be implemented as corresponding operations that update stored data. The transformations and rearrangements must be such as to ensure consistency with the original conceptual model is continued. The requirements of ensuring consistency limit the types of rearrangements that can be allowed and implemented. The data structure seen by an application or query language program is called an external data model.

The types of external data model allowable for updating are more restricted than those allowed for retrieval. The various restrictions and their justification are explained later in the chapter.

Considerations of computer efficiency may further limit the types of transformations between the external models and the internal model.

The stages of limitations are
- what is theoretically possible
- what within that is technically feasible on the available computers and using the available DBMS
- what within that is cost-effective, i.e worthwhile.

This book covers the first. Particular DBMSs may have particular facilities, giving a particular subset implementable. What from that is worthwhile depends on the particular organization's needs, costs, resources and other management considerations.

The plan of this chapter is as follows.

Section 6.1 presents the three types of data structures that are most promising as external data models, the hierarchical, network and relational approaches. A DBMS that has facilities for external data models of two or more of these types to exist together is said to provide structure type coexistence.

Briefly, a relational model is a collection of relations. A hierarchy is where there are a collection of record types with relationships between them, where all the relationships are functional in one direction and where the data structure is a tree with the functional relationships each being towards the root record type. Any structure of record types with relationship types is essentially a network. CODASYL-based DBMSs have network structures both for the global logical model of the internal realm and for every external model.

Generally the DBMSs of the 1970s have not provided facilities for external models of different structural types from the internal model. The designer should however understand structure type coexistence since it may be needed to provide convenient models for users and application programmers, for example where they are familiar with a particular type of structure for a particular kind of application.

Section 6.2 explains the problems which may occur when superimposing data models. Important restrictions have to be observed when designing external data models, especially where applications include updating operations. These restrictions are because every updating operation is specified on data structured according to the external model but has to be implemented by corresponding operations on data stored according to the internal model. Of course any such storage operation (whether specified on the external level or realized on the internal level) has always to be consistent with the conceptual model. The system should prevent users from accidentally or deliberately making the data inconsistent with the conceptual model.

The conceptual data model was derived from analysis independent of any computer constraints. It can be expressed as elementary relations corresponding to the functional dependencies and other mappings between the information types such as entity types. However the DBMS works on a particular computer system, using a global logical model and corresponding physical structure of stored data that fit the system's rules. The design of the external models must both fit the particular DBMS facilities and contribute to ensuring consistency with the independent conceptual data model.

In what follows we discuss what is theoretically possible, not what is available with current (1980) hardware and software.

6.1 HIERARCHIES, NETWORKS AND RELATIONS AS EXTERNAL DATA MODELS

The organization of data as seen by a database query or application program is described by means of an external data model. Since there are usually many applications each viewing the data in a different way there are usually many external data models. A DBMS has several types of users

- the database administrator and similar control staff
- job trained routine users, e.g. users in operational departments of the organization
- casual users, e.g. unexpected or infrequent requests for information are becoming more feasible and important and the design must cater for such
- application programmers
- people researching the computer system performance e.g. with ideas of tuning or improvement
- assurance staff concerned with reliability, quality, accuracy, integrity, recovery, privacy and security, e.g. to change passwords and to verify that jobs have been done correctly.

But only the users in operational departments are proper users. The database administrator, programmers, researchers and analysts are using the system only in the sense of providers of a service to the real users of the information system. The real end-users of current systems do not directly use the DBMS, they use it through other programs that provide to them more satisfactory interfaces than the DBMS interfaces. This could change in the future.

The external data models are the specifications of the data types available through interfaces between the application programs and query language processors on the one hand and the DBMS on the other.

In the future external models may be available to casual users working directly as in Fig. 6.0.1. In most current systems these external interface specifications fit to the internal global logical model which is the specification of the relevant aspects of the internal model. But in the future the specification of the external data models may interface to the conceptual data model as in Fig. 1.1.11, page 12.

In CODASYL-based systems the coded specification of the data types available in a particular external model is called a subschema (or external subschema). Two or more application programs can use the same subschema. As information systems evolve over the years the requirements of different applications tend to change in different ways and so drift apart. So it is usually simplest in the long run to start with differently named subschemas for each application program then each can be independently changed.

Some database researchers have proposed that DBMSs should provide facilities for external models that can be any of three types of structures. These are
- hierarchical models
- network models, based on the CODASYL recommendations
- relational models, i.e. using relations.

Sufficient examples of relations have been given earlier that the relational architecture needs little more explanation, so we briefly cover that first. The principles of the hierarchical and network approaches are then described in the rest of the chapter.

The essence of a relational database is that
- the external models are in terms of relations, so each application manipulates relations by operations such as project, join, select (to select only those tuples that satisfy a condition such as 'Year = 1981') and each such operation produces a new relation as its result. So the user thinks in terms of relations, operations on relations to produce new relations, and has all results printed like relations. The operations such as project, join, select that take relations as operands and produce new relations as results are called relational algebra. The procedure for doing each is a straightforward algorithm. It is also possible for the user to think in terms of specifying the relation that is required but without specifying exactly how it should be computed. For example a user might want a table giving all parts that use part number 1234 as a component or as a component of a component and so on and that have been manufactured between 17 February and 3 March 1980, because a fault has been reported and its effects must be investigated. Such a request is said to be specified in a relational calculus form. It is possible for a program to work out a way of calculating the required relation and indeed to make near optimum choices of method where there are alternative ways of computing the required relation.
- the internal global logical model is expressed as relations
- the physical model implementation is structured to make the required manipulations efficient.

Basic Notions

Consider the attribute name/value pairs Name/Brown, Location/London and Occupation/Analyst. If there is an individual (i.e. an entity) whose name is Brown, whose location is London and whose occupation is analyst, then the three pieces of information are logically related.

We say that two or more pieces of information are logically related when they are related through the way they occur in the real world.

If n attribute/value pairs A_i/v_i with i = 1, 2, ... n are properties of an entity occurrence, then they are said to be logically related {6.4}.

Similarly two or more data item name/value pairs are logically related if they occur in the stored data and correspond to logically related information.

An application program needs to receive from the DBMS and hand back to the DBMS collections of logically related data items. Their structure must conform to the external data model for which the application program was written. Current external models all assume the same structures are handed across in the two directions from DBMS to application and from application to DBMS. These directions correspond to retrieval and to updating.

The term <u>segment</u> is used in some data description languages for a collection of one or more data values handed across together and corresponding to a particular structure of data item names. The structure of named data item types is called a segment type. In most current DBMSs the segment types used at the interfaces to application programs must correspond fairly closely to the structure of the stored record types. For example a segment type might include the data item types

Employee#,Employee-surname,Employee-initials,Occupation.

In CODASYL-based subschema descriptions the term <u>record</u> is used for what we call a segment here. Thus record is used both in describing the record structures of the internal global logical model (i.e. the schema) and for the corresponding structures in the subschemas. A <u>segment type</u> denotes a collection of data item types representing attributes whose names and values participate in a logical relation. A segment type is symbolically denoted by

$$S_1 (A_1, A_2, \ldots A_n)$$

where S_1 = segment name and A_1, A_2, $\ldots$, A_n = names of attributes whose values participate in each logical relation occurrence. Here the word <u>attribute</u> means the representation to the application program of what internally was the name of a data item type, i.e. it may internally be a role name and a domain name, but these names may be changed to present to the application program the data values in association with the attribute name in the user's local view of the conceptual data model. The same applies to a query program. Alternatively the application program can be responsible for any change of names from an external model using the same names as the internal model to the names the user expects.

A segment type can be considered as a framework into which attribute values can be fitted yielding <u>segment occurrences</u> (or segment instances). It is segment occurrences that are handed between the DBMS and the application program. The application program or query language program may further rearrange the data item values of the segments in presenting them to the user.

Some authors who omit the word "type" in other contexts write "segment" for segment type and for segment occurrence.

A segment occurrence is symbolically denoted by

$$S_1 (A_1/v_1, A_2/v_2, \ldots A_n/v_n)$$

or simply

$$S_1 (v_1, v_2, \ldots v_n)$$

where v_1, v_2, $\ldots$ v_n = attribute or data item values.

It is possible that attribute name/value pairs corresponding to a single entity occurrence are located in different segment occurrences such as

$$S_1 (A_i/v_i, A_{i+1}/v_{i+1}, \ldots A_{i+m}/v_{i+m})$$
$$S_2 (A_k/v_k, A_{k+1}/v_{k+1}, \ldots A_{k+n}/v_{k+n})$$
$$S_3 (A_1/v_1, A_{1+1}/v_{1+1}, \ldots A_{1+o}/v_{1+o})$$

For example details of an order might in an external model be in several segments such as
Order(Order-no, Order-date, Total-price)
Line-item(Quantity,Part-no, Price)
Supplier(Supplier-no, Supplier name, Supplier-address).
The fact that three such segment occurrences belong to the same entity (i.e. the fact that they are logically related) has to be reflected in the external data model in some way. Similarly, since an entity may act as a property of another entity, it is possible that segment occurrences corresponding to different entities are related. For example a line item segment is also logically related to a part and to a supplier. Again the external data model has to reflect these relationships in some way. Thus an external data model expressed in terms of segment types must also represent the relevant relationship types between these segment types.

Hierarchical Data Structures

Here is an example of an external data model that is a hierarchical relationship, i.e. a tree structure.

Example 6.1.1

The external data model consists of the segment types
Department (D#, D-name, Manager)
Employee (E#, E-name, Salary, D#).
For example the stored data at some instant could include data that is rearranged into the following two occurrences for the segment type Department
Department (D1, Operation, Brown)
Department (D2, Programming, Smith).
and the following five occurrences for the segment type Employee
Employee (E1, Watson, 10K, D1)
Employee (E2, Jones, 12K, D2)
Employee (E3, Atkins, 9K, D2)
Employee (E4, Jones, 13K, D2)
Employee (E5, Cohen, 15K, D1).
The external model must also cover the relationship between the segment types. This is the directed relation
$$R \text{ (Department, Employee)} = R \text{ (D.D\#, E.D\#)}.$$
D. and E. are abbreviated role names for Department and Employee. This relation associates the values of D# in Department segment occurrences with D# values in Employee segment occurrences.

In this example no employee works in more than one department so we call the relation R an elementary hierarchical relation. The next two figures show

- the hierarchical structure type (showing just the segment types and their relations)
- two hierarchical structure occurrences (showing the associations between the above segment occurrences).

The structure type is the general picture valid for all departments and employees. It is the external data model.

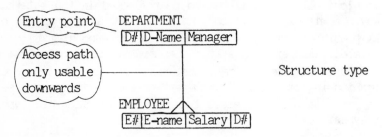

Structure type

Figure 6.1.1

A structure occurrence covers the information about a particular department and its particular employees only. One structure occurrence consists of one Department segment occurrence and its several related Employee segment occurrences.

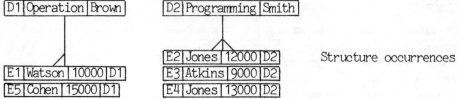

Structure occurrences

Figure 6.1.2

Using this external model the user and the application program must use the Department segment type as entry point. In other words if the application has not previously found a segment occurrence it can only first find a Department segment occurrence. It can do this for example by quoting a valid D# value, such as D2 and asking the DBMS for the segment occurrence for that value. In general an entry point is a type of segment that an application can find an occurrence of directly, i.e. without having previously found a related segment occurrence. After finding a segment occurrence the application can request occurrences of logically related segments. For example after finding a Department segment occurrence it is possible to find the first Employee segment or to find in sequence all Employee segments for that department. We say an access path is available from Department to Employee. The logical order in which the Employee segment occurrences are accessed is part of the specification of the external

data model. Usually for efficiency the internal model and external models will
use the same order, chosen to fit the most frequently used applications. For
example the order might be ascending alphabetical order within each department.
But the user of the above external data model cannot directly find the segment
occurrence for say Employee E3 as an entry point. That would need a different
external model, e.g. a hierarchy with Employee as the root.

We next restate the above in general terms. Suppose that D_1 and D_2 are two
domains (i.e. sets of attribute values) with the elements $\{d_{1i}\}$ and $\{d_{2j}\}$
respectively. The two domains are said to be <u>directed logically related</u> if
between their elements there exists a <u>directed logical relation</u> (i.e. a simple,
conditional or complex association) {6.4}. A directed logical relation is symbolically denoted by

$$R\ (D_1,\ D_2)$$

where D_1 represents the <u>parent</u> and D_2 the <u>child</u> of the relation. The domains
here could be composite.

A directed logical relation is an <u>elementary hierarchical relation</u> if for
every d_{2j} belonging to D_2 there exists one and only one parent of d_{2j} in D_1
{6.4}. For an elementary hierarchical relation the child-parent relation is always functional.

Elementary hierarchical relations can be used to define a <u>hierarchical</u>
<u>relation</u> between n domains.

Suppose there are n domains D_1, D_2, ..., D_n and n-1 elementary hierarchical
relations

$$R_i\ (Dp_i,\ Dc_i)$$

with i = 1, 2, ..., n-1 and

Dp = parent domain, each Dp_i being a different one of D_1 to D_n
Dc = child domain, similarly, so one domain (the root) is not a child domain.

Each elementary hierarchical relation defines exactly one parent for each
domain with the exception of one domain (the root) in which no element has a
parent. The set

$$\{R_i\ (Dp_i,\ Dc_i)\}$$

then defines a hierarchical relation. A <u>hierarchical relation</u> is a collection
of elementary hierarchical relations in which no element of the root domain has
a parent and the elements of all other domains have exactly one parent each
{6.4}. Data that is thus structured conforms to a <u>hierarchical data structure</u>.

The terms used with hierarchical data structures (or trees) were introduced
in Section 4.3. The <u>root</u> of a hierarchical relation is the domain whose elements have no parents. The <u>leaves</u> of a hierarchical relation are the domains
whose elements have no children. The root of a hierarchical relation is said to
lie on the first <u>level</u> and a child which lies at the end of a path of length j-1
from the root is on the jth level.

Example 6.1.2

Assume an external model consists of segment types
Division (DV#, DVName, Manager)
Department (D#, DName, Manager, DV#)
Employee (E#, E-name, Salary, D#)
Building (B#, Location, DV#).
Assume the following segment occurrences
Division (DV1, Management-Services, Davis)
Department (D1, Operation, Brown, DV1)
Department (D2, Programming, Smith, DV1)
Employee (E1, Watson, 10K, D1)
Employee (E2, Jones, 12K, D2)
Employee (E3, Atkins, 9K, D2)
Employee (E4, Jones, 13K, D2)
Employee (E5, Cohen, 15K, D1)
Building (B1, North, DV1).
The directed logical relations (i.e. associations) are
R1 (Division, Department) = R1 (DI.DV#, DP.DV#)
R2 (Department, Employee) = R2 (DP.D#, E.D#)
R3 (Division, Building) = R3 (DI.DV#, B.DV#).
DI., DP., E. and B. are role names for Division, Department, Employee and
Building. The meanings of these relations are
- each department belongs to one division
- each employee works in one department
- each building holds one division.
R1, R2 and R3 are elementary hierarchical relations. The three relations
{R1, R2, R3} form a hierarchical relation.
The Division segment type does not have any parent: it is the root of the
hierarchical data structure. The Employee and Building segment types do not
have any children: they are leaves of the hierarchical data structure. The
Division segment type lies on the first, the Department and Building segment
types on the second and the Employee segment type on the third level of the
hierarchical data structure.

Fig. 6.1.3 shows
- the hierarchical structure type (valid for all divisions, departments, employees and buildings) which is the external data model

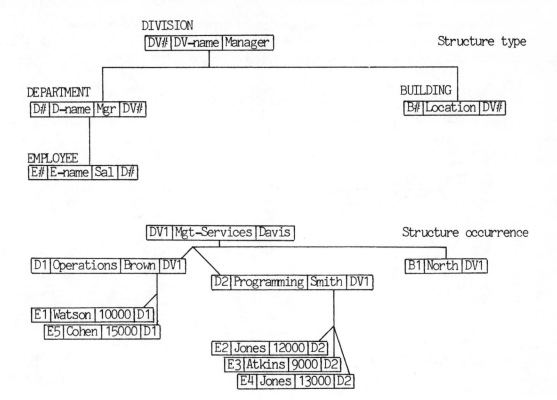

Figure 6.1.3

   – a hierarchical structure occurrence (valid for a particular division, particular departments and employees and a particular building only).

    A hierarchical data structure occurrence represents facts for only a single entity, i.e. the entity determined by the key of the root segment. The content of any dependent segment characterizes the entity as determined by the key of the root segment and hence acts essentially as an entity property. The occurrence in Fig.6.1.3 shows the division with the division number DV1. The structure occurrence indicates that that division (entity) has a certain organization (departments and employees) and is located in a certain building. A department, an employee or a building just characterizes the entity DV1 and hence here each acts as an entity property rather than acting as a pure entity. Relating an entity (such as division) to another entity (such as department) has the general consequence that the second entity appears as an entity property.

To obtain details of each employee in E# order would need an external data model with E# as an available entry point. Such an external model could use the same segment types as above and with Employee as the entry point.

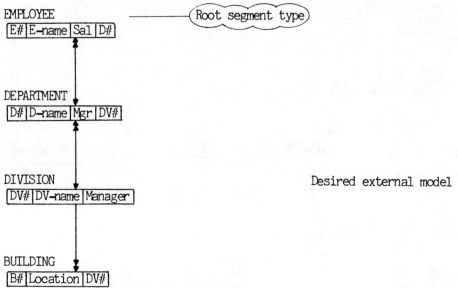

Desired external model

Figure 6.1.4

Strictly this is not a tree because it is not a tree structure of one to many relationships going away from the root segment entry point. But some DBMSs allow the following near equivalent as an external data model, where the absence of an arrowhead in the direction towards the root means the relationship cannot be used as an access path in that direction.

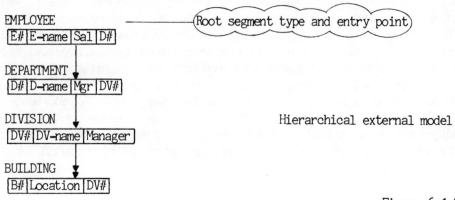

Hierarchical external model

Figure 6.1.5

Each employee has one occurrence of this structure, such as the following.

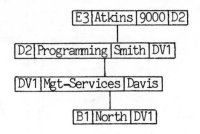

Figure 6.1.6

The application program could ask the DBMS to find the segment for employee E3 and thus access this structure occurrence and display required information to the user.

An application where users quote either Division numbers or employee numbers and request facts about either of the entities might require both a hierarchical structure with Division as root and a hierarchical structure with Employee as root. It is possible for an application to use two or more external models concurrently.

Network Data Structures

A set of logical relations that satisfies the rules above for tree structures can be classified as a hierarchical relation. Many information structures of entity types and relationship types are not trees or hierarchies. They are called networks. A hierarchy is a special case of a network. Thus a collection of arbitrarily connected logical relations is called a network relation. The data structure defined by such a network is called a network data structure {6.4}.

A hierarchical data structure becomes a network data structure if a functional child-parent relation is changed into a non-functional relation. For example if a building may hold several divisions then the hierarchical structure is destroyed (but that would correspond to a change in the conceptual data model). In general it is possible to make a hierarchical data structure non-hierarchical by adding new segment types and new directional logical relations.

Example 6.1.3

For the university example in Fig. 5.2.7, page 214, the following directed logical relations can be defined

PS (Professors, Students) = PS (P#, S#)
PL1 (Professors, L1) = PL1 (P#, (P#, C#))
CL1 (Courses, L1) = CL1 (C#, (P#, C#))
PL3 (Professors, L3) = PL3 (P#, (P#, R#))

RL3 (Classrooms, L3) = RL3 (R#, (P#, R#))
RL4 (Classrooms, L4) = RL4 (R#, (S#, R#))
SL4 (Students, L4) = SL4 (S#, (S#, R#))
RC (Classrooms, Courses) = RC (R#, C#)
CL5 (Courses, L5) = CL5 (C#, (S#, C#))
SL5 (Students, L5) = SL5 (S#, (S#, C#))
CL7A (Courses, L7) = CL7A (C#, (Before.C#, After.C#))
CL7B (Courses, L7) = CL7B (C#, (Before.C#, After.C#)).

Here each directed logical relation is functional in at least one direction. Suppose the external data model for some application includes the complete structure. Each segment type has either a parent or a child. Also they are interconnected in a single network, as opposed to being two or more networks. This does not matter, as most DBMSs that handle networks can handle structures that can be separated into two or more discrete networks. The relations

{PS, PL1, CL1, PL3, RL3, RL4, SL4, RC, CL5, SL5, CL7A, CL7B}

form a network relation.

A network relation is said to be _simple_ if each directed logical relation is functional in at least one direction.

In contrast a network relation is said to be _complex_ if at least one directed logical relation is non-functional in both directions. But any complex structure can be made simple by replacing each many-to-many relationship by two one-to-many relationships with the original record types as owners and a new record type as member of both. This new record type is sometimes called the _intersection_. For example the intersection between the entities Student and Course will give an extra record type called say Enrolment in a CODASYL-based model even if Enrolment has no data item types. (More usually the replacement will have been done during the development of the conceptual data model, e.g. where there are relationship attributes such as Grade, Opinion.) So in a DBMS that can handle only simple structures the non-availability of many-to-many relationship structures is not a significant restriction.

Example 6.1.4

In a CODASYL-based data structure the relationship from any member to its owner is a total or partial function (Section 5.2). Hence any CODASYL-based data structure (such as the structure in Fig. 5.2.8, page 215) is a _simple network data structure_.

Example 6.1.5

Suppose in the same university example that a user wanted the following external data model.

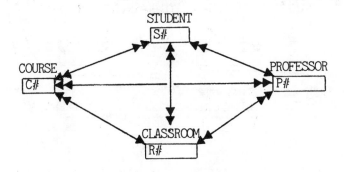

Figure 6.1.7

The following directed logical relations can be defined
PS (Professors, Students) = PS (P#, S#)
PC (Professors, Courses) = PC (P#, C#)
PR (Professors, Classrooms) = PR (P#, R#)
SC (Students, Courses) = SC (S#, C#)
SR (Students, Classrooms) = SR (S#, R#)
RC (Classrooms, Courses) = RC (R#, C#).
The relations
$$\{PS, PC, PR, SC, SR, RC\}$$
define a complex network data structure since several directed logical relations are non-functional in both directions.

It can be resolved into a simple network by replacing each many to many relationship by two one to many relationships to a newly introduced extra record type. That would give an external data model like Fig. 5.2.8, page 215, as might be needed for application software that required a simple network structure.

Thus the equivalent CODASYL subschema would have the following structure. Any similar structure with, for example, changes of names or any sensible subset of these record and set types would also be feasible.

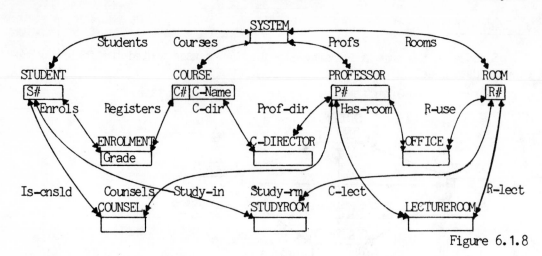

Figure 6.1.8

The <u>system</u> record type is a special CODASYL facility so that for example all Course records can belong to one set occurrence of the Courses set. It is called a <u>singular set type</u>. It can be used in applications that access each Course record one after another in logical order.

Data Manipulation Language

The application programs are written in a high level language such as Cobol, Fortran, PL/1, Algol. Extra kinds of declarations and statements are included which extend the high level language. These declarations and statements
- specify which subschema of which schema is used
- specify the various actions to retrieve, update and interact with the stored data. You can think of the manipulation statements as calls of procedures or subroutines in the database control system. In practice there may be slight variations of syntax between implementations of the data manipulation language to fit the different syntaxes of Cobol, Fortran and so on. But the same facilities in terms of database manipulations should be available. These facilities are summarized next. A designer of a CODASYL-based system would need to be aware of their effects and to discuss them.

The central concept of CODASYL DML is that each application program run unit is at any instant interested in one record and one set of each of the types in its subschema. There is one record which is the current record of the run unit. Usually this is the record most recently found or stored.

The database control system keeps a note of which record of the database is each of
- the current record, i.e. the last found or stored
- the current record of each of the record types in the subschema
- the current record of each set type, i.e. the last found or stored record that belongs to a set occurrence of the set type; there is one such current record for each set type in the subschema
- the current record of the realm, where a _realm_ is a logical area of stored records; this idea is less important.

Application program run units each have a work area of the main store of the computer. This working area is called the User Work Area (UWA). A term such as run unit work area might have been better since the contents of the area are under the control of the application program and the database software, so the end user may be unaware of the existence of the UWA.

The UWA has locations for one record of each type in the subschema normally. Suppose an application will want to find a Student record for which the user has supplied the S# value, say 4728, as input data. There will be in the UWA a place for a Student record and this will have a place for a S# value within it. So the application coding can move (in Cobol) or assign the value 4728 to that location.

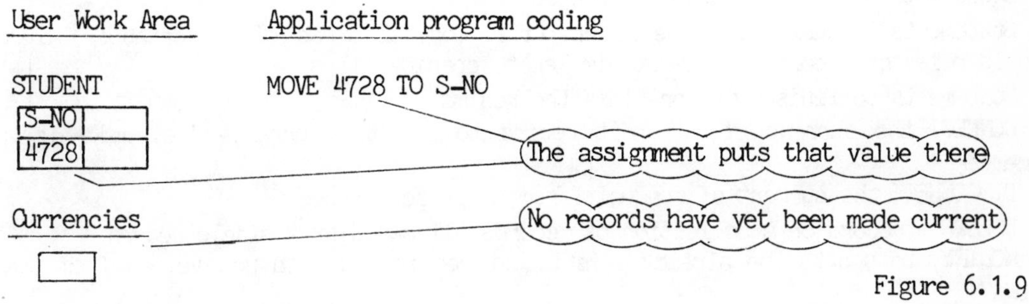

User Work Area   Application program coding

STUDENT   MOVE 4728 TO S-NO
[S-NO]
[4728]

                          (The assignment puts that value there)

Currencies   (No records have yet been made current)
[   ]

Figure 6.1.9

The next statement executed will be a DML statement to find the database Student record with that value of S#. The effect of the FIND statement is to make the found record current, but - for efficiency in the more general case - not to copy it to the Student record location in the UWA. The copying is done by a GET statement that is executed after the FIND statement.

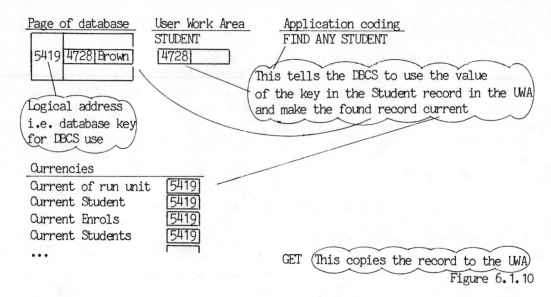

Figure 6.1.10

There are about 20 other kinds of DML statements, including several other kinds of FIND statement. It would not be appropriate to explain them all in detail here. Briefly, some of the other DML statements are

FIND FIRST/LAST/NEXT/PRIOR Enrolment WITHIN Enrols

FIND OWNER WITHIN Enrols

STORE - to store a new database record

Statements to make ready the realms (i.e. logical areas of the database) that hold relevant records, somewhat similar to opening files

Statements to finish with or close the realms

CONNECT the current of run unit record to a set occurrence i.e. make it a member

DISCONNECT the current of run unit from a set occurrence

DELETE a record or a collection of records all owned by a single record

MODIFY, to update the already existing stored record with new values from the UWA.

Structure Type Coexistence

A Data Base Management System supports structure type coexistence if it can derive from a given stored data representation at least two of hierarchical, network and relational data structures. The basic idea behind the concept of structure type coexistence is to enable the database administrator to make an appropriate data structure available to any potential database application or user. Structure type coexistence may simplify transition from two or more current incompatible DBMSs to some new DBMS. This means that existing application programs will require (almost) no adaptations.

If a network structure (not necessarily CODASYL-based) is used for the physical structure, then all three types of external models can theoretically be made available. For example for this the global logical model could be relational and the physical structure could be a network structure. As far as we know no currently available DBMS (1980) provides such. However, several pilot and research systems have shown that structure type coexistence is feasible.

The purpose of the discussion is to illustrate that – with the convertibility between the different structure approaches – structure type coexistence is achievable if a simple network data structure, e.g. a CODASYL-based structure, is used on the internal level. If the global logical model is a network the physical structure can be very similar.

Being simple is no restriction since, as stated above, any complex network data structure can be transformed into a simple network data structure by replacing each (M:M)-mapping by an intermediate intersection record type, and two (M:1)-mappings from it to the two owner record types.

There are three external model types to consider transforming a simple network internal model into
- simple network
- relations
- hierarchies.

We first discuss the procedure required to transform simple network data structures (internal level) into simple network data structures (external level).

If the internal-external mapping procedure involves no structure adaptations (e.g. changes of segment layouts, modifications in directed logical relations), in other words if the external structure represents an immediate image of the internal structure, then the mapping procedure is trivial and requires no further explanation. Mappings which involve structure adaptations will be discussed in Section 6.2.

Similarly the transformation of simple network data structures (internal level) into relations (external level) is trivial (of course again only if no adaptations of the external structure are required) since the tuples of a set of relations can be arranged in the form of a simple network structure. Thus a set of relations represents so to speak an immediate image of a simple network structure.

The transformation of simple network data structures (internal level) into hierarchical data structures (external level) requires explanation.

1 Since any hierarchical data structure starts with a root segment one has first of all to determine which record of the network data structure (internal level) has to correspond to the root segment of the hierarchical structure (external level). The root segment contains the key of the entity for which facts

have to be shown. Hence the record of the network structure belonging to the
entity in question becomes the root segment of the hierarchical structure. The
coresponding record type must be an entry point in the network global logical
model.

2 Once the root segment type is chosen the hierarchical structure is built
up by simply following the record to record relationships of the network structure. Each record encountered thereby becomes a dependent in the hierarchical
structure.

3 An intersection record type in the internal model acts as a link element
between the owners. There has to be a satisfactory way of selecting the appropriate intersection record occurrence and making it the retrieved segment occurrence when the application demands. For example Fig. 6.1.11 left side illustrates the case where the (M:M)-mapping

Suppliers $\ll\!\!-\!\!\gg$ Products

has been replaced by an intermediate link record L and two (M:1)-mappings.

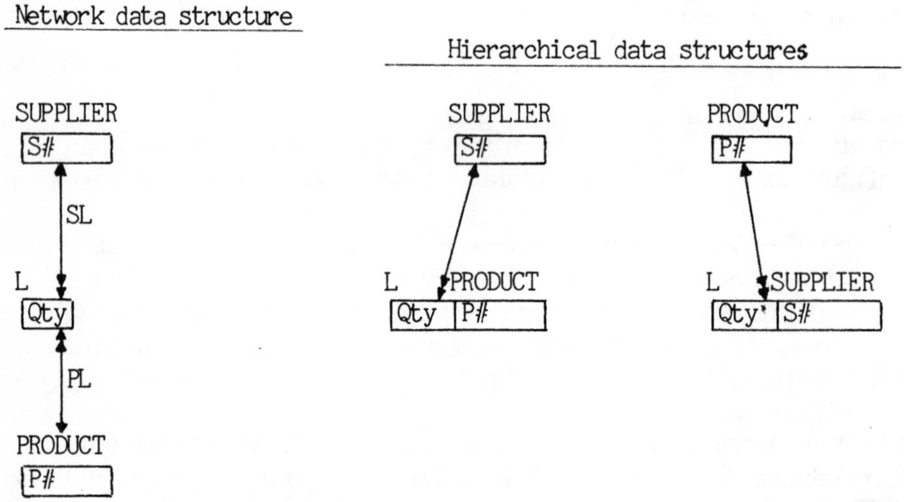

Network data structure

Hierarchical data structures

Figure 6.1.11

Note that L is the member of two owners in two different sets and hence acts
as a link element between the owners in question.

In the internal network L includes the attribute Qty containing details concerning the relationship between a particular supplier and a particular product.

In each hierarchical structure obtained by transformation of the network
structure a dependent level segment type includes the link element L concatenated with the other owner.

Fig. 6.1.11 middle shows the hierarchical structure required to consider a
supplier as an entity (the products supplied by a supplier are then considered

as entity properties). Fig. 6.1.11 right shows the hierarchical structure required to consider a product as an entity (the suppliers supplying a product are then considered as entity properties).

Fig. 6.1.12 illustrates network and hierarchical structure occurrences.

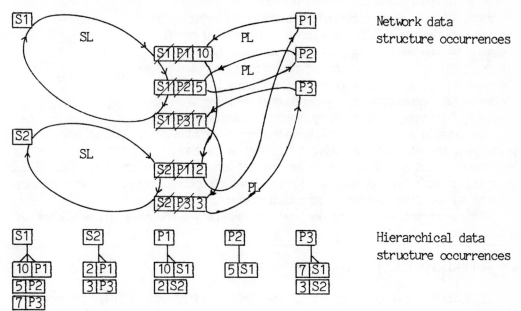

Network data
structure occurrences

Hierarchical data
structure occurrences

Figure 6.1.12

Example 6.1.6

Here is a hierarchical structure using Student as entry point and derived from the network structure of the university example of Fig. 5.2.8, page 215.

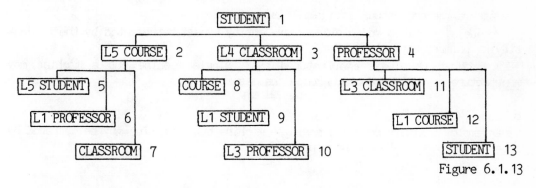

Figure 6.1.13

The segments show the following facts
Segment 1: General facts for an entity, say student S1,

Segment 2: Courses attended by S1,
Segment 3: Classrooms occupied by S1,
Segment 4: Professor advising S1,
Segment 5: Attendees of courses attended by S1,
Segment 6: Professors of courses attended by S1,
Segment 7: Classrooms occupied by courses attended by S1,
Segment 8: Courses taught in classrooms occupied by S1,
Segment 9: Students occupying classrooms occupied by S1,
Segment 10: Professors occupying classrooms occupied by S1,
Segment 11; Classrooms of professor advising S1,
Segment 12: Courses taught by professor advising S1,
Segment 13: Students advised by professor advising S1.

The example network structure can never be exhausted and it is possible, in principle, to determine an infinite number of dependent segments. If a network structure contains a cycle (such as the network structure shown in Fig. 5.2.8) then the transformation into a hierarchical structure always allows determination of an infinite number of dependent segments.

Similar structures can be derived for professors, courses and classrooms.

6.2 SUPERIMPOSITION OF DATA MODELS

Limitations have to be observed when rearranging data from an internal data structure to an external data structure. The limitations are because an internal data structure has to be and has to remain consistent with the conceptual model. This means that any storage operation (i.e. retrieve and update) specified on the external model but reflected by corresponding operations on the internal model has to take this consistency into consideration.

Example 6.2.1

Assume the conceptual data model is as follows.
1 Products, machines and employees are entity types, represented by their identifying primary keys.
2 A product is always manufactured by a single machine but a machine may manufacture several products. Hence the mapping

$$P\# \longleftrightarrow M\#$$

holds.
3 An employee always operates a single machine but a machine may be operated by several employees. Hence the mapping

$$E\# \longleftrightarrow M\#$$

holds.

4 Products and employees have names, i.e. dependent attributes P-name and E-name respectively.

The perception of the real world can be represented by the following elementary relations ER1 (P#, P-name) ER2 (P#, M#) ER3 (E#, E-name) ER4 (E#, M#).

These elementary relations represent the conceptual data model and correspond to the following functional dependencies

P# $\longrightarrow$ P-name

P# $\longrightarrow$ M#

E# $\longrightarrow$ E-name

E# $\longrightarrow$ M#.

The next figure shows this model.

Functional dependencies	Conceptual model elementary relations	Attributes	Entity types
P# $\longrightarrow$ P-name	ER1(P#, P-name)	P#	PRODUCT
$\searrow$ M#	ER2(P#,M#)	P-name	
E# $\longrightarrow$ E-name	ER3(E#, E-name)	E#	EMPLOYEE
	ER4(E#,M#)	E-name	
		M#	

Figure 6.2.1

The elementary relations ER1, ER2, ER3 and ER4 are all in 4NF but not in optimal 4NF. The optimalization procedure discussed in Section 5.1 yields the following optimal 4NF relations

Product (P#, P-name, M#),

Employee (E#, E-name, M#).

These two relations determine immediately the record layouts of the internal data structure. For a relational global logical model they would be the same as illustrated below. For a CODASYL-based internal model the global logical model would be equivalent and as follows.

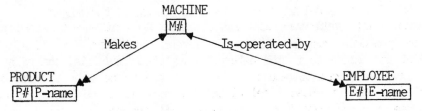

Figure 6.2.2

The next figure shows the models.

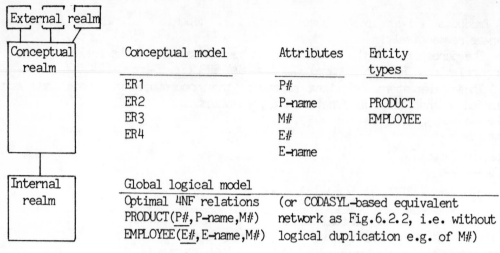

Conceptual model	Attributes	Entity types
ER1	P#	
ER2	P-name	PRODUCT
ER3	M#	EMPLOYEE
ER4	E#	
	E-name	

Global logical model	
Optimal 4NF relations	(or CODASYL-based equivalent
PRODUCT(P#,P-name,M#)	network as Fig.6.2.2, i.e. without
EMPLOYEE(E#,E-name,M#)	logical duplication e.g. of M#)

Figure 6.2.3

Suppose the following records occur (with the relational internal model for simplicity).

Record type ⎯ PRODUCT(P#, P-name, M#)   EMPLOYEE(E#, E-name, M#)

Record
occurrences ⎯

P1	Nut	M1
P2	Bolt	M1

E1	Brown	M1
E2	Smith	M1

Figure 6.2.4

The two record structures are consistent with the conceptual model. They guarantee that each product always has a single product name and a single machine number and each employee always has a single name and a single machine.

Now suppose an end user would like to know which machines and employees are required to produce a certain product. The external view

Manufacture (P#, M#, E#)

presented in the form of a relation could be used to derive the answer.

The external view Manufacture contains elements from different records; in other words the procedure required to map the internal data structure (i.e. the records Product and Employee) to the external data structure (i.e. the relation Manufacture) involves a rearrangement of data. It was to be able to make this point more clearly that we chose a relational internal model: it would be more difficult to see from the CODASYL internal model with its Machine record type.

For this end-user's enquiry only retrieval is needed. The rearrangement is therefore only from the internal global logical model to the external model. The mapping procedure can be formulated by the following natural join and project operations

Manufacture ⟵ (Product * Employee) [P#, M#, E#].

This algorithm yields

MANUFACTURE (P#, M#, E#)

P#	M#	E#
P1	M1	E1
P1	M1	E2
P2	M1	E1
P2	M1	E2

Figure 6.2.5

The key of the relation Manufacture (i.e. the external model) is the compound key (P#, E#).

Fig. 6.2.6 illustrates the perception of the real world, the elementary relations required as the conceptual data model, the record types of the internal global logical model allowing physical implementation of the conceptual model, and the external view Manufacture obtained by rearranging data located in Product and Employee records.

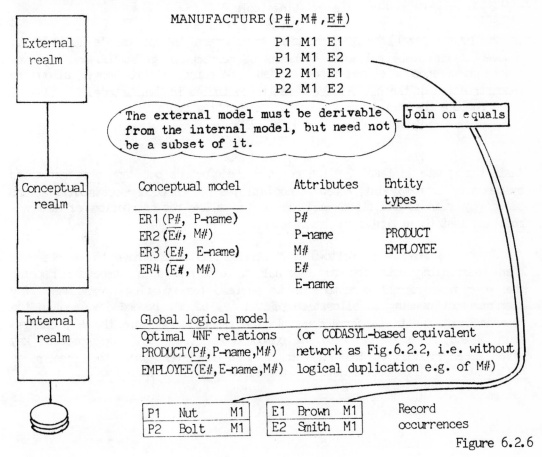

Figure 6.2.6

For <u>retrieval</u> operations the relation Manufacture is perfect and really permits the user to determine the machines and employees required to produce a particular product.

Now suppose that the relation Manufacture is also used for <u>storage updating</u> operations. The three situations to consider are insert, delete and modify.

1 Suppose Manufacture is made available and the user tries to insert a new tuple

<P2, M2, E3>.

This insertion is absolutely legal for the relation Manufacture since the user really tries to insert a tuple with the key P#/P2, E#/E3; that is to say a key value that does not yet exist in Manufacture. However the insertion is not consistent with the conceptual model which postulates that the production of any product requires a single machine (P2 requires the machine M1 already). This restriction is correctly reflected by the internal model since the Product record with key P# will never allow an insertion causing duplicated key values. Thus the above (invalid) insertion operation cannot be reflected by means of corresponding operations on the internal model.

2 A request to delete the existing tuple

<P2, M1, E2>

is absolutely legal for the relation Manufacture in the user's local view. However it cannot be reflected by means of corresponding Product and Employee record occurrence deletions since any such deletion will no longer allow the reconstruction of the not-deleted first three tuples in Manufacture.

3 Suppose the user tries to modify the existing tuple

<P1, M1, E1>

to

<P1, M2, E1>.

Again the update is legal for the relation Manufacture but cannot be reflected by means of corresponding Product and Employee record occurrence modifications since any such modification will no longer allow reconstruction of the unmodified last three tuples in Manufacture.

From this example it follows that strong limitations have to be observed when rearranging data for an internal to external data structure mapping whereever the external structure is to be used for updating operations. Any rearrangement causing an alteration of the key of any record involved in the rearrangement has to be forbidden. In the preceding example the key changed from P# and E# respectively to the compound key (P#, E#). The compound key gives more freedom but this freedom is not consistent with the freedom as defined by the conceptual model. So the software should not allow it.

This leads to the question whether it is possible to formulate the conditions under which a rearrangement will cause problems. In the following we present these conditions assuming that any rearrangement consists of a natural join followed by a project operation. Perhaps we ought also to explain the procedures used in the opposite direction, from external to internal, but they do not lead to any stronger conditions than are reached below.

Case 1

Suppose the following records occur

R1 (A, B, X)   and   R2 (A, Y)

A	B	X
A1	B1	X1
A1	B2	X2
A1	B3	X1
A2	B2	X1
A2	B3	X3
A2	B4	X2
A3	B1	X2

A	Y
A1	Y1
A2	Y2
A3	Y1

Figure 6.2.7

The natural join (preceding the rearranging project operation) R ← R1 * R2 yields

R (A, B, X, Y)

A	B	X	Y
A1	B1	X1	Y1
A1	B2	X2	Y1
A1	B3	X1	Y1
A2	B2	X1	Y2
A2	B3	X3	Y2
A2	B4	X2	Y2
A3	B1	X2	Y1

Figure 6.2.8

The key of the new relation (or segment) is the compound key A, B. Hence the key of the external model equivalent of record R2 altered from A to (A, B). Thus any restriction implied by the fact that A alone is the key of R2 is withdrawn. Thus the rearrangement may cause serious problems when used for updating operations.

Case 2
Suppose these records occur

$$R1 \ (\underline{A}, \ X) \qquad \text{and} \qquad R2 \ (\underline{B}, \ X)$$

A	X
A1	X1
A2	X2
A3	X1
A4	X1
A5	X3

B	X
B1	X3
B2	X1
B3	X2
B4	X1
B5	X1

Figure 6.2.9

The mappings

$$A \longleftrightarrow X$$
$$B \longleftrightarrow X$$

are assumed in R1 and R2 respectively.

The natural join (preceding the rearranging project operation) $R \leftarrow R1 * R2$ yields

$$R \ (\underline{A}, \ \underline{B}, \ X)$$

A	B	X
A1	B2	X1
A1	B4	X1
A1	B5	X1
A2	B3	X2
A3	B2	X1
A3	B4	X1
A3	B5	X1
A4	B2	X1
A4	B4	X1
A4	B5	X1
A5	B1	X3

Figure 6.2.10

The key of the new relation (or segment) R is the compound key (A, B). Hence the keys of the two records R1 and R2 changed from A and B respectively to (A, B). The consequence of this alteration is non-enforcement of any restriction implied by the fact that A and B are the keys of R1 and R2 respectively. Thus the rearrangement may cause serious problems when used for updating operations. (This case corresponds to the example at the beginning of this section.)

Case 3

Suppose these records occur

R1 (A, X)   and   R2 (B, X)

A	X
A1	X1
A2	X2
A3	X3
A4	X4
A5	X5

B	X
B1	X3
B2	X1
B3	X2
B4	X1
B5	X1
B6	X3

Figure 6.2.11

The mappings

$$A \longleftrightarrow X$$
$$B \lleftarrow\!\!\longrightarrow X$$

are assumed in R1 and R2 respectively.

The natural join (preceding the rearranging project operation)

R ← R1 * R2

yields

R (A, B, X)

A	B	X
A1	B2	X1
A1	B4	X1
A1	B5	X1
A2	B3	X2
A3	B1	X3
A3	B6	X3

Figure 6.2.12

The key of the new relation (or segment) R is B. Hence the key of the record R1 altered from A to B. So any restriction implied by the fact that A is the key of R1 is withdrawn. Thus the rearrangement may cause serious problems when used for operations that update stored data.

Case 4

Suppose these records occur

R1 (A, X)   and   R2 (B, X)

A	X
A1	X1
A2	X2
A3	X3
A4	X4
A5	X5

B	X
B1	X4
B2	X3
B3	X2
B4	X1

Figure 6.2.13

The mappings assumed to be enforced are

$$A \longleftrightarrow X$$
$$B \longleftrightarrow X$$

in R1 and R2 respectively.

The natural join (preceding the rearranging project operation) R ← R1 * R2 yields

R (<u>A</u>, B, X) or R (A, <u>B</u>, X)

A	B	X
A1	B4	X1
A2	B3	X2
A3	B2	X3
A4	B1	X4

A	B	X
A1	B4	X1
A2	B3	X2
A3	B2	X3
A4	B1	X4

Figure 6.2.14

The keys of the new relation (or segment) are A and B (i.e. two candidate keys). Hence the keys of the records R1 and R2 did not change which means that any rearrangement specified by a project operation will not cause problems in connection with updating operations provided that the keys A and B appear within the rearrangement. (Otherwise the system is not able to reflect storage operations specified on the external model by means of corresponding operations on record occurrences.)

From the preceding discussion it follows that a rearrangement of data for an internal to external data structure mapping causes no problems in storage updaing operations except in a very particular case. The rules are as follows.

1 For pure retrieval operations a rearrangement never causes problems. This applies to external models for query language programs. We have shown this only for examples with a natural join followed by a project operation, but more complicated external models are equivalent to rearranging using several join and project operations and possibly selection of certain tuples that have particular data item values, so the same applies. Alternatively this can be seen from thinking that retrieval does not alter any stored values so cannot make the stored data inconsistent, so it is only necessary to avoid the design allowing the user to retrieve from an inconsistent structure. Join and project operations cannot give any such trouble.

2 Relations (or segments) used for storage operations (i.e. updates – inserts, deletes and modifications) have to be created according to the following rules

(a) The set of data item types in a single relation (i.e. segment type) occurring in an external model has to correspond to a subset of the data item types in a single record type of the internal global logical model. This assumes that the global logical model is in optimal 4NF when expressed as relations, or is the appropriate equivalent simple network (e.g. with Machine and the two set types in the product and employee example above). For CODASYL-based network internal models this rule is saying that each external segment type for updating must correspond to a subset of the data item types in the relational optimal 4NF form, i.e. it can include the appropriate key data items of owning record types.

(b) The subset in the segment type has to include at least the record key (otherwise the system is not able to reflect a storage operation specified on the external model by means of corresponding operations on the internal model).

Summary

Strong limitations have to be observed when rearranging data for an internal to external data structure mapping where the external data structure is to be used for storage updating operations. Any rearrangement causing an alteration of the key of any record involved in the rearrangement has to be forbidden. The reason is that such alterations lead to an apparent increased freedom which is not consistent with the conceptual data model. The problem can be solved by the designer ensuring that the set of attributes in each single relation (or segment type) occurring in an external model has to correspond to a subset of the data item types in a single record wherever the external model is to be used for storage updating operations. The subset must include at least the record key because otherwise the system is not able to reflect a storage operation by means of corresponding operations on the internal model.

EXERCISES

1 Suppose in a CODASYL-based DBMS an external model (i.e. a subschema) is exactly the same as the global logical model (i.e. schema) in Fig. 6.2.2. Draw the record and set occurrences that would be available to an application program if the stored data were as in Fig. 6.2.4.

2 Does an external model that is used only for retrieval have to be fully normalized?

3 If the internal model is fully normalized is it possible to derive from it external data models that are not fully normalized and yet that cannot lead to anomalies in storage operations? If so, give an example. If not so, explain why not.

4 Fig. 4.0.1, page 97, showed a table for data about students, teachers and courses which could become inconsistent if it was an external model and used for updating because the meaning included that each teacher only did one course.

Could this table be provided as an external model for a query program which then provided the same model as local conceptual model to users making enquiries? Briefly justify your answer.

REFERENCES AND BIBLIOGRAPHY

6.1 Codd, E.F.: 'Recent Investigations in Relational Data Base Systems', Proc. IFIP Congress 74, August 5-10, Stockholm Sweden, Pages 1017-1021

6.2 Date, C.J.; Hopewell, P.: 'File Definition and Logical Data Independence', Proc. 1971 ACM-SIGFIDET Workshop on Data Description, Access and Control, obtainable from ACM, New York

6.3 Date, C.J.; Hopewell, P.: 'Storage Structure and Physical Data Independence', Proc. 1971 ACM-SIGFIDET Workshop on Data Description, Access and Control, obtainable from ACM New York

6.4 Ghosh, S.P.: 'Data Base Organisation for Data Management', Academic Press, New York, 1977

7

Generalized Design Procedure

Aims

This chapter represents a consensus of the preceding chapters and consolidates their content. It is based on an idea presented in {7.4} and describes a generalized database design procedure with the following objectives

1 The procedure is a systematic derivation of an internal model from an appropriate conceptual model

2 the internal model is consistent with the conceptual model

3 no anomalies in storage operations may occur (i.e. all normalization criteria are complied with)

4 the internal model guarantees efficient operation

5 the internal model corresponds as closely as possible to the enterprise's most crucial external models thus minimizing of the effort required for the internal to external data structure transformations.

It is usually possible to model a specific mini world by several non-redundant models (i.e. minimal covers). The database administrator must find the minimal cover that fits the enterprise's needs in an optimum manner. In Section 7.1 we assume that the optimum solution is represented by the minimal cover whose physical implementation requires the fewest machine operations for applications. This means executing the fewest operations in the database software while performing the manipulations for the commonest applications.

The design procedure does not necessarily require a database management system with a three level architecture as proposed by the ANSI/X3/Standards and Planning Committee (SPARC). Most DBMS currently (1980) available support a two level architecture only. But even in such cases it is still essential to obtain an internal model which adequately reflects the right model of the mini world and which requires relatively few machine operations when mapping the internal model to the organization's most crucial external models. The procedure discussed in Section 7.1 satisfies these objectives, regardless of whether or not a three level DBMS architecture is available.

7.1 CONSOLIDATION PHASE

In this section the various considerations discussed in preceding chapters are shown to give a consolidated and generalized database design procedure. This procedure involves the following phases

Phase 1: Real world conceptualization (as in Chapter 3 and Section 4.1)

Phase 2: Determination of irreducible units (as in Section 4.2)

Phase 3: Determination of a transitive closure and elimination of semantically meaningless compositions (as in Section 4.3)

Phase 4: Determination of the minimal cover which fits the enterprise's needs in an optimum manner (as in Section 4.4)

Phase 5: Transforming the minimal cover into a consistent internal data model (as in Chapter 5).

These phases are illustrated in the following example which is based on {7.1} but extended to show all kinds of dependency cases.

Assume that the real world portion to be modelled consists of the entity sets, entity attributes, relationship sets and relationship attributes below.

Domain	Relationship attribute	Relationship set	Entity set	Entity attribute	Domain

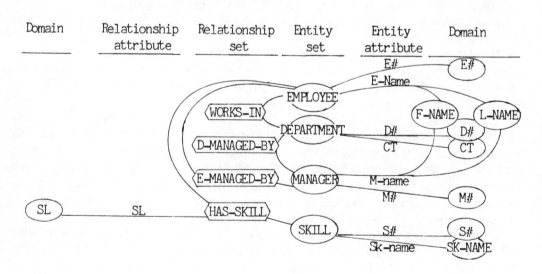

Figure 7.1.1

The procedure followed by the analyst and database designer goes as follows.

Phase 1: Real world conceptualization (discussed in Chapter 3 and Section 4.1)

Step 1

The analyst finds the real world portion consists of the following entity sets

EMPLOYEE
DEPARTMENT
MANAGER
SKILL.

In other words users say they would like to collect and store data about employees, departments, managers and skills as soon as at least the value of the identifier of such an entity is known.

This requires that each entity set is represented by an independent record type in the eventual internal model.

Step 2

The analyst distinguishes the following domains

E#	(employee number)
D#	(department number)
M#	(manager number)
S#	(skill number)
F-name	(first name)
L-name	(last name)
Sk-name	(skill name)
SL	(skill level)
CT	(contract type: either government or non-government)

Step 3

The entity key domains are

E#	(for the entity set EMPLOYEE)
D#	(for the entity set DEPARTMENT)
M#	(for the entity set MANAGER)
S#	(for the entity set SKILL).

Step 4

The analyst replaces the entity sets defined in Step 1 by their primary key domains and determines the following entity attributes (defined in terms of relations)

For the entity set EMPLOYEE: EMP-NAME (E#, F-name, L-name)
For the entity set DEPARTMENT: D-CT (D#, CT)
For the entity set MANAGER: MANAGER-NAME (M#, F-name, L-name)
For the entity set SKILL: SKILL-NAME (S#, Sk-name).

Step 5

The analyst distinguishes the following relationship sets (note that the entity sets participating in a relationship set have been replaced by their primary key domains)

WORKS-IN (E#, D#)
E-MANAGED-BY (E#, M#)
D-MANAGED-BY (D#, M#)
HAS-SKILL (E#, S#).

Step 6

For the relationship sets defined in Step 5 the analyst distinguishes the following relationship attribute (defined in terms of a relation)

SL (E#, S#, SL).

Phase 2: Determination of irreducible units (discussed in Section 4.2)

The following abbreviations are used

CK: Candidate Key
ER: Elementary Relation
FD: Functional Dependence
FFD: Full Functional Dependence
PK: Primary Key.

For the relations obtained in Phase 1 the analyst derives the following elementary relations

1   Relation: EMP-NAME (E#, F-name, L-name)
     CK and PK: E#
     FDs: E# $\longrightarrow$ F-name, E# $\longrightarrow$ L-name (Each employee has a single first name and a single last name)
     ERs: ER1 ($\underline{E\#}$, F-name), ER2 ($\underline{E\#}$, L-name)

2   Relation: D-CT ($\overline{D\#}$, CT)
     CK and PK: D#
     FD: D# $\longrightarrow$ CT (Each department is associated with a single contract)
     ER: ER3 ($\underline{D\#}$, CT)

3   Relation: MANAGER-NAME (M#, F-name, L-name)
     CK and PK: M#
     FDs: M# $\longrightarrow$ F-name, M# $\longrightarrow$ L-name (Each manager has a single first name and a single last name)
     ERs: ER4 ($\underline{M\#}$, F-name) ER5 ($\underline{M\#}$, L-name)

4   Relation: SKILL-NAME (S#, Sk-name)
     CK and PK: S#
     FD: S# $\longrightarrow$ Sk-name (Each skill has a skill name)
     ER: ER6 (S#, Sk-name)

5   Relation: WORKS-IN (E#, D#)
    CK and PK: E#
    FD: E# $\longrightarrow$ D# (Each employee works in a single department)
    ER: ER7 (E#, D#)
6   Relation: E-MANAGED-BY (E#, M#)
    CK and PK: E#
    FD: E# $\longrightarrow$ M# (Each employee has a single manager)
    ER: ER8 (E#, M#)
7   Relation: D-MANAGED-BY (D#, M#)
    CK: D#, M#
    FDs: D# $\longrightarrow$ M#, M# $\longrightarrow$ D# (Each department has a single manager and
each manager manages a single department)
    ERs: ER9 (D#, M#) ER10 (M#, D#) (The fact that departments and
managers are entities requires two elementary relations)
8   Relation: HAS-SKILL (E#, S#)
    CK and PK: E#, S#
    FD: - (Each employee possesses several skills and each skill is
held by several employees)
    ER: ER11 (E#, S#)
9   Relation: SL (E#, S#, SL)
    CK and PK: E#, S#
    FFD: E#, S# $\Longrightarrow$ SL (An employee may possess several skills and a
skill may be held by several employees. For a particular skill an employee has
at any time a single level)
    ER: ER12 (E#, S#, SL)

Phase 3: Determination of a transitive closure and elimination of meaningless compositions (as in Section 4.3)

The elementary relations obtained in Phase 2 define a digraph.

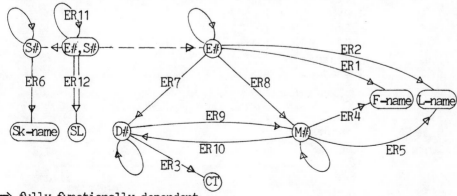

$\Longrightarrow$ fully functionally dependent
$\longrightarrow$ functionally dependent
$-\ -\ \longrightarrow$ trivially dependent

Figure 7.1.2

This digraph can be represented in a compatible form by a connectivity matrix M.

M	CT	D#	E#	E#, S#	F-name	L-name	M#	S#	SL	Sk-name
CT										
D#	1	1					1			
E#		1	1		1	1	1			
E#, S#			1	1				1	1	
F-name										
L-name										
M#	1				1	1	1			
S#									1	1
SL										
Sk-name										

Figure 7.1.3

Applying the transitive closure procedure (as in Section 4.3) to this connectivity matrix M yields a connectivity matrix MT that represents the transitive closure.

MT	CT	D#	E#	E#, S#	F-name	L-name	M#	S#	SL	Sk-name
CT										
D#	1	1			1	1	1			
E#	1	1	1		1	1	1			
E#, S#	1	1	1	1	1	1	1	1	1	1
F-name										
L-name										
M#	1	1			1	1	1			
S#									1	1
SL										
Sk-name										

Figure 7.1.4

The connectivity matrix MT defines a digraph as below.

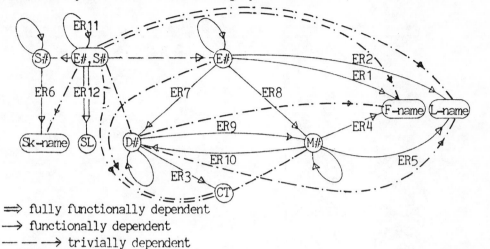

$\Longrightarrow$ fully functionally dependent
$\longrightarrow$ functionally dependent
$-- \longrightarrow$ trivially dependent
$-\cdot-\cdot \longrightarrow$ composition

Figure 7.1.5

A comparison of the connectivity matrices M and MT shows that the transitive closure procedure produces the following dependencies.

Dependency		Composition of			Semantically meaningful
D#	$\longrightarrow$ F-name	D#	$\longrightarrow$ M# $\longrightarrow$ F-name		no
D#	$\longrightarrow$ L-name	D#	$\longrightarrow$ M# $\longrightarrow$ L-name		no
E#	$\longrightarrow$ CT	E#	$\longrightarrow$ D# $\longrightarrow$ CT	or	yes
		E#	$-\cdot\longrightarrow$ M# $\longrightarrow$ CT	***	
E#, S#	$\longrightarrow$ D#	E#, S#	$\longrightarrow$ E# $\longrightarrow$ D#		no
E#, S#	$\longrightarrow$ CT	E#, S#	$\longrightarrow$ D# $\longrightarrow$ CT	***	no
E#, S#	$\longrightarrow$ F-name	E#, S#	$\longrightarrow$ E# $\longrightarrow$ F-name		no
E#, S#	$\longrightarrow$ L-name	E#, S#	$\longrightarrow$ E# $\longrightarrow$ L-name		no
E#, S#	$\longrightarrow$ M#	E#, S#	$\longrightarrow$ E# $\longrightarrow$ M#		no
E#, S#	$\longrightarrow$ Sk-name	E#, S#	$\longrightarrow$ S# $\longrightarrow$ Sk-name		no
M#	$\longrightarrow$ CT	M#	$\longrightarrow$ D# $\longrightarrow$ CT		yes

Figure 7.1.6

The compositions marked *** in the fourth and sixth lines above are each a composition of a composition.

The analyst should recognize that many dependencies produced by the transitive closure procedure are meaningless. Eliminating these meaningless dependencies gives the following modified connectivity matrix MM.

MM	CT	D#	E#	E#, S#	F-name	L-name	M#	S#	SL	Sk-name
CT										
D#	1	1					1			
E#	1	1	1		1	1	1			
E#, S#			1	1				1	1	
F-name										
L-name										
M#	1	1			1	1	1			
S#									1	1
SL										
Sk-name										

Figure 7.1.7

The modified connectivity matrix MM defines a digraph as below. The semantically meaningful compositions $E\# \longrightarrow CT$ and $M\# \longrightarrow CT$ are represented by the elementary relations ER13 and ER14 respectively.

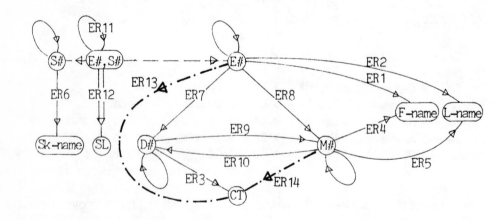

$\Longrightarrow$ fully functionally dependent
$\longrightarrow$ functionally dependent
$- - \longrightarrow$ trivially dependent
$\cdot - \cdot \longrightarrow$ meaningful composition derived by the transitive closure procedure

Figure 7.1.8

Phase 4: Determination of the best minimal cover (as in Section 4.4)

In the following discussion we assume that the optimum solution is represented by the minimal cover whose physical implementation requires the fewest machine operations when transforming the internal data model to the organization's most crucial external data models.

The analyst should proceed as follows. Let

$$S^z = \{ER1, ER2, ..., ER_z\}$$

represent the list of elementary relations obtained in Phase 3 and let

$$MC \{S_n^m\}$$

represent the best set of minimal covers. Here z and m represent the cardinality of S and MC respectively, and n stands for a running number. Also MC is empty at the beginning of the procedure.

Step 1

Each elementary relation in S^z has a longest distance.

Step 2

The analyst associates a weight with each elementary relation with distance greater than 1. The weights are used to control the elimination of elementary relations where several have equal distance.

Each weight denotes the relative frequency of use together of the combination of attributes in the corresponding elementary relation. This means how often an external model segment containing them together is retrieved or stored, summed over all the applications of all the external models. Higher weight means the attributes in that elementary relation are likely to be frequently used together. Then it is better to structure the database so the data item types corresponding to these attributes are stored together. This minimizes the machine operations to transform between the internal model data structure occurrences and the external structure occurrences. Transformations are needed in both directions. Transformations from internal to external are for retrieval; those from external to internal are to update, e.g. store new occurrences.

Step 3

Remove ER_r from S^z where it is a composition of say ER_i and ER_j, i.e.

(a) ER_i, ER_j, ER_r belong to S^z
(b) $ER_r = C'(ER_i, ER_j)$
(c) ER_r possesses maximum distance
(d) In the case where there are several with equal maximum distance remove the ER_r with minimum weight.

Condition (c) has priority over condition (d). The weights are used to control the elimination of elementary relations in the case where several elementary relations have equal maximum distance. This guarantees that the minimal covers obtained are optimal in the sense that they do not contain any insignificant redundant elementary relations. Call the remaining set S_n^{z-1}. If no element can be removed from S^z, place S^z in the set MC and terminate the process. In the case where there are several maximum distances and several minimal weights one can find a family of collections S_1^{z-1}, S_2^{z-1} ... S_n^{z-1} each containing z-1 elements.

Note that $ER_r \; \mathbf{v} \; S_n^{z-1} = S^z$.

Step 4

Repeat Step 3 for each S_n^{z-1} to obtain a family of S^{z-2} collections. If no element can be removed from S_n^{z-1} form the union of this with MC and assign the result to MC. Hence perform

$$MC \longleftarrow MC \; \mathbf{v} \; S_n^{z-1}.$$

Step 5

Repeat Step 4 until no element can be removed from any collection then terminate. Then

$$MC \; \{S_n^m\}$$

represents the best set of all minimal covers. MC does not contain any elementary relation that represents the composition of other elementary relations.

We apply the procedure to the example.

Example 7.1.1

From the digraph in Fig. 7.1.7 the analyst derives the following elementary relations

ER1 (E#, F-name)
ER2 ($\overline{\text{E\#}}$, L-name)
ER3 ($\overline{\text{D\#}}$, CT)
ER4 ($\overline{\text{M\#}}$, F-name)
ER5 ($\overline{\text{M\#}}$, L-name)
ER6 ($\overline{\text{S\#}}$, Sk-name)
ER7 ($\overline{\text{E\#}}$, D#)
ER8 ($\overline{\text{E\#}}$, M#)
ER9 ($\overline{\text{D\#}}$, M#)
ER10 $\overline{\text{(M\#}}$, D#)

ER11 $(E\#, S\#)$
ER12 $(E\#, \overline{S\#}, SL)$
ER13 $(E\#, \overline{CT})$
ER14 $(\overline{M\#}, CT)$.

    Thus $S^{14} = \{ER1, ER2, ..., ER14\}$.

    Then

ER13 = C (ER7, ER3) with distance $d_{13} = 4$ (because $E\# \longrightarrow D\# \longrightarrow M\# \longrightarrow D\# \longrightarrow$ CT). Also ER(13) = C (ER8, ER14).

ER3 = C (ER9, ER14) with $d_3 = 2$
ER7 = C (ER8, ER10) with $d_7 = 2$
ER8 = C (ER7, ER9) with $d_8 = 2$
ER14 = C (ER10, ER3) with $d_{14} = 2$
ER1 has $d_1 = 1$
ER2 has $d_2 = 1$
ER4 has $d_4 = 1$
ER5 has $d_5 = 1$
ER6 has $d_6 = 1$
ER9 has $d_9 = 1$
ER10 has $d_{10} = 1$
ER11 has $d_{11} = 1$
ER12 has $d_{12} = 1$.

    From discussions with users the analyst should associate weights with each elementary relation of maximum distance greater than 1, in accordance with expected use from functional analysis. E.g. suppose users most frequently will need $(E\#, CT)$ and so on, the weights may be as follows.

ER13 $(E\#, CT)$ weight $W_{13} = 10$
ER7 $(E\#, D\#)$ weight $W_7 = 7$
ER3 $(\overline{D\#}, CT)$ weight $W_3 = 5$
ER8 $(E\#, M\#)$ weight $W_8 = 4$
ER14 $(\overline{M\#}, CT)$ weight $W_{14} = 1$

    Provided that no normalization criteria are violated it is best to store the most often used combinations within single record types. This reduces the number of machine operations required to transform between the internal data structure and the organization's most frequently used external data structures.

    The derivation of the best minimal cover is tabulated next.

Iteration	S_n^z	ER,s	$C(ER_i, ER_j)$	d_r	W_r	ER_r removed	S_n^{z-1}	MC
0	S^{14}	ER13	C(ER7, ER3) C(ER8, ER14)	4	10	<-	S_1^{13}	
		ER3	C(ER9, ER14)	2	5			
		ER7	C(ER8, ER10)	2	7			
		ER8	C(ER7, ER9)	2	4			
		ER14	C(ER10, ER3)	2	1			
		ER1	-	1	-			
		ER2	-	1	-			no
		ER4	-	1	-			
		ER5	-	1	-			
		ER6	-	1	-			
		ER9	-	1	-			
		ER10	-	1	-			
		ER11	-	1	-			
		ER12	-	1	-			
1	S_1^{13}	ER3	C(ER9, ER14)	2	5			
		ER7	C(ER8, ER10)	2	7			
		ER8	C(ER7, ER9)	2	4			
		ER14	C(ER10, ER3)	2	1	<-	S_1^{12}	
		ER1	-	1	-			
		ER2	-	1	-			
		ER4	-	1	-			no
		ER5	-	1	-			
		ER6	-	1	-			
		ER9	-	1	-			
		ER10	-	1	-			
		ER11	-	1	-			
		ER12	-	1	-			

Ite-ration	S_n^z	ER,s	$C(ER_i, ER_j)$	d_r	W_r	ER_r removed	S_n^{z-1}	MC
2	S_1^{12}	ER3	–	2	5			
		ER7	C(ER8, ER10)	2	7			
		ER8	C(ER7, ER9)	2	4	<–	S_1^{11}	
		ER1	–	1	–			
		ER2	–	1	–			
		ER4	–	1	–			
		ER5	–	1	–			no
		ER6	–	1	–			
		ER9	–	1	–			
		ER10	–	1	–			
		ER11	–	1	–			
		ER12	–	1	–			
3	S_1^{11}	ER3	–	2	5			
		ER7	–	2	7			
		ER1	–	1	–			
		ER2	–	1	–			
		ER4	–	1	–			
		ER5	–	1	–			yes
		ER6	–	1	–			
		ER9	–	1	–			
		ER10	–	1	–			
		ER11	–	1	–			
		ER12	–	1	–			

Figure 7.1.9

After the third iteration MC (i.e. the best set of minimal covers) consists of MC $\{S_1^{11}\}$
with

$$S_1^{11} = \{ER3, ER7, ER1, ER2, ER4, ER5, ER6, ER9, ER10, ER11, ER12\}.$$

That is the final minimal cover, equivalent to the following directed graph.

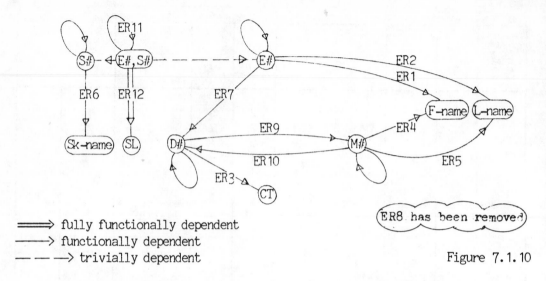

⟹ fully functionally dependent
⟶ functionally dependent
— — ⟶ trivially dependent

Figure 7.1.10

As an exercise you may show that the weight of the elementary relation ER13 has no influence and that different solutions may result with other weights.

Phase 5: Transforming the minimal cover into a consistent internal data model (as discussed in Chapter 5)

In Section 5.1 we showed that any elementary relation is in 4NF. However the collection of all elementary relations, CER, is in general not in optimal 4NF; it is usually possible to find a smaller collection of 4NF relations retaining the essential information of the relations in the CER. The procedure to find this smaller collection consists of creating subsets S_j of the relations in the CER such that each subset S_j contains only elementary relations with identical keys K_j

$$ER_i (\underline{K_j}, A_i).$$

The next step consists in combining the elementary relations of a subset S_j such that the resulting relation, R_j, contains the key K_j and all non-key attributes A_i of the elementary relations ER_i in S_j. In other words we create for each subset S_j a single relation of the form

$$R_j (\underline{K_j}, A_1, A_2, \ldots A_i, \ldots A_n).$$

We now show this procedure applied to the example. From the digraph in Fig. 7.1.10 (representing the optimal minimal cover) the analyst derives the following elementary relations

ER1 ($\underline{E\#}$, F-name)
ER2 ($\underline{E\#}$, L-name)
ER3 ($\underline{D\#}$, CT)

ER4 ($\overline{M\#}$, F-name)
ER5 ($\overline{M\#}$, L-name)
ER6 ($\overline{S\#}$, Sk-name)
ER7 ($\overline{E\#}$, D#)
ER9 ($\overline{D\#}$, M#)
ER10 ($\overline{M\#}$, D#)
ER11 ($\overline{E\#}$, S#)
ER12 ($\overline{E\#}$, $\overline{S\#}$, SL).

The subset creation yields

S_1 (with K_1 = E#)   =   {ER1, ER2, ER7}
S_2 (with K_2 = D#)   =   {ER3, ER9}
S_3 (with K_3 = M#)   =   {ER4, ER5, ER10}
S_4 (with K_4 = S#)   =   {ER6}
S_5 (with K_5 = E#, S#) =   {ER11, ER12}.

The combining of the elementary relations in each subset yields

R_1 ($\overline{E\#}$, F-name, L-name, D#)
R_2 ($\overline{D\#}$, CT, M#)
R_3 ($\overline{M\#}$, F-name, L-name, D#)
R_4 ($\overline{S\#}$, Sk-name)
R_5 ($\overline{E\#}$, $\overline{S\#}$, SL).

The combining of elementary relations does not produce transitive dependencies in any resulting relation (Section 5.1). This follows because the set of elementary relations produced by the minimal cover procedure (Phase 4) does not contain any elementary relation representing the composition of other elementary relations. Hence the relations R_1, R_2, R_3, R_4, R_5 are in 4NF. As usual the relations R_1, R_2, ... R_5 are associated by means of primary keys and foreign keys. R_1.D# and R_3.D# are foreign keys because they are not the primary keys of R_1 and R_3 respectively, but their values are values of the primary key of the relation R_2. This means that a particular tuple in R_1 (respectively R_3) is always associated with a single tuple in R_2 and that a particular tuple in R_2 is usually associated with several tuples in R_1 (respectively R_3). That is

$R_1 \longrightarrow R_2$
$R_3 \longrightarrow R_2$.

Similarly R_5.E# is a foreign key because E# is not the primary key of R_5 but of R_1. Hence the functional dependence

$R_5 \longrightarrow R_1$

holds. Finally R_5.S# is a foreign key because S# is not the primary key of R_5 but of R_4. Hence the functional dependence

$R_5 \longrightarrow R_4$

holds.

Since every link involving two relations is functional in at least one direction it is possible to implement the relations R_1, R_2, ... R_5 by means of CODASYL sets. Fig. 7.1.11 shows an appropriate internal global logical model.

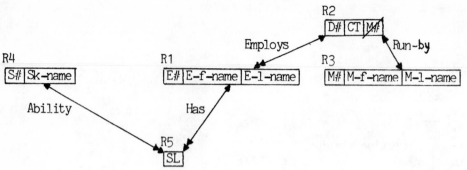

Figure 7.1.11

7.2 CONCLUSION

In this book we have shown how it is possible to replace the intuitive approach actually used for the design of databases by a much more rigid and
systematic procedure. Certain parts of the design process can be computerized
{7.2}, {7.3}. This allows the analyst and designer to concentrate more on the
semantic problems for which no mechanized solution is available. Alternative
designs can be evaluated.

If use is monitored by the DBMS software then weights might be automatically
computed and the designer alerted if the pattern of use suggested a better internal model. The designer can then decide whether to allow the automatic ad-
justment of the internal model. Some future database management systems may include, possibly via an attached data dictionary system, algorithms which allow
systematic derivation of an internal data structure from an appropriate conceptual data structure.

A conceptual schema is a specification of what is allowable in the mini
world. It covers
- all the types of information allowed, including rules about occurrences.
- all the rules about types of operations allowed, for example that the employees of an insurance organization cannot access any information about their
own policies or other employee's in the ways that their normal jobs require them
to handle similar information about other people's.

The conceptual schema should be complete in the sense of specifying all the
rules about all the types of information and operations envisaged. This implies
including many kinds of rules that cannot be coded in existing data description
languages.

Perhaps future conceptual models may include all such rules derived from
functional analysis as well as the kinds of data analysis rules and functional
rules we have described in this book.

For further reading you may like to consider {5.20, 7.5 to 7.7} and the references of {5.20, 7.6}.

EXERCISES

1 For the example of Section 7.1 assume that the pattern of use has changed so the elementary relations should have the following new weights.

ER14(M#,CT) has W_{14} = 8
ER13($\overline{E\#}$,CT) has 7
ER8(E#,M#) has 6
ER3($\overline{D\#}$,CT) has 5
ER7($\overline{E\#}$,D#) has 4.

Determine the new minimum cover to best serve users needs. Transform it into a suitable internal model. Represent the internal model to conform to a CODASYL-based DBMS, i.e. using set types and record types.

REFERENCES AND BIBLIOGRAPHY

7.1 Codd, E.F.: 'Further Normalization of the Relational Model', in 'Data Base Systems', Courant Computer Science Symposium 6, 1971, Rustin, R.: Ed., Prentice-Hall Inc., Englewood Cliffs, New Jersey, 1972, Pages 33-64

7.2 DBDA (Data Base Design Aid), Designer's Guide, IBM Form Number: GH20-1627

7.3 Thievent, G.; Stoltz, B: 'An APL Program for Database Design', IBM ESRI (European Systems Research Institute), Study Project Class 28, 1977, (limited distribution)

7.4 Vetter, M: 'Data Base Design by Applied Data Synthesis', Proc. of the 3rd International Conference on Very Large Data Bases, Tokio, Oct. 6-8 1977.

7.5 Maddison, R. N. (Editor): Data analysis for information system design: Conference at Loughborough, 29 June 1978. About 75 pages. (During 1980 this was available from R. N. Maddison, Mathematics Faculty, Open University, Walton Hall, Milton Keynes, MK7 6AA, price £3.00 payable to BCS(DAFISD).)

7.6 Deen, S. M.: A canonical schema for a generalised data model with local interfaces. Computer J. Vol. 23 No. 3 Aug 1980 pages 201-206.

7.7 The Open University: M352 Computer-based Information Systems. 1980. The correspondence element includes four course text Blocks (ISBN 0-335-14000-9 ...), two case studies (LOLA and STC (ISBN 0-335-14004-1 ...)) and four Activity Booklets. Available from OUEE, 12 Cofferidge Close, Stony Stratford, Milton Keynes MK11 1BY, Great Britain; and their distributors. This book is not based on the M352 course.

Appendix 1

Coding Details

Appendix 1.1

(See page 152.) The whole of this procedure can be specified in APL by means of the following boolean inner matrix product

$$C \leftarrow M \vee . \wedge M$$

Appendix 1.2

(See page 153.) In APL we create MM by multiplying M with a matrix, say J, having the same dimension as M (i.e. n x n). The elements on the diagonal of J, i.e. $J_{i,i}$ for $1 \leqslant i \leqslant n$, are 0. The other elements of J are 1. The matrix J may be obtained by either of the expressions

$$J \leftarrow (\rho M)\rho 0, (\rho M)[1]\rho 1$$

or

$$J \leftarrow (\iota(\rho M)[1]) \circ . \neq \iota(\rho M)[1]$$

MM then is determined by

$$MM \leftarrow M \times J$$

Appendix 1.3

(See page 153.) One way to do this in APL is to multiply the matrix C by the matrix J

$$C \leftarrow C \times J$$

282

Appendix 1.4

(See page 154.) The following APL-function CLOSURE may be used to determine
a transitive closure.

```
        ∇CLOSURE[□]∇
        ∇ TC←CLOSURE M;I;MM;C
[1]     ⍝ CREATE MATRIX I SUCH THAT I[i;i] = 0
[2]     ⍝ FOR 1 ≤ i ≤ n AND 1 OTHERWISE
[3]     I←(ρM)ρ0,(RM)[1]ρ1
[4]     ⍝ DERIVE MODIFIED CONNECTIVITY MATRIX FROM
[5]     ⍝ ORIGINAL CONNECTIVITY MATRIX M
[6]     MM←M×I
[7]     ⍝ DETERMINE THE COMPOSITIONS FOR MM
[8]     COMP:C←MM∨MM∨.∧MM
[9]     ⍝ REMOVE ERRONEOUS COMPOSITIONS OBTAINED
[10]    ⍝ BY THE CONDITION N_i → N_j → N_i
[11]    C←C×I
[12]    ⍝ NEW COMPOSITIONS OBTAINED?
[13]    →END×ι(∧/∧/C=MM)
[14]    ⍝ CREATE NEW MODIFIED CONNECTIVITY MATRIX MM
[15]    ⍝ INCLUDING THE NEW COMPOSITIONS DETERMINED
[16]    ⍝ IN [8]
[17]    MM←C
[18]    ⍝ DETERMINE COMPOSITIONS OF COMPOSITIONS
[19]    →COMP
[20]    ⍝ COMBINE THE COMPOSITIONS OBTAINED IN [8]
[21]    ⍝ WITH THE ORIGINAL CONNECTIVITY MATRIX M
[22]    END:TC←M∨MM
        ∇
```

Appendix 1.5

(See page 163.) The following APL-function REDUCE may be used to determine
the ERs belonging to the different subsets. The function accepts a connectivity
matrix and presents the result in table form. The table has the same dimension
as the connectivity matrix and indicates rowwise the ERs constituting a subset.

```
      ∇REDUCE[[]]∇
      ∇ R←REDUCE M
[1]   A CONDITION C1:
[2]   A DETERMINE ER'S SUCH THAT FOR EACH ER ITS NON-KEY
[3]   A ATTRIBUTE DOES NOT OCCUR AS A KEY ATTRIBUTE IN
[4]   A ANY OTHER ER:
[5]     R←M>(ρM)ρ∨/M
[6]   A CONDITION C2:
[7]   A DETERMINE ER'S SUCH THAT FOR EACH ER ITS NON-KEY
[8]   A ATTRIBUTE DOES NOT OCCUR AS A NON-KEY ATTRIBUTE IN
[9]   A ANY OTHER ER AND C1 IS SATISFIED:
[10]    R←R≥(ρM)ρ+/M
[11]  A DETERMINE ROWWISE IF THERE ARE AT LEAST TWO ER'S
[12]  A SATISFYING C1 AND C2:
[13]    R←R×⍉(ρM)ρ(+/R)>1
      ∇
```

Appendix 2

Solutions to Exercises

Solutions to Exercises of Chapter 1

1 Information must be communicated (i.e. actually received by the right staff) and at an appropriate time. It must be understood by the user and be in a suitable form for this (e.g. laid out as a sensible table or display with headings that the user understands for the various items. The information must be relevant to the user's function in the organization. The information should be accurate, otherwise mistakes may be compounded.

2 A database is a collection of stored data structured so <u>all</u> user's needs can be met without restructuring or sorting. A traditional file has a structure of similar records in some physical sequence such as ascending order of some key data item values.

Database users are unaware of physical sequence, two different users can view the same data with different structures each appropriate to their needs and without file processing operations such as sorting and merging. In a database each fact is normally stored only at one place (except for backup copies for recovery from errors). With files the same data item values may occur in several records in different files.

See also the six design aims, page 7.

3(a) Logical
(b) Global. The word local means for one user or application
(c) Conceptual or canonical
(d) Integrity
(e) Accuracy
(f) Privacy
(g) Security
(h) Retrieve
(i) Update.

4 Logical data independence means existing application programs do not need maintenance when new applications are added or other existing ones are changed. They also do not need attention when new types of data are defined and added to the database (provided their functional specifications remain the same).

Physical data independence means the physical structure of the stored data can be changed without attention to the application programs, whether or not they use the data items whose structure has been changed.

(In some current (1980) DBMSs existing application programs have to be recompiled when new irrelevant data types are added or when the physical data is restructured.)

5 Storing each item of information once means consistency and the avoidance of extra processing to update many copies at updates. Storage space is also saved.

Solutions to Exercises of Section 2.1

1 Yes, the sets are disjoint. Each project has a set of programmers. No programmer belongs to two sets at any instant.

2 Customers may be grouped into sets with one set per sales person and one extra set for those who are postal customers. These sets are disjoint. Their union is not empty; it is the set of all customers. Their intersection is empty.

3 With P = paid, D = delivered, L = loaded, the meanings are

A $P \cap (D \cup L) = (P \cap D) \cup (P \cap L)$
B $(P \cap L) \cup D = (P \cup D) \cap (L \cup D)$
C $(P \cap D) \cup (L \cap P)$
D $(D \cap P) \cup L = (D \cup L) \cap (P \cup L)$
E $(P \cap L) \cup D = (P \cup D) \cap (L \cup D)$

Thus A = C, B = E.

4 D: F and G or H = $(F \cap G) \cup H$.

5 Yes, "not" binds tighter than "and".
A and not B or C = $(A \cap (B')) \cup C$.
Not B and A or C = $(B' \cap A) \cup C$ is the same.

6 With the meaning "This needs that" the table is a binary relation.

THIS	THAT
Paste	Water
Wallpaper	Paste
Rooms	Wallpaper
Windows	Paint
Houses	Rooms
Houses	Windows
Houses	Walls
Walls	Bricks
Walls	Wallpaper
Ceilings	Paint
Paint	Brushes	⎯(Care
Paste	Brushes	⎯(here

7 The calendar as a relation is of degree 2 because as below there are two columns and it has cardinality 21 because there are 21 rows.

DAY	DATE
Monday	1
Tuesday	2
Wednesday	3
Thursday	4
Friday	5
Monday	8
Tuesday	9
Wednesday	10
Thursday	11
Friday	12
Monday	15
Tuesday	16
Wednesday	17
Thursday	18
Friday	19
Monday	22
Tuesday	23
Wednesday	24
Monday	29
Tuesday	30
Wednesday	31

8 (i) A - B = {x| x ∈ A and x ∈ B}.
(ii) BLDGS - OFFICES - HOUSES is the set required.

9 The drawings should show the two sets in (a) are the same and the two sets in (b) are the same.

10 If you choose ⟨Ann, Bob⟩ and ⟨Su, Paul⟩ you get

GIRL	BOY
Ann	Bob
Su	Paul

The reverse exists. It is {⟨Bob, Ann⟩, ⟨Paul, Su⟩}. It is a partial function. The product Has-boy-friend x Has-boy-friend^{-1} exists and is the identity transformation. It transforms Ann into Ann and transforms Su into Su.
(ii) The alternative Has-boy-friend2 is also a function. But its reverse is not a function because Bob associates to two girls.

Solutions to Exercises of Section 2.2

1 The proper subsets are {}, {a}, {b}, {a,b}, {c}, {a,c}, {b,c}. The subsets are the same plus {a,b,c}.

2 (a) is correct.
(b) is meaningless because b is an element and ∈ must have a set to its left. The statement {b} ∈ A would be correct.
(c) is correct.
(d) is correct.
(e) is correct.
(f) is correct.

3 Using initials e.g.T = Tom for brevity
(a) {A,M,S,T}
(b) {A,M,P,S,T}
(c) {A,B,M,P,S,T}
(d) {A,B,M,P,S}
(e) = (f) = {A,B,M,P,S,T}
(g) {M,S}
(h) = (i) = {M}
(j) = A ∪ (B ∩ C) = {A,M,P,S,T} because intersection binds tighter than union.
(k) {S,T}
(l) {B,P}
(m) {}.

4 (a) and (b) are true.
(c) is meaningless because the codomain of f (i.e. B) is not the domain of g (i.e. A). So (c) is false.

5 (a) Girls1 $\longleftrightarrow$ Boys1
(b) Girls2 $\longleftrightarrow\!\!\!\rightarrow$ Boys2
(c) Girls3 $\longleftrightarrow$ Boys3
(d) Girls4 $\longleftrightarrow\!\!\!\rightarrow$ Boys4.
(ii) (a) and (c) are functions in the direction stated.

6 Assume each supplier supplies many products, where many means none or one or several. Each product is supplied by many suppliers. Hence the mapping is many to many.
(b) and (c) could similarly be many to many.
(d) Assuming each employee belongs to one department and every employee does gives Employee $\longleftrightarrow$ Department. But assuming each employee belongs either to one or to no department gives Employee $\longleftrightarrow\!\!\!-$ Department.
(ii) Yes, e.g. for (c) different employees may service each machine from those who operate it. This gives two mappings, each mapping is many to many.

7 (a) A larger product, e.g. chair, is made from several smaller products, e.g. leg, as components. This gives
        Made from: Larger.PRODUCT $\longrightarrow\!\!\!\rightarrow$ Smaller.PRODUCT
(b) {<Chair, Back>, <Chair, Leg>, <Chair, Seat>, <Stool, Leg>, <Stool, Seat>}.
(c) Where-used: Smaller.PRODUCT $\longrightarrow\!\!\!\rightarrow$ Larger.PRODUCT
(d) {<Back, Chair>, <Leg, Chair>, <Leg, Stool>, <Seat, Chair>, <Seat, Stool>}.
(e) Structure: Larger.PRODUCT $\longleftrightarrow\!\!\!\rightarrow$ Smaller.PRODUCT. Methods of modelling the quantity, e.g. 4 legs, are covered in later chapters.

8 (a) Taught-by: STUDENTS $\longleftrightarrow\!\!\!\rightarrow$ PROFESSORS. Occurrences could be {<S1, P2>, <S1, P4>, <S2, P2> ...}.
(b) Advised-by: STUDENTS $\longleftrightarrow\!\!\!-$ PROFESSORS with suitable occurrences.
(c) Examined-by: STUDENTS $\longleftrightarrow\!\!\!\rightarrow$ PROFESSORS with suitable occurrences. Here a group of students all doing the same course would have the same examiners; the way to model this comes in Chapter 4.
(d) Taught-by[-1]: PROFESSORS $\longleftrightarrow\!\!\!\rightarrow$ STUDENTS has {<P2, S1> ...}.
(e) Advised-by[-1]: PROFESSORS $\longleftrightarrow\!\!\!\rightarrow$ STUDENTS has the reverse pairs to those occurring for (b).
(f) Examined-by[-1]: PROFESSORS $\longleftrightarrow\!\!\!\rightarrow$ STUDENTS has the reverse ordered pairs to those in (c).

Solutions to Exercises of Chapter 3

1 Analysis to derive a conceptual data model is done independent of computer constraints, i.e. there is no consideration of the eventual structure of the stored data as sequentially accessed or randomly accessed files and so on.

2 (a) information subject areas give the boundaries of the kinds of information to be analysed in detail. For example the analysis may be plannned to include manufacturing, purchasing, sales, bill-of-materials and stores but not personnel or payroll areas.

(b) The situations where entities are created must be analysed to model correctly how entities are identified. Users may want to store information about a created entity as soon as its identifying attribute value is known. Deletions can only occur when dependents no longer exist, e.g. a course cannot be deleted while there are students enrolled for it. Thinking about such helps analysis, e.g. how is the course identified at the last stage before deletion.

(c) the types of information that users have about an entity suggest attributes of the entity. Similarly relationship attributes may be suggested.

(d) Retrievals and updates arise in uses of the information for various operational functions. The information system must be based on models that allow all the use requirements.

3 (i) The entities are automobile, case, box, Rentout Inc. The entity properties are

An automobile has registration number, contents.

A case and a box have color.

Property values are

Color has values grey, brown.

Registration number has values ABC 123.

Relationship occurrences are

The automobile has the case in it.

The automobile has the box in it.

The automobile was rented from Rentout Inc. This relationship has the relationship attributes of Start-date-and-time, Duration; with attribute values July 1 at 1830, one week. An example fact is 'The case is grey'.

(ii) There is an association from an entity set Automobiles to a domain Registration-number. There is an association from the entity set Package to the domain Color, and so on. There is an association from the entity set Automobile to the entity set Package meaning that an Automobile contains a package. An automobile may be empty or be loaded with packages. A package can only be in either one automobile or none.

4 A person might be identified by any of the following candidate identifiers in different contexts

Social Security Number
Surname and first names
Name and address
Employee number
Passport number
Identifiers of parents and whether first, second ... child
Occupier of a room or building.

For employees Passport number would not be suitable because some employees do not have passports. There may be two or more employees with the same name. When information is first created about a person the person's social security number may be unknown, so cannot be used to identify the person. Each person can be assigned a unique employee-number.

5 (i) First one has to identify the entity types, i.e. Ship, Port, Container, Voyage, Consignment. The types of relationships are

A ship makes many voyages.

Ship $\longleftrightarrow\!\!\!\longrightarrow$ Voyage

Voyage is related to Stop, a ship makes a stop at each of the ports on the voyage. So one voyage is related thus to many ports. Each port has many ships that make a stop there. So

Port $\longleftrightarrow\!\!\!\longrightarrow$ Stop

Stop $\longleftrightarrow\!\!\!\longleftrightarrow$ Voyage

A container may conditionally be in a Consignment

Container $\longleftrightarrow\!\!\!\longleftarrow\!\longrightarrow$ Consignment

A container goes from origin port to destination port

Container $\longleftrightarrow\!\!\!\longrightarrow$ Origin.port

Container $\longleftrightarrow\!\!\!\longrightarrow$ Destination.port. Here Origin and Destination are role names to distinguish the attributes.

(ii) The entity and relationship types may either be drawn as above or listed as a collection of relations as below that specify the model to which occurrences will conform.

PORT(Ship#, ...)
SHIP(Ship#, ...)
STOP(Voyage#, Ship#, Arrival-date, Departure-date)
CONSIGNMENT(Consignment#, Consignment-date ...)
CONTAINER(Container#, ...)
CONT-CONS(Container#,Consignment#)   (This has a row for each container that belongs to a consignment.)

6 Yes, they are based on the principles in Sections 3.1 and 3.2.

7 To be able to recognize and discuss occurrences.

8 This example is used in later chapters (e.g. page 214).

Solutions to Exercises of Chapter 4

1 The four kinds of conceptual objects are given at the top of page 99
- entity sets (or entity types)
- relationship sets (or relationship types)
- entity attributes
- relationship attributes.

The analyst assigns names to all four types. The steps used by the analyst are on pages 100 to 101. These steps form part of the procedures outlined on pages 96 to 97. The details of conceptual objects were given in Section 3.2, starting page 79.

2 The entity types are those that users will want to store information about. These appear from the description to be Airline, Flight, Airport, Passenger and Trip.

The key for Airport can be the three letter code as implied. The key for a flight can be its number: this occurs daily so the key for a particular flight on a particular day will be the composite Flight-number and Date. Presumably Airlines can be identified by their letter codes, e.g. BA. How to identify trips and passengers is not explained, further analysis or investigation may be needed.

3 Elementary relations are important because they cannot be further subdivided without loss of information. They ensure a model with only one occurrence of each primitive. Hence a collection of elementary relations ensures that each more complex fact or association occurs only once in the conceptual object occurrences. This gives a clean structure that can ensure consistency.

Most elementary relations correspond to functional dependencies, i.e. associations that at each instant are either total or partial functions, but where values that occur can instantaneously change from one value to another when being updated. Some elementary relations correspond to many to many relationships which have no relationship attributes; these ERs are all key. Some ERs correspond to the one to one mappings between the chosen primary key and some other candidate key.

4 Employee as stated is not an ER because presumably Employee# is the primary key so there are two other dependent attributes.

Town could be an ER with Name as the primary key, assuming town names are distinct.

Grey-trousers-in-stock has both its attributes together forming the composite key, so it is all key, as case 1 at the foot of page 134, so is an ER.

Order is not an ER because if Order# is the key there are two non-key attributes, rather like Employee above.

Part has only one attribute so is all key so is an ER.

5 A project operation selects certain columns, not rows, so it is not A or B. It gives one new relation from one existing relation so cannot be F. Options C, D and E are operations that can be project operations.

6 A join is as option F. It is also as G. The columns used for the join do not have to have the same names as in H but could have; so H is also correct sometimes.

7 Full functional dependence means depending on the whole of a collection of two or more attributes. Functional dependence means depending on one attribute or else depending on either a subset or the whole of a collection of attributes.

8 If the correct ERs have been derived then the original relation can be constructed (except in the obscure case of an original relation that is not in first normal form because it has elements that are themselves decomposable structures as described later - in Fig. 5.1.6 page 81).
Assuming Passport# is the primary key, the ERs are
PASSPORT-SURNAME (Passport#, Surname)
PASSPORT-GIVEN-NAMES (Passport#, Given-names) assuming Given-names is regarded as a string that is not decomposable
PASSPORT-ADDRESS-CITY (Passport#, Address-City) assuming that Address-city is not decomposable
PASSPORT-DATE (Passport#, Date) assuming Date is not decomposable.
The PASSPORT relation can be calculated from the natural join of these relations.

9 Multivalued dependence is a fairly rare situation that must, however, be modelled correctly. In a relation of at least degree three there may be further structure which the relation itself does not show because the relation is all key. This additional structure can be of the form that the same collection of occurrences of certain attributes appears with every occurring set of values of some other collection of the attributes of the relation. This means that the collection of values is essentially a function of only some of the other attributes.
Multivalued dependencies must be modelled correctly in the conceptual data model otherwise the consistency of eventual stored values with the additional structure cannot be ensured by the DBMS software.

10 The diagram shows a transitive dependence.

11 The nodes correspond to attributes or to collections of attributes. The arcs correspond to dependencies, either functional, full functional, or trivial dependencies.

A node can correspond to more than one attribute where these appear together, e.g. as a composite key. The key attributes have a loop.

12 Matrices are used to represent directed graphs corresponding to the dependencies. They are a convenient notation both when working by paper and also for computer processing.

13 A minimal cover is a minimal set of ERs from which the transitive closure can be derived. In general it is not unique, there can be several. Where there are several candidate keys can lead to alternative minimal covers.

If a designer derives all possible minimal covers then the best can be chosen, in the sense of the one most appropriate to the organization's applications.

The rest of the question requires you to work through the procedure. We will summarize. The dependencies are as follows.

Next the analyst must investigate each situation which appears to be a transitive dependency to find out whether or not it really is. E.g. does A ⟶ c have the same meaning as the composite a ⟶ b ⟶ c ? For example if a ⟶ b is person to mother and a ⟶ c and b ⟶ c are both person to political party if they belong to such, then a ⟶ c does not mean the composite to the person's mother's party. However if they really mean the compositions then the analyst can develop the equivalent of the transitive closure, remove those with longest distance, and so on. Assuming these are compositions gives the following.

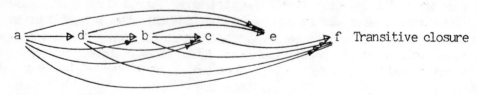

Transitive closure

Then, in summary, the analyst removes all those except the following.

Minimal cover

The elementary relations are thus
ER1 (a, d)
ER2 (d, b)
ER3 (b, c)
ER4 (b, e)
ER5 (c, f)
    Some b values in ER4 may perhaps not occur in ER3 at times during the eventual use.

    14 If also e ⟶ c the ERs are
ER1 (a, d)
ER2 (d, b)
ER3 (b, e)
ER4 (e, c)
ER5 (c, f).

    15 (i) Ans1 ⟵ Select Course tuples satisfying C# = C12
(ii) Ans2 ⟵ Join Ans1, Enrolment where Ans1.C# = Enrolment.C#
(iii) Ans3 ⟵ Project Ans2 [S#]
(iv) Ans4 ⟵ Join Ans3, Student where Ans3.S# = Student.S#
(v) Ans5 ⟵ Select Enrolment tuples satisfying S# = S45
(vi) From R3, page 121, Physics is course C3, hence
Ans6 ⟵ Select Enrolment tuples satisfying C# = C3 and Grade = C
    If this Ans6 is empty then no student got C for physics.

    16 (i) The elementary relations are
ER1 (S#, S-name)
ER2 (S#, S-year)
ER3 (C#, C-title)
ER4 (C#, C-year)
ER5 = ENROLMENT (S#, C#, Grade).
(ii)

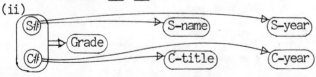

(iii)

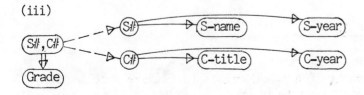

(iv)

	S#,C#	Grade	S#	C#	S-name	S-year	C-title	C-year
S#,C#	1	1	1	1				
Grade								
S#			1		1	1		
C#				1			1	1
S-name								
S-year								
C-title								
C-year								

17 No multivalued dependencies are shown, so assume they do not occur.

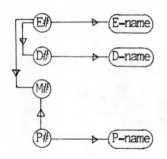

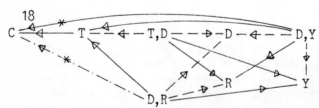

* These compositions are not needed for a minimal cover

Solutions to Exercises of Chapter 5

1 (i) The important ones are 3NF and 4NF.

(ii) Being in 3NF is a property of a single relation. Each of a collection of relations may or may not individually be in 3NF.

(iii) Optimal 3NF is a property of a collection of relations as a whole.

2 (i) Yes if it is by itself and not part of a larger collection of relations, no otherwise.

(ii) As (i).

(iii) Yes, the procedure for obtaining optimal 4NF relations is given starting half way down page 205. Every ER is individually in 4NF but an arbitrary collection of ERs is in general not in optimal 4NF.

3 (i) The degree of a relation is the number of columns or attributes.

(ii) A domain is a set of values. An attribute is a list of occurring values.

(iii) A primary key is the one chosen because users may want to store information about an occurrence as soon as its value is known. Tuples cannot exist without a value for the primary key attribute or attributes, but null values can exist for other attributes.

(iv) A prime attribute participates in at least one candidate key of the relation being discussed. A non-prime attribute does not. See page 177.

(v) A determinant is one or more attributes on which some other attribute is functionally or fully functionally dependent as appropriate. See page 177. If it is a collection of attributes then there must be another attribute that is fully functionally dependent on the collection.

(vi) The anomalies in storage operations are update (i.e. insert, delete or modify) operations that appear to be valid to a user with a local view but are not consistent with the conceptual data model or the internal model somehow. Alternatively they can be situations where a user with a local view cannot do something which in principle could be done, e.g. inserting information about a student could anomalously be done only if the user knew of a course that the student was attending.

(vii) Most relations in this book have atomic (i.e. non-decomposable) elements. The relations on page 191 satisfy the question, but those on page 181 do not.

(viii) Redundancy in the global logical model may lead to possible inconsistency or to extra storage space being needed.

(ix) No, far from it. There are many internal model logical record occurrences stored together on one physical block. A logical page may correspond to say three physical blocks instead of to one block, thus giving larger logical pages but making most transfers physically to be three adjacent blocks.

4 (i) A and B, 2NF (Kent's, page 190), and D, 3NF (BCNF page 197).

(ii) A, B, D, 3NF (page 198 line1).

(iii) Nothing in particular other than A. Compare page 185 definition of 2NF.

(iv) 2NF if dependent means fully functionally, 1NF otherwise.

(v) 1NF

(vi) 2NF (Kent's, page 190)

(vii) 3NF

(viii) 4NF

(ix) 3NF

None of the parts (i) to (ix) describe the requirements of optimal collections.

5 Yes, this proposal could give difficulties, because although every non-primary key data item type is fully dependent on the primary key, Emp#, there is a transitive dependency through M# to Machine-name. E.g. it is impossible to store the M# and Machine-name for a newly acquired machine for which as yet there are no employees as trained operators.

6
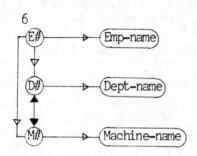

There are several alternative minimal covers since D#, Dept-name and M# can all be interchanged. One possibility is as follows.
ER1 (E#, Emp-name)
ER2 (E#, D#)
ER3 (D#, D-name)
ER4 (D#, M#)
ER5 (M#, M-name)

However if in the future each department may perhaps instead have several machines then that could be modelled by ER42 (M#, D#) instead of ER4.

Using ER4 leads to the following global logical model for a CODASYL-based DBMS.

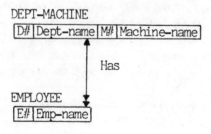

7 The relationships are C $\ll\longrightarrow\!\!\!\!\gg$ T and C $\ll\longrightarrow\!\!\!\!\gg$ B so the ERs are
ER1 ($\overline{C\#}$, $\overline{T\#}$)
ER2 ($\overline{C\#}$, $\overline{B\#}$)
The CODASYL-based model is

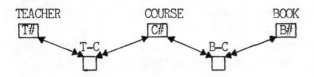

T-C and B-C have no data item types in their record types.

8 The proposed model is not satisfactory, because for example the first Hampton could be changed without changing the second, thus giving stored data that is inconsistent with the assumption that Roy and Sue Conn were both children of the same marriage which could only have occurred at one town on 5 Jan 1936.

Solutions to Exercises of Chapter 6

1

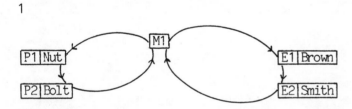

2 No.

3 Yes if the external model is used only for retrieval. No if used for updating, because then every external model record type (i.e. segment type) must include its primary key data item type.

4 Yes because the enquires will not lead to anomalies. To provide it would need join (and possibly project) operations.

Solutions to Exercises of Chapter 7

1 ER13 has the largest distance, so as implied in the question in the text on page 278 it will be removed first, whatever its weight. So iteration 1 in the solution to Exercise 1 will give the same $S_1{}^{13}$ as page 276.

With the new weights ER7 has lowest weight 4 from {5, 4, 6, 8} for {ER3, ER7, ER8, ER14} so ER7 is removed next.

Then Er8 is no longer a composition. Of the remaining ER3 and ER14 that have longest distance, it is ER3 that has lower weight so that is removed.

Index

|	Such that, 25	
{...}	Set, 25	
<...>	List, 25	
∈	Belongs to, 26	
{}, ∅	Empty set, 26	
⊂	Contained in, 26	
⊆	Contained in or equal to, 26	
∪	Union, 27	
∩	Intersection, 28	
n-ary	Relation with n columns, 38	
⟶	Type 1, to one, 47	
⟶)	Type C, Conditional, 50	
⟶»	Type M, to many, 50	
Tr	Type reverse, 54	
Tf	Type forward, 54	
(1:M)	Mapping type, 54	

←	Assignment, 62
||	Concatenation, 63
θ	Equals or similar comparison, 63
[ ]	Join, 63
⟶⟶	Multivalued dependency, 123
C	Composition, 151
CK	Candidate key, 177
D	Determinant, 177
NPA	Nonprime attribute, 177
PA	Prime attribute, 177
PK	Primary key, 177
NF	Normal form, 179
BCNF	Boyce-Codd Normal form, 197
CER	Collection of elementary relations, 205